MELISSUS AND ELEATIC MONISM

In the fifth century BCE, Melissus of Samos developed wildly counterintuitive claims against plurality, change, and the reliability of the senses. This book provides a reconstruction of the preserved textual evidence for his philosophy, along with an interpretation of the form and content of each of his arguments. A close examination of his thought reveals an extraordinary clarity and unity in his method and gives us a unique perspective on how philosophy developed in the fifth century, and how Melissus came to be the most prominent representative of what we now call Eleaticism, the monistic philosophy inaugurated by Parmenides. The rich intellectual climate of Ionian enquiry in which Melissus worked is explored and brought to bear on central questions of the interpretation of his fragments. This volume will appeal to students and scholars of early Greek philosophy, and also those working on historical and medical texts.

BENJAMIN HARRIMAN is Leverhulme Fellow in Classics at the University of Edinburgh.

CAMBRIDGE CLASSICAL STUDIES

General editors

R. G. OSBORNE, W. M. BEARD, G. BETEGH,
J. P. T. CLACKSON, R. L. HUNTER, M. J. MILLETT,
S. P. OAKLEY, T. J. G. WHITMARSH

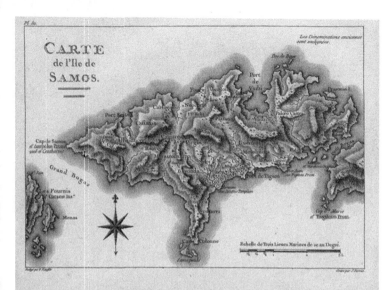

Pl. 54.

CARTE
de l'Ile de
SAMOS.

Echelle de Trois Lieues Marines de 20 au Degré.

Pl. 55.

VESTIGES DU TEMPLE DE JUNON A SAMOS.

A.P.D.R.

MELISSUS AND ELEATIC MONISM

BENJAMIN HARRIMAN
University of Edinburgh

CAMBRIDGE
UNIVERSITY PRESS

University Printing House, Cambridge CB2 8BS, United Kingdom

One Liberty Plaza, 20th Floor, New York, NY 10006, USA

477 Williamstown Road, Port Melbourne, VIC 3207, Australia

314–321, 3rd Floor, Plot 3, Splendor Forum, Jasola District Center, New Delhi – 110025, India

79 Anson Road, #06–04/06, Singapore 079906

Cambridge University Press is part of the University of Cambridge.

It furthers the University's mission by disseminating knowledge in the pursuit of education, learning, and research at the highest international levels of excellence.

www.cambridge.org
Information on this title: www.cambridge.org/9781108416337
DOI: 10.1017/9781108236324

© Faculty of Classics, University of Cambridge 2019

First published 2019

Printed and bound in Great Britain by Clays Ltd, Elcograf S.p.A.

A catalogue record for this publication is available from the British Library.

ISBN 978-1-108-41633-7 Hardback

CONTENTS

Contents

PREFACE

This book offers a reconstruction of the preserved textual evidence for Melissus of Samos, along with an interpretation of the form and content of each of his arguments. One of the upshots of the reconstruction I offer is the contention that Melissus' fragments constitute a far higher proportion of his original book than is the case for any other Presocratic philosopher, including Parmenides. This situation makes Melissus' work uniquely valuable for the insights it provides into Eleatic thought and philosophical method in the Presocratics, more generally speaking.

The surviving fragments, two preserved paraphrases of his book, and the evidence of ancient commentators indicate that Melissus adopted a rigorously deductive method of argumentation. By 'deductive' I mean that he clearly identifies the premises of his arguments, the methods by which he proceeds from them, and the conclusions he establishes. The conclusions established, in turn, act as premises for arguments that follow, forming a neat, pellucid (within reason) chain of argumentation. So the structure of the treatise permits us to reconstruct the original arrangement by following the pattern of deduction to which Melissus adheres closely.

In addition, I tackle a number of interpretative problems that have emerged in the scholarly reception of Melissus. I argue that his treatise begins from an assertion of the hypothesis 'something is'. It is from this foundational claim that he proceeds to deduce that this 'something', which he identifies with 'nature', is sempiternal (i.e. temporally infinite in both directions), spatially infinite, unique, unchanging, incorporeal, and indivisible. It is how each of these predicates relates to the demonstration of the others that I have attempted to identify. In addition, I offer an interpretation of the argument for spatial infinity that preserves its validity in the face of vigorous criticism from Aristotle and subsequent critics. The reconstruction of the argument for monism, i.e. the thesis that what-is (nature) is unique and unified, significantly rearranges the order of the relevant fragments, with the upshot that each now has its own

ix

easily identifiable role within the argument. Also developed is a proposed solution to Melissus' difficult demonstration of the assertion that what-is is without a body, a solution which preserves the whole of the quoted material in the face of demands for excision.

The above list should give some idea of the specifics of the interpretation this book aims to offer. There are a number of puzzles, including those philological and philosophical, that demand our attention when examining Melissus' fragments. I hope, however, to provide something more than a series of micro-arguments for the reader's consideration. This project began with a simple question: If Parmenides' poem is as significant an achievement in the history of philosophy as commentators maintain, why is Melissus, so clearly his early (if not earliest) advocate and expounder, so neglected? This question is made all the more immediate when we note that early reports in Plato and Aristotle closely associate the two philosophers, and that it is not unreasonable to think that it is Melissus' version of Eleaticism which becomes the dominant one in that philosophy's early reception.

If Melissus' claim to historical prominence is correct, and Parmenides' poem so fragmentary and often downright obscure, why is there no English monograph dedicated to Melissus and his fragments? This book is an attempt (however partial) to rectify an imbalance and give an oft-maligned philosopher his rightful due.

Yet a narrow focus on Melissus is not the exclusive aim of what is to follow. I have adopted a deliberate policy of avoiding taking positions on the many controversies in Parmenides' poem. In this task, I have not always been successful, but my hope is that readers concerned with Parmenides, wherever their loyalties may reside, will find there is more to learn from Melissus than they may have suspected. What Melissus contributes to Eleaticism may not definitively answer any puzzles in the study of Parmenides, but his work is far from irrelevant in this regard. Melissus' book, on any account, amounts to a provocative and suggestive response to Parmenides' monism. In this respect, I hope those with interests in Eleaticism and its reception in Plato and Aristotle will find something here enticing (even if it is only to disagree with).

Melissus' fragments also touch on the intellectual culture of the fifth-century Mediterranean, both inside and outside of what we would now classify as the strictly philosophical. His fragment B9, for example, devoted to demonstrating that what-is is without a body, has long been a centre of controversy. The difficulties of construing both the Greek and the structure of the argument we will examine in detail; however, the discussion of the nature of bodies and, in B7, the non-susceptibility of what-is to pain and anguish, suggest clear links with the Hippocratic corpus and, I will submit, with considerations about the divine nature of the world. Melissus' work then has a broad scope which touches on much within and outside of traditional philosophical concerns.

Partly this is the result of the intellectual context in which, I will argue, Melissus is properly situated: this is the world of the broad-ranging fifth-century enquiries by Ionic Greek speakers. Melissus is a product of the culture that produced not just the natural philosophers Anaximander, Anaximenes, and Anaxagoras, but also Herodotus, Hecataeus, and the Hippocratics. As such, Melissus has much to offer even to those interested in fifth-century intellectual life outside of philosophy, and this book is intended to embrace readers with concerns not primarily philosophical, as well as those whose are.

The nature of Melissus' place in the development of philosophy outside of Eleaticism is difficult to discern. In the Introduction to follow, we will have the opportunity to examine the relevant evidence of the details of Melissus' life; however, whatever tentative conclusions we may reach there, the details are too uncertain to make any confident claims about Melissus' chronology relative to figures such as Anaxagoras, Empedocles, and the atomists. My conclusions will echo Reale's contention that, to make good sense of the arguments, we need not assume these non-Eleatic philosophers to have influenced Melissus. The question will be considered closely in the chapter devoted to Melissus' fragment B8 on sense experience and plurality.

What I will suggest is that this conclusion is not a suggestion of Melissus' ignorance or an indication of the absence of historical relationships or influence. Rather my suggestion will be that a deliberate *diagnostic* strategy is in play, with the intention of exposing the failure of rival philosophical positions, and ordinary practice, to come to grips with the danger of relying on the evidence of sense experience. It is here, in the discussion of B8, that further strategic connections between the Eleatics will be explored, and where I will suggest what I take to be crucial strands that tie Parmenides and Zeno with Melissus. B8, in any case, offers a fascinating case of philosophical practice and method with implications well beyond those associated with the philosophy of Elea.

Thus it is my hope that readers take away not only some ideas about Melissus and the philosophical strategy he adopted in his book but something more as well. This is my suggestion that the study of Melissus opens up a window on to fifth-century intellectual enquiry that enriches our understanding not only of the philosophical developments of the period but also of the the broader-ranging pursuit of knowledge that is its hallmark.

This book is a product of my PhD research and its existence is due to the extremely generous community working on ancient philosophy in Cambridge. I arrived in Cambridge with enthusiastic but wholly jejune thoughts on Greek philosophy and have benefited from innumerable seminars both within the Faculty of Classics and throughout the university. Members of the 'B' caucus, including Nick Denyer, Robert Wardy, and Myrto Hatzimichali, have provoked and inspired many thoughts that find their final form here. Gábor Betegh and Catherine Rowett examined my thesis, suggested helpful clarifications and additions, and saved me from many errors. I am indebted to them. James Warren helped supervise my doctoral work and raised a practised eyebrow at much that was loose or ill-considered, or needed rethinking. Malcolm Schofield had the highly dubious privilege of supervising my work when I first arrived in Cambridge. He provided a model of clarity, wisdom, and good humour, and didn't laugh when I suggested Melissus as a topic for my research.

David Sedley acted as my primary supervisor throughout my time in Cambridge. Most of those reading this will know the contribution David has made to the study of ancient philosophy and to the progress of his students; I am very grateful for this because it would be exceedingly difficult to express how much he has given to me over the years.

As the manuscript for this book was being completed, the publication of Jaap Mansfeld's lectures on Melissus at *Eleatica* 2012 appeared in print.[1] Unfortunately, I have not been able to take account of his stimulating arguments in the following. However, it is worth remarking that we arrive at strikingly similar conclusions on several issues, including the interpretation of Melissus' B9 – a long-standing puzzle in the fragments. I have committed further thoughts to print on Mansfeld's book in a forthcoming issue of *Archiv für Geschichte der Philosophie*. I hope the following work plays some small part in the renewed interest in Melissus.

---

[1] Mansfeld 2016.

INTRODUCTION

In the first book of *De Generatione et Corruptione* (325a13–25), Aristotle criticises philosophers who follow arguments to conclusions in palpable contradiction with the evidence of the senses. From the context, it is clear that it is the Eleatics, and Melissus in particular, that Aristotle has in mind.[1] In what follows, we shall be chiefly concerned with how Melissus assumes his premises and from them, stubbornly on Aristotle's account, deduces his conclusions, which act to characterise Melissus' subject, i.e. nature, or what-is. The sophistication with which Melissus develops his picture of his subject and the importance of his disciplined deductive strategy are a large part of what I hope the reader takes away from what follows.

Aristotle's remark is hostile and Melissus would surely object to his insistence on the importance of the senses in philosophical enquiry. Yet in one very important respect, Aristotle recognises what will prove to be a fundamental contention of the present work: Melissus, beginning from the twin hypotheses that there is something and that *generatione ex nihilo* is impossible, pursues arguments to seemingly outrageous conclusions with a dogged determination that only one who not only ignores the evidence of the senses, but positively dismisses such data from his philosophical tool kit, could muster.

Aristotle's remark suggests something else important as well: philosophical positions specifically attributable to Melissus on the evidence of the extant fragments were often taken to be representative of the 'Eleatics' or 'Eleaticism' from the fifth century onwards.[2]

---

[1] Aristotle claims that these philosophers maintain that the whole is one, unmoved, and infinite. From this description, it seems highly likely that Melissus is the most relevant representative of the group. See Williams 1982: 128 and Rashed 2005: 138.

[2] See Reale 1970: 31–2 and Palmer 2009: 218–24. Brémond (2016: 23–48; see 47–8 in particular) argues strongly for the thesis that Aristotle takes Melissus to be the prime representative of Eleaticism and the main advocate of its signature monism.

This raises a host of questions about Melissus' connections, philosophical and otherwise, with the Eleans (i.e. those from Elea itself, modern-day Velia in southern Italy) Parmenides and Zeno, both in historical fact and in the depictions of these thinkers in our major sources from antiquity, e.g. Plato and Aristotle.

The outsized role, then, that Melissus seems to have played in the reception of the so-called 'Eleatics' in antiquity means that the philosopher must be taken seriously, if we are to get a fuller picture of any of those figures (Parmenides, Zeno, and Xenophanes) that are associated with the philosophy of Elea. We will soon have the opportunity to take a closer look at these associations in Plato and Aristotle.

First it is worth asking what we can say, if anything, with a fair degree of certainty about the historical details of Melissus' life. Three details are uncontested: he came from the island of Samos, fought valiantly and successfully (for a time) as an admiral in a battle against the Athenians in 441 BCE,[3] and wrote a philosophical treatise in Ionic prose. These facts, though few in number, do reveal something of Melissus' character and philosophy. That he wrote in prose immediately sets him apart from Parmenides, while Melissus' role as an admiral, a position won as a result of his political acumen according to Diogenes Laertius,[4] perhaps suggests a similarity, if we are to believe Diogenes' report (IX.23) of Speusippus' claim in his lost *On Philosophers*, that Parmenides was also a politically active citizen, in his case a law giver.[5]

The date of Melissus' philosophical work is more difficult to establish. Apollodorus (*apud* Diogenes, IX.24) gives Melissus' *floruit* as the 84th Olympiad (444–440 BCE), suggesting that his philosophical output was roughly contemporaneous with his position as admiral in the Samian fleet. Such a dating does, however,

---

[3] The battle was a part of a larger struggle with the Athenians, who, when approached by the Milesians, enemies of the Samians, sailed to Samos and established a democracy. The following year (probably 441) Melissus and other disaffected Samians attacked the Athenian navy, with great success, until the arrival of Pericles, who crushed the navy and besieged Samos. The Samians surrendered in 439. See Thucydides 1.115–17.

[4] IX.24.

[5] For this aspect of Parmenides' biography, see Cosgrove 2014: 18–22. Cosgrove compares Parmenides' civic role with the tradition of Heraclitus' refusal to engage within the polis; this contrast takes on a particular relevance for Melissus if he did indeed come into contact with Heraclitus and the Ephesians, as Diogenes claims.

seem to demand an account of the relationships Melissus' work has with two groups of pluralists, the post-Parmenideans (Anaxagoras and Empedocles) and the atomists, both of which are reasonably understood to have been active by this date. For the former group, we might ask whether Melissus was aware of the pluralist response to Parmenides and, if so, how his work fits in within the debate. For the latter, the relative chronology seems crucial for assessing the veracity of two vital historical links: (a) the significant influence Melissus is often held to have had on the recognition of void as a precondition for motion; and (b) the impact of the supposed challenge Melissus issues at the conclusion of his B8, εἰ πολλὰ εἴη, τοιαῦτα χρὴ εἶναι οἷόν περ τὸ ἕν (if there were many, they ought to be of just the same sort as the One is), which is widely thought to have been accepted by Democritus.[6]

Giovanni Reale, seeking to interpret Melissus' work as entirely Parmenidean in influence, i.e. innocent of any trace of the pluralist response, moves to eliminate the motivation for such puzzles by proposing to date Melissus' birth to roughly 500 BCE. This attempt relies on a reading of Plutarch's *Life of Themistocles* 2, where the fifth-century historian and biographer Stesimbrotus is said to have claimed that Themistocles studied with Anaxagoras and interested himself in Melissus. Plutarch accuses Stesimbrotus of confusing Themistocles with the significantly younger Pericles, whom Melissus opposed in battle. Reale, taking Stesimbrotus to be a contemporary witness, and thus more reliable, dismisses Plutarch's criticism.[7] As Themistocles died in 459 BCE, Reale takes this as good evidence that Apollodorus' *floruit* is at least twenty years off the mark.

In principle, we might be sympathetic to Reale's criticism of Plutarch's correction; after all, Stesimbrotus is reputed to have written a biography of Themistocles (included in his Περὶ Θεμιστοκλέους, καὶ Θουκυδίδου καὶ Περικλέους) and Plutarch himself makes free use of this material in his *Lives*. The assumption that

---

[6] The direction of influence between Melissus and the atomists is openly contested. Those in favour of Melissus' priority include Kirk and Stokes 1960, Guthrie 1965: 117–18, and Furley 1967: 79–103; and, tentatively, Graham 2010: 462. See Long 1976: 647 for some reservations.

[7] Reale 1970: 8–9.

Melissus' age as admiral was approximately sixty years, making him only slightly older than Pericles (born *c*. 495 BCE), is also plausible.

We might ask, though, two questions about Reale's use of Stesimbrotus' contention. First, is it reasonable to believe that it was Themistocles and not Pericles who was the first Athenian statesman to come into contact with Anaxagoras?[8] The date of Anaxagoras' arrival in Athens and the length of his stay are both controversial. If we follow Jaap Mansfeld's (plausible) reconstruction of the Apollodorean evidence, Anaxagoras' arrived in Athens in 456/5 BCE and stood trial and left in 437/6.[9] This makes an Athenian acquaintance impossible, but it does not immediately discount Stesimbrotus' claim. Themistocles, of course, was ostracised from Athens in the late 470s and, after some time in Argos, made his way to Asia Minor and was made governor of Magnesia by Artaxerxes, the Persian king. As Magnesia was only a short distance from Anaxagoras' native Clazomenae, it is possible, although not likely, that Themistocles came into contact with the philosopher before Anaxagoras' move to Athens.

A more significant worry is whether Stesimbrotus' claim, even if true, does the work of eliminating a pluralist response from the context of Melissus' work, as Reale thinks it does. This is no hint, for instance, that Themistocles was specifically familiar with Melissus' book, as we have it today. Indeed, it is perfectly possible that Themistocles' association with Melissus, if accepted, involved discussion of ideas yet to take their final form, making the connection less telling about relative chronology than Reale seems to think. We might also wonder whether dating Melissus' book to the 460s is sufficiently early to entitle one to a confident claim that pluralist responses to Parmenides had yet to be formed.[10] Even if we were to accept Reale's dating of Melissus' birth, this would make him roughly coeval with Anaxagoras (on Mansfeld's reconstruction) and thus not give Melissus any significant claim to chronological priority.[11]

---

[8] Long (1976: 646) very much doubts that this is a reasonable claim.

[9] Mansfeld 1979.   [10] Long (1976) also suggests points along these lines.

[11] I leave aside here Aristotle's puzzling remark in *Metaphysics* A (984a11–13) that Anaxagoras was *proteros* to Empedocles in age, but *husteros* in works. Whether Aristotle intends to claim that Anaxagoras wrote after Empedocles is a long-standing

Provisionally, I suggest that Reale's dating of Melissus' birth to 500 BCE is plausible enough, but that it in no way justifies his claim that this guarantees his work was free from a context in which Parmenides' work had already generated a pluralist response. My contention will be that nowhere in Melissus' fragments do we find something that is an obvious indication of a familiarity with a *specific* rival philosophical position. This is not to say that Melissus was unaware of the likes of Anaxagoras and Empedocles. Rather, I will maintain that Melissus' procedure (on my view, very much akin to what Parmenides does in the second half of his poem) is to diagnose what he takes to be the flaw in *any* pluralist account, philosophical or lay. Thus, in B8, pluralists of all stripes are taken to task for holding the results of sense perception to be philosophically relevant. Such a method need not involve a direct response to any one philosopher and perhaps benefits, dialectically speaking, from a refusal to distinguish the opinions of 'expert' theorists from those of ordinary people.

Melissus' connection with philosophers associated with Elea in antiquity is a more trying issue and one unlikely to be settled with any great confidence. Claims of influence, even in contexts where the evidence is clearer, are difficult to assess. It is worth, however, simply marshalling the evidence we have from Plato and Aristotle and deciding whether any provisional conclusions might be drawn. I intend this not as an exhaustive or novel examination, but rather as an overview that may help flesh out the character of the reception of Melissus.[12] I do claim, however, that too often a

controversy. Some, beginning with Alexander of Aphrodisias *in Met.* 27–8, have interpreted *husteros* qualitatively as 'inferior' with no temporal element implied. Curd (2007: 96 n.17 and 133–4) suggests that Aristotle is using the adjectives to explain why Empedocles is considered before Anaxagoras, even though the latter was older. On such an account, we need not assume either one's chronological priority in activity. Kahn (1960: 163–5) offers a similar explanation of Aristotle's text, though without drawing the same conclusion about either's chronological priority.

[12] Brémond (2016: 23–48) covers much the same ground with a helpful survey of Aristotle's presentation of Parmenides, Melissus, and the nature of Eleaticism. There is much to say for her conclusion that it is Melissus who should properly be considered the prime representative of Eleatic monism for Aristotle. I avoid, however, taking her strong position (at 34–5) that the sort of monism attributed to Melissus by Aristotle is improperly retroactively ascribed to Parmenides. It is certainly true that, as Jonathan Barnes has argued, Parmenides' B8 does far less to commit him to numerical monism than many interepreters would have us believe. This is different, however, from saying

polarising tendency is evident in attempts to assess the relationship between Melissus and Parmenides. Melissus is presented either as slavish imitator, or an eristic charlatan perverting the majesty of Parmenides' innovative metaphysics. The evidence suggests a more nuanced picture.

In modern accounts the philosophical association between Parmenides and Melissus is often said to be characterised, generally speaking, by doctrinal consistency.[13] The understanding that Melissus and Zeno were faithful followers and defenders of Parmenides is a familiar claim found throughout standard histories of Greek philosophy.[14] This consensus has more recently been challenged, in some respects persuasively. In the case of Zeno, for instance, Jonathan Barnes has argued that Plato's suggestion in his *Parmenides* that Zeno defended Parmenides from the mockery his counterintuitive claims provoked should be countered. Zeno *did* attack those who mocked Parmenides by arguing that the implications of pluralism are as absurd as or even more absurd than those of monism; however, it was not for any substantive doctrinal reason. Zeno is an intellectual dazzler on Barnes' account, a thinker more attracted to the bright spark of eristic debate than to a systematic, consistent philosophy.[15]

John Palmer has suggested a reading of Melissus and his relationship with Parmenides along similar lines. He helpfully catalogues the formal differences between their fragments, e.g. the use of prose and the absence of a proem and of a cosmological section in Melissus,[16] and points out that the evidence of Plato and Aristotle does *not* confirm or even suggest, on his account, that the views of Parmenides and Melissus were assimilated by them.

---

that Parmenides is not, in the final analysis, so committed, or that Melissus did not believe him to be so.

[13] Reale (1970) for instance finds no substantial philosophical divergence from Parmenides in Melissus' work. He even goes so far as to argue that the usual view of Melissus' B1 and B2, as maintaining that what-is is sempiternal, should be overturned in favour of a reading of a sort of non-durational eternity akin to what is found, on Reale's account, in Parmenides' B8.

[14] See Guthrie 1965 and Burnet 1930 for two prominent examples. See Makin 2014 for a more recent example.

[15] Barnes 1982: 234–7. See his *Zenone e l'infinito* (2011: chapter 1) for the further claim that Zeno is 'a philosopher without philosophy'.

[16] Palmer 2009: 208–10.

He suggests that 'the characterization of Melissus' purpose as essentially one of eristic controversy has the ring of truth' and that 'it is at any rate clear that he belongs to an intellectual milieu quite different from that of Parmenides'.[17] I take it that there are, at least, two distinct claims here that ought to be investigated: (1) Plato and Aristotle make a clear and unequivocal distinction between the positions of Parmenides and Melissus; (2) The differences between the two are so prominent that we should think that the latter pursued a project very much apart from, and perhaps at odds with, what the former aimed to achieve. It is clear enough, as well, that Palmer's second claim is meant to follow, at least partially, from the first.[18]

On the first claim, at least, Palmer does make an important point, although his conclusions extend beyond the letter of the text. Both Plato and Aristotle make it clear that there are differences between the two; whether these amount to the substantial divide Palmer sees, we shall have to investigate. Consider Plato's discussion of Parmenides and Melissus in the *Theaetetus*. At 183e–184a, Socrates responds to Theaetetus' insistence that they discuss the partisans of the view that the universe is at rest, a position attributed to certain 'Melissuses' and 'Parmenideses' at 180e. Socrates dismisses Theaetetus' demand in the following celebrated passage:

I respect those who say that the universe is one and at rest, so I wouldn't want to investigate them in a crude way – and still more than Melissus and the rest, I respect one being, Parmenides. Parmenides seems to me to be, as Homer puts it, venerable and awesome. I met the great man when I was quite young and he was very old, and he seemed to me to have a sort of depth which was altogether noble. So I'm afraid, not only that we'll fail to understand what he said, and get still more left behind on the question of what he had in mind when he said it; but also – this is my greatest fear – that the theories that keep jostling in on us will, if we listen to them, make us lose sight of what our discussion has been aimed at, the question what, exactly, knowledge is. (Trans. by J. McDowell)

---

[17] Palmer 2009: 217. See Brémond 2016: 23–4 for the important point that Palmer is, of course, considering the historical relationship between Parmenides and Melissus primarily, if not exclusively, for the sake of interpreting the former and not the latter.

[18] It is, of course, not only on their characterisation in Plato and Aristotle that Palmer grounds his account. Alleged differences, contestable or not, in the fragments themselves are also prominent.

Socrates is clearly made here by Plato to pick out Parmenides as of an especial philosophical interest that Melissus does not merit, though, if it is intended in earnest, Socrates does encourage us to give the latter our respect. Yet there seems to be no hint that Socrates' hesitancy indicates a concern that the positions of the venerated Parmenides might be conflated with Melissus and the rest of the monists, as Palmer suggests. It is not that, were we to take up and criticise Melissus, Parmenides would, in turn, be tarnished by association. Is it not rather that, were we to consider Parmenides' position, we might fail to grasp him properly and thus fail to live up to his nobility? Conflation or assimilation does not seem to be the most pressing concern for Socrates, but the respect due to Parmenides, first won by the personal acquaintance between the two depicted, fictionally or not, in the *Parmenides*.

Indeed the treatment of Parmenides and Melissus in the *Theaetetus* points to the very opposite conclusion. In the passage containing the striking pluralisation of their names, we learn that these philosophers maintain 'that everything is one and motionless, having no place in which to move'.[19] This argument, tackling the impossibility of motion through the impossibility of void, is a distinctively Melissan contribution.[20] Those who hold that such an argument is to be attributed solely to Melissus face the difficulty of explaining why Parmenides, even if the pluralised names are to be taken as roughly equivalent to 'those like Parmenides and Melissus', would be associated with an argument not original to him. It is noteworthy, as well, that Aristotle follows suit. In the passage from *De Generatione et Corruptione* discussed above, Aristotle marshals the same argument targeting motion and attributes it to some of the ancient thinkers (ἐνίοις τῶν ἀχραίων), suggesting a similar assimilation between the positions of Parmenides and Melissus.[21]

[19] ὡς ἕν τε πάντα ἐστὶ καὶ ἕστηκεν αὐτὸ ἐν αὑτῷ οὐκ ἔχον χώραν ἐν ᾗ κινεῖται (180e3–4).

[20] I will maintain that this sort of argument is original to Melissus, without insisting that Parmenides' fragments indicate that he had *no* conception of void, as Kirk and Stokes (1960) and Tarán (1965: 110–13 and 196) claim.

[21] Edward Hussey (2004: 249) makes this point. Aristotle is quick to note, at 325a15–16, that some add that the universe is infinite (i.e. Melissus).

The pattern that the *Theaetetus* suggests is that Parmenides is to be distinguished from Melissus but not dissociated. Crucially, as well, Melissus is nowhere made to be a pupil or follower of Parmenides in any obvious way. This is significant if we put this omission in context with Aristotle's report, at *Metaphysics* A5 (986b22), that Parmenides *is said* to have been Xenophanes' pupil.[22] In the passage, Xenophanes, Parmenides, and Melissus are all considered as advocates of the One and, though Aristotle repeats the qualitative distinction between Parmenides and Melissus familiar from *Physics* 1, the three receive what appears to be their closest association anywhere in Plato or Aristotle. That Melissus is not, in turn, mentioned as Parmenides' pupil is significant, and suggestive of the former's independence. Yet this confirmation of independence is only found within a context in which the relations, however they are to be characterised, between the philosophers of Elea are taken for granted.

This passage from the *Metaphysics* offers a further example of the assimilation of 'Eleatic' thinking that finds no support in the extant fragments. We learn that Xenophanes maintained, 'with his eye on all of heaven', that the One is god, suggesting quite clearly that god is to be taken to be coextensive with the world. This is done, according to Aristotle, despite Xenophanes' failure to grasp either Parmenides' conception of the 'One' as being so in account,[23] or Melissus' understanding as it being so materially. Such a view is in palpable tension with Xenophanes' extant fragments,[24] but is a plausible interpretation (as I shall suggest) of the positions of both Parmenides and Melissus. What we find, then, once again is an Aristotelian confirmation of a Platonic assimilation, this time following on from Plato's claim in the *Sophist* 242d5–6 that Xenophanes was the founder, or at least an early representative, of the 'Eleatic Tribe': τὸ δὲ παρ' ἡμῖν

---

[22] Brémond (2016: 32–3) rightly notices how unusual such a claim is in Aristotle: 'Aristote offre l'image d'une école au sens plus strict d'une succession de maître à disciple, démarche pour le moins rare dans le corpus aristotélicien.' She offers *Meteorology* 342b36–343a1 on Hippocrates as a rare parallel.

[23] This points to Aristotle's criticism in *Physics* 1.3 that Parmenides fails to understand that being is said in many ways and not simply in the category of substance.

[24] It is difficult to see, for example, how God can both remain stationary perpetually (B26) and shake things with his thought (B25), if he is identical with the world.

Ἐλεατικὸν ἔθνος, ἀπὸ Ξενοφάνους τε καὶ ἔτι πρόσθεν ἀρξάμενον (And the Eleatic tribe in our region, beginning from Xenophanes and even earlier ...). Yet, as in the case of Melissus, Aristotle's assimilation is far from total. Parmenides is picked out as being of considerably more worth than either Xenophanes or Melissus, both of whom are said to be a bit crude or rustic (μικρὸν ἀγροικότεροι).

The question now is whether the associations, suggested by Plato and Aristotle, between Xenophanes, Parmenides, Melissus, and Zeno are historical or classificatory. What I mean by this is to ask whether any of these four were working within an intellectual context where the influence of one or more of the others played an active role, acknowledged or not. One might think, alternatively, that the associations and assimilations we have canvassed are the product of the imposition of an interpretative schema, intended to group disparate philosophers into dichotomous classifications.[25] Thus, we might think, as Palmer argues, that such a schema structures Aristotle's division of earlier thinkers in *Physics* I.2 (184b15–25).[26] Here Aristotle divides the *endoxa* about *archai* into branching dichotomies: the *arche* is said either to be one or to be many; if one, it is either changeable or not; if changeable some make it air and some water. In turn, if the *archai* are many, they must be either limited or unlimited; if the latter, either they are all the same and differ only in shape, or they are different and even opposed.

This schema, traceable back to Gorgias' *On What-Is-Not, or On Nature*, on Palmer's account,[27] certainly has the potential to obscure or to conflate philosophical positions. Yet, even if we were to agree that such a classification is a relevant element behind the association of Parmenides and Melissus in Aristotle (or Plato),

---

[25] See Mansfeld 1986, for his classic study of early, pre-Platonic, classificatory schemata, based on the number and nature of philosophical principles. See also Brémond 2016: 30–1.

[26] Palmer 2009: 220–1.

[27] Palmer (2009: 220) argues that this classification is original to Gorgias, on the evidence of what he calls the 'doxographical preface' to *On What-Is-Not, or On Nature* found in *MXG* 979a15ff. Certainly the *form* of the classification is dichotomous in both, but it is not so clear that Aristotle's classification, which makes different distinctions than those found in Gorgias, is destructive in the same manner. Indeed Aristotle, at 184b22–5, fits his own project of natural philosophy within the terms of the classification.

we might wonder whether this indicates anything of substance about the question of historical relations. In order to come to the conclusion that the associations apparent in the texts we have considered are *only* or even largely the product of such an inherited and misleading classificatory programme, we would need to accept two highly implausible claims. First, the connections between Parmenides, Melissus, and (on my account) Xenophanes evident in their verbatim texts are only apparent or, at least, much weaker than they have understood. Second, Plato and Aristotle, in suggesting associations between Parmenides, Melissus, Zeno, and Xenophanes, that go beyond mere superficial similarities classified after the fact, must themselves be falling to the reductive classification.

Our look at the reception of the so-called 'Eleatics' in Plato and Aristotle suggests something else, less certain, but perhaps more helpful. There is a clear attempt to mark out Parmenides as being worthy of peculiar interest, but *not* an effort to make his philosophical views entirely distinct from either Xenophanes or Melissus. What I take this to suggest is that a nexus of philosophical connections between the figures is assumed, but that this nexus does not contain elements of a unidirectional intellectual authority, beginning from Xenophanes and continuing through Parmenides to Melissus. Xenophanes is, of course, said to be Parmenides' teacher by Aristotle, but it is clear that Aristotle understands Parmenides' genius to have quickly surpassed any philosophical clout the elder philosopher may have had.

This state of affairs is confirmed by the influence Melissus appears to have had as the chief representative of 'Eleatic' thought, as evidenced by his appearance by name in the Hippocratic treatise *On the Nature of the Human Being*, and by the strong possibility that it is Melissus who is Gorgias' primary target in his *On What-Is-Not, or On Nature*.[28] If Parmenides were the central, authoritative figure of what we call 'Eleaticism', it

---

[28] This point is made by Reale (1970: 24 n.97) and Palmer (2009: 218–21). That Melissus is the intended target is suggested by Gorgias' parody of Melissus' title, *On Nature, or On What-is*, and his first hypothesis 'nothing is' (*MXG* 979a11), which I take to correspond, again in a parodic manner, to Melissus' hypothesis 'something is'.

would be exceptionally odd that Melissus appears so prominently in these texts.

What we may say, then, is that there is good reason to think that Parmenides and Xenophanes figured within the intellectual context in which Melissus worked but, crucially, not as philosophical authorities. Melissus is associated with the philosophy of Elea, but he is never made to be philosophically bound by it. We find further confirmation of this point if we recall how Plato uses the suggestive adjective 'Ἐλεατικός'. The word is far rarer than one might expect; it is entirely absent from Aristotle and rare, if prominent, in Plato. Intriguingly, it is nowhere to be found in any of Plato's descriptions of the interlocutor often termed by modern scholars and translators the 'Eleatic Stranger'. For Plato, the stranger (ξένος) is an Elean (Ἐλεάτης), but not an Eleatic (Ἐλεατικός). This distinction is suggestive, not least because of what it indicates about the relationship between the so-called 'Eleatic Stranger' and his 'father' Parmenides in the *Sophist*.[29] For our purposes, it is surely remarkable that it is Xenophanes in the *Sophist* and Zeno in the *Phaedrus* (261d6), and *not* Melissus in the *Theaetetus*, that are called 'Ἐλεατικός' by Plato.

With this in mind, I shall take both Parmenides and Xenophanes to be relevant for the reconstruction and interpretation of Melissus' fragments, but without the assumption that any philosophical coherence among them must be sought. Thus, for example, I will suggest that Xenophanes' criticism of popular views of the gods is a helpful analogue to Melissus' discussion of pain and grief in B7 and the bodilessness of what-is in B9. Yet I will not take such a connection to suggest that various incompatibilities between their positions ought to be dissolved or explained away. I do not seek doctrinal coherence but rather evidence of the sparks that drove a response from Melissus as found in the work of earlier thinkers. My claim is both that those sparks are both there to be found and that they help to illuminate Melissus' fragments.

If such an account of Melissus and his relations with 'Eleaticism' is along the right lines, we might ask what it is that

---

[29] The distinction might, for instance, confirm that the famous 'parricide' discussed at *Sophist* 241d5ff. suggests that Plato is making the Stranger progress beyond, and perhaps in contradiction with, his Eleatic heritage.

Melissus contributes to this family of positions, and why he became peculiarly associated with and representative of their thinking. In short, what is it that makes Melissus an Eleatic? We must keep in mind, of course, not only the differences noted in the secondary reports considered above but also the very real divergences apparent in the fragments themselves. Melissus, it is important to remember, is nowhere associated with the town of Elea (as Parmenides and Zeno are) or with travel to Italy and Elea itself (as in the case of Xenophanes).[30] Melissus argues for positions that are *prima facie* incompatible with what Parmenides avers in his fragments: Melissus, for example, is committed to the claims that what-is is sempiternal and spatially infinite. Both seem to be in flat contradiction with Parmenides' denial of past and future tenses in B8.5, his talk of a limit in B8.30–1 and B.42, and his comparison of what-is to a sphere at B8.42–4. Strikingly, as well, as many recent interpreters have noticed, Parmenides' rejection of plurality, a position universally associated with him in antiquity, receives rather scant support from his fragments.[31] Melissus' commitment to monism, meanwhile, is clear from the fragments and uncontested in the secondary literature.

Although these differences appear profound, I will suggest that they are best interpreted as developments and clarifications of Parmenides' positions and not adversarial reworkings. This will be justified partly, in the case of sempiternity and spatial infinity, on the basis of Melissus' Ionian background and his place within its tradition of natural philosophy. Thus, I take it that Parmenides' suggestion of a limit and Melissus' claim of spatial infinity are not so very different, insofar as both are aiming to prove that what-is is complete and invariant, though each is working with different assumptions as regards how to demonstrate such a point.

The issue of the sorts of monism that Parmenides and Melissus adopt and what, if anything, they share in common outside of the

---

[30] For an explicit connection of Xenophanes with the city of Elea, see his *testimonium* A13.

[31] Jonathan Barnes' work is pioneering in this area; see 1982: 204–13, in particular. Barnes claims that Parmenides' fragments commit him to neither one of the crucial two aspects of what I call the 'Eleatic One', namely uniqueness (that what-is is numerically singular) and homogeneity (that what-is is unified and qualitatively uniform). Various proposals, building on Barnes' scepticism of the previous *communis opinio*, have been raised. See Palmer 2009: 19–32 for a helpful survey.

generic term, is difficult to determine, but goes some way towards answering one of the central questions I have raised: why is it that Melissus became the dominant representative of Eleaticism? I do not, here, take a view on Parmenides' position except to say that there is a difference between claiming that there is nothing in his fragments themselves that absolutely commits him to what is often called in the literature 'strict' monism (namely the thesis that what-is is numerically one) and the thought that he advocated a monistic ontology that was explicitly in contradiction with such a thesis.[32] One might be happy to agree to the first and be strongly sceptical of the second.

Whatever we make of Parmenides' view, it should be uncontroversial to say that Melissus adopts a far more transparent position in advocating something along the lines of the 'strict' understanding canvassed above. This fact itself, perhaps, helps to explain Melissus' prominence. I will suggest, however, that Melissus' contribution goes further than mere clarification. It will be, on my account, because of Melissus' argument for monism, which establishes a tight connection between the primary attributes of what I shall call the Eleatic 'One', that Melissus seems to emerge as the spokesman for Eleaticism. His argument itself, which will be reconstructed using his fragments B4, B5, and B6 (though not in that order), marks a significant development beyond Parmenides by eschewing a reliance on the impossibility of not-being or what-is-not. Instead we find an argument that begins from the premise of spatial infinity and demonstrates that what-is is both unique and unified (homogeneous). It will be with these two predicates in place that change in all its forms (alteration, rearrangement, and motion) will be eliminated in his B7. This is to be contrasted with Parmenides' procedure in his B8, where it is the elimination of not-being that is repeatedly invoked as the fundamental premise used to eliminate such changes from his picture of what-is. This is not to suggest that Melissus intentionally diverges from Parmenides, or that he understood his conclusions to be in tension with the latter. I take it as possible, and

---

[32] One might think here of the thesis of 'predicational' monism advanced by Curd (1998) or the 'modal reading' of Palmer (2009).

perhaps plausible, that Melissus took his monism to be in conformity with what he understood Parmenides to argue. Rather we find the development of a demonstration that is clearer and more transparently deductive (its premises and the means by which conclusions follow are clearer) than what Parmenides' fragments contain. It is this conclusion that will emerge repeatedly as we reconstruct Melissus' fragments.

It is this function of the 'Eleatic One' in Melissus' work that suggests why he quickly became the dominant representative of the 'Eleatics'. The connections between the characteristic, counterintuitive positions associated with their philosophy from antiquity onward are given definite shape. The thesis that what-is is one (both unique and homogeneous) leads directly and necessarily to changelessness. One might find compatible positions in Parmenides. Certainly, he says that what-is is ἓν συνεχές in B8.6, and much of that fragment is devoted to eliminating various species of change. What we don't find is any intrinsic connection between monism and changelessness other than the fact that both are demonstrated on the basis of the impossibility of what-is-not. Indeed it is characteristic of the attributes Parmenides attempts to predicate of what-is in B8 that they are argued independently of each other and do not form a deductive chain.[33] This is in striking contrast with Melissus' procedure in B7 where alteration, rearrangement, and motion are explicitly said to threaten the previous proof of the twin attributes of the 'Eleatic One', which in turn had been demonstrated on a clear deductive basis from spatial infinity.

Thus it is Melissus' methodology that I will maintain is the key for understanding not only his fragments and how they fit together, but also his role in the reception of Eleatic thought. His method also provides the vital support for the project of reconstruction undertaken here. The deductive strategy that is apparent throughout the surviving fragments gives us a unique insight into the structure of Melissus' book and allows for the reconstruction of the individual arguments into a coherent and continuous run of text. Indeed I will maintain that *every* fragment surviving from

---

[33] Sedley (1999: 122) makes this point. The exception is the argument denying motion at B8.26–30, which is grounded on the impossibility of generation and coming-to-be. This argument itself though is reliant on the denial of what-is-not (see B8.7–10).

Melissus can be fitted, with only the occasional and minimal assumption of transitional elements, into such a text.

This is a bold claim and it provides us with a respect in which Melissus' fragments are unique among Presocratic philosophical texts.[34] There are a number of facts (peculiar in their conjunction to Melissus) that encourage such a thesis. First, there is strong evidence that Melissus composed a single work and that all our fragments are portions from that one book. Secondly, all of the extant quotations are given by Simplicius in his commentaries on Aristotle, suggesting that all fragments derive from the same copy of Melissus' text. Thirdly, our secondary evidence about Melissus, including the two paraphrases of his book (found in Simplicius and the *MXG*), is either confirmed by the verbatim fragments or obviously derived from them, with a single exception from Diogenes Laeritus that we shall consider in detail.

All of this suggests that we have a strong basis on which we may begin our reconstruction and that we are in the fortunate position of possessing a greater proportion of Melissus' book than anyone has dared to suggest thus far. It even raises the tempting thought that what we possess is something close to the whole of his book. In the final chapter, I consider this possibility by comparing the length of the total sum of the extant fragments with our evidence for the books of Parmenides and Zeno. While I do not adopt the strong conclusion that there is absolutely no lost Melissan material of significance, I do maintain that our secondary evidence nowhere unequivocally suggests that such material has been lost (e.g. there are no *testimonia* attributing positions to Melissus that are not directly traceable to the fragments themselves). Certainly, the introduction to B8, which offers the fragment as a secondary σημεῖον for the claim that what-is as one, suggests further proofs or

---

[34] This is, of course, not to say that global reconstructions of a Presocratic thinker's fragments have not been attempted before. Serge Mouraviev in his vast project on Heraclitus, for example, pursues a similar aim by arranging some 248 separate items from Heraclitus into a full-scale sequence intended to reflect the original ordering of Heraclitus' book. See the reconstruction found in his (2011) book (the eleventh volume of the project, *Heraclitea* 4.A). What makes Melissus unique is that such a reconstruction can be conducted using fragments derived from the *same source*, i.e. Simplicius' commentaries on Aristotle's works. This allows for the thesis that Simplicius was quoting from a copy of Melissus' book, which puts such a reconstruction on far firmer ground than anything similar that could be attempted for Heraclitus.

arguments of similar status may have been offered in addition to B1–7. B8 itself is presented as secondary insofar as it does not directly further our understanding of what-is, but rather targets the assumptions about sense experience that rival conceptions entail. Thus it is possible that further methodological arguments, understood to be complementary to the main business of deductively describing what-is, were provided. This, however, is no guarantee that they were.

What I suggest, then, is that our reconstruction will yield a continuous run of text that provides an unparalleled insight into the construction and defence of Eleatic arguments. The reconstruction itself will be broken down into individual nodes that together form the chain of deductions Melissus makes. The chain, on my account, begins from Melissus' title and the establishment of nature, or what-is as the subject of his work.

The Historical Context of Melissus

The above remarks suggest something about Melissus' place among his fellow 'Eleatics' and the character of the arguments I shall make as we go forward. Much of what I shall offer is firmly on the 'micro' side of things. Many small arguments must be offered in favour of the reconstruction of Melissus' text that I propose. But what I hope emerges is a larger picture of Melissus as a philosopher and of his unique contribution to the logic of arguments and the history of Eleaticism. If we are to take Eleatic thinking seriously as a major, if not *the* major, philosophical contribution of the Presocratics, Melissus' work and its reception are absolutely crucial.

It is in this area of arguments that Melissus, Parmenides, and Zeno make what I take to be their most influential advance, and indeed it will be here that we find what ties them most closely together. This achievement is the development of a series of strategies that develop arguments in favour of theses in direct contradiction with the evidence of the senses and of experience. Melissus proceeds from a hypothesis (that there is something and we can speak about it) that would be acceptable to anybody, bar the committed nihilist (e.g. Gorgias?). That such a hypothesis leads to the conclusions that what-is is one, unchanging, and motionless is shocking and evidence of an exceptionally clever and daring philosophical project. One can (and indeed must) find fault with many, and perhaps all, of his arguments. Yet what I attempt to show is that these arguments are not as feeble as many have thought and are a central aspect of the development of early Greek philosophy.

Even if such a favourable opinion about the quality of Melissus' arguments is not shared by the reader, it is worth pointing to one salient fact that has not received the attention it deserves. Melissus takes it that arguments *alone* are sufficient to demonstrate his conclusions. His work is presented in the workaday prose of Ionian intellectual enquiry (whether philosophical, historical, or otherwise) without the adornment of divine revelation and Epic language that characterise Parmenides' poem. He does not claim any special access to truth outside of the results of his arguments. He does not shape his thought into oracular, aphoristic pronouncements in the manner of Heraclitus nor clothe himself as a mystic as Empedocles did. His conclusions stand or fall by the quality of his arguments.

Melissus' commitment to arguments as his means of persuasion places him firmly within the Ionian intellectual climate of the period and suggests that his treatise is worth considering alongside this rich tradition consisting of thinkers as varied as Herodotus and the Hippocratic medical writers. Indeed I will maintain that taking the wider background of the period seriously allows us crucial interpretative tools denied if we were to limit our scope to the traditional canon of philosophical thinkers.

Rosalind Thomas has drawn attention to intellectual connections of the period and put particular emphasis on the similarities between Herodotus and Melissus in their use of sustained deductive reasoning[35] and emphasis on 'truth, certainty, and correct knowledge'.[36] This is not to suggest that the differences between

---

[35] Thomas 2000, particularly 174, where the Eleatics are linked with Herodotus in the wider trend of the development of deductive argument and its persuasive value, and 189 n.48, where Melissus is picked out as sharing 'the most immediate similarity' with Herodotus in their respective method of logical deductive proof.

[36] Thomas 2000: 228–35.

Melissus' project, very much a work of natural philosophy, and Herodotus' book are not profound. Rather it is to say that there is a striking overlap in that both take it that persuasion is, at least in part, the result of convincing argumentation and need not demand the seal of an unquestioned authority.

For Thomas, an emphasis on correctness, signified by the word ὀρθῶς and its cognates, apparent throughout Herodotus and evident in heavy concentration in Melissus' B8, and on certain truth brings the well-known first chapter of the Hippocratic *On the Nature of the Human Being* into view. That Melissus is specifically named in this chapter sheds a particularly bright light on his influence on the broad intellectual currents of the day.

The medical writer declares of those who illicitly exploit the results of natural speculation in relation to the nature of the human being: δοκέουσι μέντοι μοι οὐκ ὀρθῶς γινώσκειν οἱ τὰ τοιαῦτα λέγοντες ('those who say this do not know correctly, it seems to me'). This epistemological use of ὀρθῶς is connected by Jouanna with Anaxagoras' B17 and is said by him to evidence the direct influence of Melissus.[37] Certainly, in B8 we find ὀρθῶς repeatedly used in relation to sense experience (ὀρθῶς ὁρῶμεν καὶ ἀκούομεν, ὀρθῶς ὁρᾶν, ὀρθῶς ἑωρῶμεν) and opinion (ὀρθῶς δοκεῖ). For Thomas, the evidence of Herodotus, who seems to have a particular fondness for talk of correctness, suggests a wide-ranging set of intellectual enquiries centred around the discussion of correctness, of which the famous Sophistic debate about the correctness of names was only a part. One would not have to agree with Thomas that 'correctness was the catch-phrase of a generation, overused as catch-phrases are, and a generation of prose writers who belonged mainly, perhaps, to the intellectual world of East Greece, arching over the *physiologoi* like Melissos, doctors and "sophists"' to think that the emphasis on correctness is at least evidence of intellectuals' broad familiarity with works and arguments we might classify as belonging to distinct disciplines.[38]

The mention of Melissus by name in *On the Nature of the Human Being* is worth considering in detail, as it is highly suggestive of the

[37] Jouanna 1975: 231.   [38] Thomas 2000: 233.

original context of his work and of the nature of the intellectual life of the period.

He who is accustomed to hear speakers discuss the nature of man beyond its relations to medicine will not find the present account of any interest. For I do not say at all that a man is air, or fire, or water, or earth, or anything else that is not an obvious constituent of a man; such accounts I leave to those that care to give them. Those, however, who give them have not in my opinion correct knowledge (δοκέουσι μέντοι μοι οὐκ ὀρθῶς γινώσκειν οἱ ταῦτα λέγοντες). For while adopting the same idea they do not give the same account. Though they add the same appendix to their idea – saying that 'what is' is a unity, and that this is both unity and the all – yet they are not agreed as to its name. One of them asserts that this one and the all is air, another calls it fire, another, water, and another, earth; while each appends to his own account evidence and proofs that amount to nothing. The fact that, while adopting the same idea, they do not give the same account, shows that their knowledge too is at fault. The best way to realise this is to be present at their debates. Given the same debaters and the same audience, the same man never wins in the discussion three times in succession, but now one is victor, now another, now he who happens to have the most glib tongue in the face of the crowd. Yet it is right that a man who claims correct knowledge about the facts should maintain his own argument victorious always, if his knowledge be knowledge of reality and if he set it forth correctly. But in my opinion such men by their lack of understanding overthrow themselves in the words of their very discussions, and establish the theory of Melissus (καίτοι δίκαιόν ἐστι τὸν φάντα ὀρθῶς γινώσκειν ἀμφὶ τῶν πρηγμάτων παρέχειν αἰεὶ ἐπικρατέοντα τὸν λόγον τὸν ἑωυτοῦ, εἴπερ ἐόντα γινώσκει καὶ ὀρθῶς ἀποφαίνεται. ἀλλ᾽ ἐμοί γε δοκέουσιν οἱ τοιοῦτοι ἄνθρωποι αὐτοὶ ἑωυτοὺς καταβάλλειν ἐν τοῖσιν ὀνόμασι τῶν λόγων αὐτῶν ὑπὸ ἀσυνεσίης, τὸν δὲ Μελίσσου λόγον ὀρθοῦν). (Text and trans. W. H. S. Jones)

This fascinating passage raises two primary questions for our immediate purposes: (1) What is the nature of the error that the author ascribes to the monistic theorisers who have conflated the enquiry into medicine with that into natural philosophy, and (2) How do they, despite themselves, 'establish the theory of Melissus'?

A prominent proposed solution to these two questions has been offered by Jacques Jouanna, closely followed by James Longrigg.[39] Their solution is to suggest that Diogenes of Apollonia is to be taken as the primary representative of the targeted monistic theorisers, on the basis of strong similarities between the arguments found in *On the Nature of the Human Being* and Diogenes' fragments, particularly his B2. A quick comparison between this fragment and the

[39] Jouanna 1965 and Longrigg 1993: 85–90.

paragraph that follows the Hippocratic passage quoted above suggests this connection is clear.

My view, in general, is that all existing things are altered from the same thing and are the same thing. And this is manifest: for if the things presently existing in this world order: earth, air, fire, and the rest, which plainly exist in this world order, if any of these was different the one from the other, being other in its own nature and not the same as it changed often and altered, in no way would it have been able to mix with another, neither would benefit nor harm <come to one from the other> . . . (Trans. D. Graham)

But I hold that if man were a unity he would never feel pain, as there would be nothing from which a unity could suffer pain. And even if he were to suffer, the cure too would have to be one. But as a matter of fact cures are many. For in the body are many constituents, which, by heating, by cooling, by drying or by wetting one another contrary to nature, engender diseases. (Chapter 2, trans. W. H. S. Jones)

The views canvassed in these two passages are striking in their diametrical opposition. Diogenes insists that harm would be impossible if there were a plurality, the Hippocratic author counters that were there a unity there would be nothing, by whose agency (ὑφ' ὅτου), pain <or benefit> could be caused. The form of the arguments, hypothetical and counterfactual, is also similar.[40]

Accepting a prominent place for Diogenes suggests, to Jouanna and Longrigg, an ingenious strategy at work in *On the Nature of the Human Being* that answers the second question posed above. The Hippocratic author is exploiting a Melissan argument to target the monistic ontology of Diogenes. Thus the author evidences the very point he makes in the first chapter of his work: the monists overturn themselves. This takes on a particular sting if you agree with Jouanna and Longrigg that Diogenes responded to Melissus and thus that *De Natura Hominis* is suggesting that Diogenes utterly fails to escape an argument that he himself must have thought he had.[41] What is the Melissan argument that is established and thereby undermines Diogenes? Jouanna and Longrigg take the discussion of pain and anguish to point towards Melissus'

---

[40] Longrigg (1993: 87) stresses this point, but perhaps too strongly. Counterfactual arguments using conditionals are familiar from the fragments of many Presocratics (Melissus chief among them).
[41] Jouanna 1965: 320ff and Longrigg 1993: 89.

arguments targeting alteration. Certainly, as we shall see, the conceptions of pain evident in all three make for a crucial and illuminating connection.[42]

I suggest that the account sketched above is largely along the right lines, but with a few needed modifications that provide for a fuller accounting of the evidence. It is certainly correct that the verbal echoes catalogued by Jouanna between the Hippocratic work and Diogenes' fragments are too similar to dismiss; however, it does not follow from this that other targets were not also intended. A larger concern is the argument by which Melissus' thesis is supposed to have been established.[43] It is far from clear from the text itself that a commitment to the alteration of whatever single and unified entity the monists hypothesise is what is at stake. This deflates the close, and nearly exclusive, connection with Diogenes the above account suggests. Rather it is a contradiction *inherent* to their positions (ἐν τοῖσιν ὀνόμασι τῶν λόγων αὐτῶν) that the Hippocratic author focuses on. On this basis, it makes more sense to turn to Melissus' B8, the very place where the language of correctness (the repeated use of ὀρθῶς connecting with the author's ὀρθοῦν) is prominent, and, crucially, where he identifies a conflict to be found within the method of his pluralist opponents.

As I will suggest in the reading of B8, I take the fragment to be truly supplemental to the other fragments and to reinforce the unity and uniqueness of what-is by identifying a weakness in the accounts of pluralists' positions. This weakness is the fundamental inconsistency of relying on sense experience as a philosophical tool for determining what is real in the world. Melissus argues:

> For if there is earth, water, air, fire, iron and gold, and one thing living and another dead, and black and white, and all the things people say are real – if indeed there are these things, and we see and hear correctly, each of these must be just as it first seemed to us, and they cannot change or become different in quality.

The point he is trying to make is that the pluralist position is fundamentally unstable because the testimony of the senses, the

---

[42] Though, as I shall maintain, Melissus' conception is far closer to that found in *On the Nature of the Human Being* than that in Diogenes.

[43] ὀρθοῦν has connotations of being set back up on one's feet in sport and martial contexts. Jouanna helpfully gives *Iliad* XXIII.695 as a parallel.

very thing that drives a commitment to pluralism, is unstable. I argue for this interpretation in detail in the section on B8; if the relevant Melissan thesis does turn on the instability of one's opponents' positions, it makes a good deal of sense of how the Hippocratic author leads into his mention of Melissus. Recall the following criticism: 'Yet it is right that a man who claims correct knowledge about the facts should maintain his own argument victorious always (αἰεί), if his knowledge be knowledge of reality and if he set it forth correctly.' We find the very same point applied *mutatis mutandis*. Melissus' pluralist thinks that sense experience serves as a guide to what is, while also accepting that it tells us that things change and become in no way like they were – the stability necessary to take the evidence of the senses seriously is entirely absent. The Hippocratic's monist faces an analogous problem: his account of whatever he calls the unity, if posited along the right lines, should permanently stand up to scrutiny and remain stable, but the monists' own debates belie this. In short, both Melissus and the Hippocratic author are identifying a contradiction inherent to their opponents' positions, i.e. a fundamental instability that needs no external disproof, but falls apart in its own terms. The upshot of such an account is that the ingenuity identified by Jouanna and Longrigg survives; the Hippocratic author is exploiting a monist's argument, intended to see off pluralists, against other monists. Yet we also make better sense of the language of correctness that closely connects this first chapter of *On the Nature of the Human Being* with Melissus' B8.

What this intriguing passage from the Hippocratic corpus suggests, whether one accepts my reading of the argument or not, is a close connection between natural philosophy and medicine, ironically coming in the very passage where the author is decrying the conflation of these two disciplines.

What, then, does this suggest about Melissus and about how we are to go about making sense of his fragments? At a minimum, I propose that we must venture beyond the traditional canon of early Greek philosophers/scientists in order to gain the best perspective on him and the nature of his intellectual project. Herodotus, Hecateaus, and Hippocratics will all find a place in the following pages.

Synoptic Overview

Title and Bɪ

In this first section, I argue for the authenticity of the title (Περὶ φύσεως ἢ περὶ τοῦ ὄντος, *On Nature, or On What-is*) ascribed to Melissus' work by Simplicius in his commentary on Aristotle's *Physics*. It is worth noting in passing here that *all* of our fragments of Melissus come from Simplicius (eight from the *Physics* commentary, two from his *De caelo* commentary). This unusual situation makes possible the reconstruction I offer, as we benefit from Simplicius' probable access to the text of Melissus and his care to distinguish verbatim quotation from paraphrase and exegesis.[44]

Our evidence for fifth-century titles of philosophical works is quite weak. For example, the title Περὶ φύσεως is routinely ascribed to the works of many Presocratic philosophers and is likely to be a generic feature of the doxographical tradition used to categorise early works of natural philosophy.[45] Yet in Melissus' case, as we shall see, the evidence for authenticity is strong.

I also make a case for the inclusion of an introductory rhetorical question,[46] which I call **Q**, found in a paraphrase of Melissus' treatise in Simplicius. I am not the first to make such an argument (Reale, Vitali, and Barnes all accept **Q** as at least indicative of something Melissus' treatise did contain), but I attempt to illustrate how well the sentence fits between the title and introductory *sphragis* and the first verbatim fragment (Bɪ), as well as to dissolve some arguments for discarding it.

For Bɪ, I offer a new text incorporating a manuscript reading (εἰ τύχοι νῦν) which I argue has better standing than what is presented in DK (Diels-Kranz) and is far more likely to be correct in view of Melissus' typical use of counterfactuals in making arguments. The reading offered does require the emendation of ἦν to the participle

---

[44] For an assessment of Simplicius' exegetical method and how his quotations of Presocratic fragments fit in with it, see Baltussen 2008: chapter 2.

[45] For example, Galen (*de elem. Sec. Hipp* ɪ 9, ɪ 487 Kühn) who indiscriminately attributes the title 'Περὶ φύσεως' to all the ancients (παλαιῶν ἅπαντα) including Melissus, Parmenides, Empedocles, Alcmaeon, Gorgias, and Prodicus.

[46] εἰ μὲν μηδὲν ἔστι, περὶ τούτου τί ἂν λέγοιτο ὡς ὄντος τινός;

ἐόν. However, it also avoids a use of τοίνυν completely out of character with its uniform role elsewhere in the fragments.

The text I offer also has the benefit of reading Melissus as giving an interesting reason why something cannot come-to-be from nothing. Parallel to Parmenides' appeal to the Principle of Sufficient Reason in B8.9–10, where he asks what could have led something to come about earlier rather than later, Melissus poses something like a thought experiment. If what-is were now nothing, he concludes that there could be no future coming-to-be.

B2 and B3

In these two fragments, Melissus moves from sempiternity to spatial infinity, and it is here that the basis of Aristotle's indictment against him is said to be found. Most commentators accept, with varying attributions of guilt, Aristotle's claim that Melissus commits an elementary logical fallacy by illicitly denying the antecedent in the following syllogism: if what-is came-to-be, what-is has a beginning and end; but what-is did not come to be, therefore what-is has no beginning and end.

I consider the range of interpretations Melissus' argument and Aristotle's subsequent criticism have received. The interpretation I offer builds on a number of important suggestions that have been made in the literature. First, I accept, with Cherniss and Verdenius, that Melissus' view of generation is absolutely critical if we are to make sense of the argument, but I disagree that this is because he has a peculiar *definition* of generation and that all B2 does is to explicate this understanding. Secondly, I proceed from David Sedley's important suggestion that the probable default understanding of the extent of the world for an Ionian natural philosopher like Melissus would be that it is unlimited or boundless. Certainly, we see such a view held by the likes of Anaximander and Anaxagoras. This goes a long way towards grasping just what Melissus aimed his argument to accomplish and how we ought to judge its success or failure.

The third string of my argument incorporates Stephen Makin's interesting work on indifference reasoning in the Presocratics, and in Melissus in particular. With these pieces in place, I adopt a hybrid account whereby Melissus holds that what-is is spatially infinite because it is not generated. This is *not* the result of his definition of generation; if it were merely this, all we would accomplish would be to shift the absurdity from the logic of Melissus' argument to his understanding of generation. Rather I suggest that, given the circumstances Melissus is considering, *only* a process of generation could explain why a spatial limit would occur in one spot rather than another. Thus there is, on my account, a lurking *ou mallon* argument hidden within his argument. I leave it up to the reader to decide whether Melissus is now absolved of Aristotle's criticism, but I think it should be clear that Melissus is the author of a far subtler argument than Aristotle allows him.

B4, B5, and B6

These three fragments, with the subsequent support of B9 and a lost, but certainly original, argument for homogeneity, constitute Melissus' argument for the 'Eleatic One'. I mean by this the view, dominant from antiquity onwards, that the Eleatics were monists or held that everything is one. As I have stressed, I do not assume any particular view on the matter in the course of my interpretation. It is clear enough, however, that Melissus does hold the view that what-is is one in a numerical sense (there is only one thing, not just, say, that there is only one *kind* of thing). My interpretation and reconstruction of his argument to this effect are novel. I place B5 prior to B4 and delete from B6 an insertion that is widely accepted. In some ways this section is likely to be the most controversial I offer. It requires the addition of transitional elements placed in angle brackets and incorporates both temporal and spatial infinity and not simply the latter. Thus, on my account, the Eleatic One has both a temporal and a spatial component. This twofold unity proves a vital development in countering alterations and rearrangements in B7, as such changes imply, for Melissus, successive iterations in time and not merely new arrangements in space.

Readers can make up their minds after they have considered the section; but here I would like to offer what I take to be some of the virtues of the account I present. First the *demonstrandum*/argument/restatement of *demonstrandum* model obviously apparent in

Melissan demonstrations is maintained and the insertion of ἄπειρον in B6 is shown to be unnecessary: so the reconstruction, despite its novelty, does make an attempt at conservatism.

The proposed reconstruction also has the benefit of setting out the final, fundamental argument around which the remainder of the fragments and arguments will orbit like satellites (I have tried to make this apparent in Appendix 3). The attributes of homogeneity and bodilessness are established jointly on the basis of monism, and B7, B10, and B8 follow naturally. Thus Melissus' chain of arguments looks like a tree: a linear trunk culminating in the Eleatic One, followed by the rich array of arguments found in B7 and B8 branching out and forming the canopy.

B9 and Homogeneity

That what-is is numerically one (spatially and temporally) grounds the arguments both for bodilessness and for homogeneity. Both are also difficult to reconstruct: the former (B9) is a compilation of two separate quotations cobbled together in DK, while the latter is not extant as a verbatim quotation and is apparent only in the paraphrase found in the *MXG*. And both are vital for the arguments that come in B7. On the proposed reconstruction, the arguments leading up to this fragment work to establish what Melissus means by 'the One'. It is crucial that it is understood to be both unique and a unity, and the arguments in B7 targeting change (including alteration, rearrangement, and motion) are best construed as turning on its prior identification as such. Thus rearrangement, for example, is eliminated not only because homogeneity would be violated but also because it requires the coming-to-be of a new iteration of what-is, illicitly necessitating plurality.

B9 and the reconstruction offered of the argument for homogeneity work to establish the 'strong' sense of uniqueness and unity that Melissus attributes to what-is. By 'strong' I mean that both these predicates apply not only synchronically but also diachronically.

In this section, B10 and its interest in division are also considered. In the reconstruction of the text, I suggest that this fragment naturally follows on from B7 and should, therefore, be placed prior to B8.

B7

This fragment is the longest extant, and the place where the purported positive elements of Melissus' reputation reside. We find clear arguments targeting alteration, rearrangement, pain and anguish and, most famously, motion. In some ways it bears a close resemblance with Parmenides' B8, where a list of the attributes of what-is is also considered. The differences, however, as I have intimated already, are important. The premises of Melissus' arguments, though occasionally obscure in their aims on first inspection (e.g. what pain and anguish are meant to signify), are far easier to identify than in Parmenides. Once it is made clear that Melissus means the Eleatic One to encompass unity and uniqueness, and not simply the latter, the emphasis on homogeneity and the threat alteration etc. pose to it is easily explained. This point is the upshot of treating the argument for the Eleatic One as not exhausted by B4, B5, and B6 but bolstered by B9 and the lost argument for homogeneity. These latter two make it plain that internal differentiation (both parthood and heterogeneity) is also eliminated.

Pain and anguish and what Melissus intends to eliminate by targeting them have often been treated as obscure.[47] Two main points emerge from the account I present. One is that it makes good sense to think that Melissus (in some ways reflecting both Xenophanes and Parmenides) considered reality to be divine and alive, and thus thought it illicit to attribute to it deficient anthropomorphic attributes like corporeality and the capacity to experience pain and anguish. Such a view explicates Melissus' motivation for what may seem to be an irrelevant argument. Second the discussion of pain and grief, when considered alongside a relevant passage from the Hippocratic text *On the Nature of the Human Being*, suggests it is not entirely distinct from the argument against alteration and rearrangement offered immediately prior in B7. If a physiological model along Hippocratic lines is indeed what Melisssus has in mind, pain and anguish can be seen to threaten the One by threatening both homogeneity and uniqueness. This makes its place in B7 not only relevant but vital for Melissus' programme.

---

[47] Barnes (1982: 216–17) canvasses some of the possibilities.

Melissus' argument targeting motion has a claim to be his most influential. It is plausible, though not absolutely certain, that it is this argument which first equates void with what-is-not and makes it a precondition for motion; both claims, for example, are fundamental to the atomist physical system. While Parmenides certainly attempted to eliminate motion (at B8.26, even if one were to concede with some commentators that he fails to make motion fully distinct from change in general), it has become a common, perhaps dominant, position that he does not do so by an appeal to the concept of the void.[48] In keeping with my general methodology, I do not assume any particular interpretation of Parmenides.[49] What is obvious, in any case, is that Melissus' argument is the first instance where such an argument is *incontestably* present.

My interpretation of the argument follows an important reading offered by David Sedley denying that Melissus had in mind motion *into* an external void outside of what-is.[50] This, the previous consensus, fails to appreciate that Melissus had already, by B7, eliminated any notion of *anything* outside of what-is. I take this line of thought one step further by arguing that it is not merely external void that is irrelevant but internal *pockets* of void as well. Melissus' concern is not with bits of what-is moving into empty spaces composed of what-is-not, but with a homogeneous mixture of what-is with void that would allow for springiness or compression. Such a reading takes into account that Melissus, at the start of B7, unambiguously states that homogeneity has been previously demonstrated[51] and thus that a heterogeneous composition of what-is with pockets of void would hardly be worth targeting.

The argument against motion also reveals something crucial about Melissus' strategy in B7. Strictly speaking, this argument, like the three previous ones (targeting alteration, rearrangement,

---

[48] Malcolm (1991) provides a summary of the spectrum of positions. Kirk and Stokes (1960) were the first to argue for this position.

[49] I do think, however, there is about equal support for the void and non-void interpretations. While motion is eliminated on the basis of the banishment of coming-to-be and perishing (B8.26–8) and void is not explicitly mentioned, it is easy enough to imagine that B8.30–1, which claims that what-is is held by necessity in the bonds of a limit, implies that it has no room to move, i.e. that there is no void.

[50] Sedley 1982: 178.

[51] Of course, we lack the verbatim fragment to this effect. But it is highly likely it is simply lost, given the evidence of the *MXG* and Melissus' recapitulation in B7.

and pain and anguish), adds no new premises or assumptions not already made. The species of change he banishes are eliminated because they violate attributes already demonstrated (homogeneity and uniqueness being the most prominent). What he is doing, then, is fleshing out what his characterisation of the Eleatic One amounts to.

B8

B8 is the final fragment in my reconstruction. B9 has been moved to follow B6 and the short B10 I take to follow the discussion of motion in B7. This fragment is unique insofar as it is explicitly supplemental. Melissus claims that the greatest σημεῖον (proof) that what-is is one has already been made and that B8 will constitute a further attempt to prove this thesis. The argument is thoroughly Eleatic in character insofar as it deliberately trades on the tension between the results of *a priori* arguments and those of sense experience. Quite how the tension works in the fragment is not as easy to determine as some commentators have assumed. A typical assumption is that Melissus is highlighting the fact that sense experience suggests change is real while B7 has firmly argued that it is not. The worry about finding the contradiction to be reliant on what has been proved in B7 is that the supplemental status of B8 is then compromised and its argumentative value diminished. I suggest that the contradiction is generated by the nature of sense-experience itself: Melissus recommends that we dismiss its testimony because its results are inherently unstable and thus useless for grasping the true nature of what-is. Melissus, on such a reading, has a real and independent argument for targeting sense-experience that does not rely on any assent to the claims of B7. On such an account, B8 delivers what its programmatic remarks promise.

RECONSTRUCTION AND COMMENTARY

PREFATORY MATERIAL

The Authenticity of the Title

Melissus' treatise is one of the earliest instances in Greek philosophy where we have good evidence for a title original to a treatise. At *In Phys.* 70.16–17, Simplicius reports that Melissus entitled his treatise Περὶ φύσεως ἤ περὶ τοῦ ὄντος (*On Nature or On What-is*).[1] Scholars have been generally quite sceptical of titles attributed to Presocratic (particularly Pre-Sophistic) treatises.[2] Certainly Περὶ φύσεως is so widely attributed by later authors to early philosophical works that it appears to be a generic description and not an indication of a genuine title given to a treatise by its creator.

In the case of Melissus too we might worry about the distorting effects of the later tradition; however, it seems safe to say that at least some fifth-century treatises *did* have titles. Despite scholarly wavering on this point,[3] it makes good sense that there would be some mechanism in place to refer to a work and, in particular, differentiate between multiple works of a single author.[4] Although Melissus himself apparently composed only a single work, two pieces of evidence point strongly in favour of the reported title's authenticity.[5] First the title reported by Simplicius is *not* the usual

---

[1] ὁ Μέλισσος καὶ τὴν ἐπιγραφὴν οὕτως ἐποιήσατο τοῦ συγγράμματος Περὶ φύσεως ἤ περὶ τοῦ ὄντος. Cf. *In De Caelo* 557.10ff.

[2] Schmalzriedt 1970. He suggests Protagoras' *Aletheia* as a potential candidate for the first titled prose work.

   See Huby 1973: 206–8, for a useful reply. See too Untersteiner 1955: CCXLII–CCL for a discussion of Xenophanes' case. Heidel (1943: 268) expresses the dominant note of scepticism.

[3] See Pendrick 2002: 32–3.

[4] The *Iliad* and the *Odyssey* are the most obvious examples. West (1995: 217 n.43) suggests that the title of the *Iliad* might be a product of its composition at Ilios and its early association with that city. If this is the case, the title would have been attached to the poem very early in its life.

[5] Diogenes Laertius, our best source for evidence about the range of a philosopher's output, is not specific about Melissus. However, his summary of Melissus' output could easily derive from a single treatise. Simplicius knows of only one title.

33

Περὶ φύσεως, being distinguished by the addition of ἢ περὶ τοῦ ὄντος. This suggests that Melissus' treatise has not been the victim of the retrojection of a generic title.

We might wonder though about the disjunctive nature of the title. Should we think Melissus' title is a deliberate unity in the manner of Stanley Kubrick's *Dr. Strangelove or: How I Learned to Stop Worrying and Love the Bomb* or F. W. Farrar's *Eric or, Little by Little*? Alternatively, was the treatise sometimes known as Περὶ φύσεως and at other times Περὶ τοῦ ὄντος? There is evidence that disjunctive titles of the kind attributed to Melissus date back at least to the fifth century. Protagoras' famous work, for instance, asserting that man is the measure of all things may have been known as Ἀλήθεια ἢ Καταβάλλοντες.[6] The second, strongest piece of evidence in favour of the acceptance of Melissus' title in the *Strangelove* camp is the likelihood that the title of Gorgias' treatise, Περὶ τοῦ μὴ ὄντος ἢ περὶ φύσεως, was a deliberate parody of the title of Melissus' work.[7] These points have already been made by a number of scholars and I concur with their conclusion that we are on firm ground in attributing the title Περὶ φύσεως ἢ περὶ τοῦ ὄντος to Melissus himself.[8] However, I suggest that we write <ἐ>όντος: Melissus would have written the Ionic form, as we can confirm from the use of τὸ ἐόν in B7. The Atticisation of Ionic forms is common in the scribal tradition. I shall revert to the Ionic form throughout this book.

Sphragis

The nature of Melissus' fragments makes the interpretation of the beginning of his treatise uniquely delicate. The work is deductive in structure; the conclusion of one argument acts as a premise for

[6] See Schmalzriedt 1970: 64–72 and Zeller 1919: 1354 n.2. Catherine Rowett (Osborne 1987: 27) has made the suggestion that the two titles associated with Empedocles in the doxography, Περὶ φύσεως and Καθαρμοί, may be two halves of a double title, much like that attributed to Melissus. The evidence is inconclusive, however, and unfortunately does not eliminate the possibility that the titles associated with Protagoras and Empedocles were alternatives used at different times and not part of a deliberately disjunctive title.

[7] Palmer 2009: 218–20.

[8] Cf. Palmer 2009: 205 n.25, Sedley 1999: 125, and Reale 1970: 22–4. See Huby 1973: 208 for a defence of Gorgias' (and, presumably, *ex hypothesi* Melissus') title.

the next argument. It is because of this that the strength of the first argument is of particular importance. If it proves to be vulnerable, the whole of Melissus' chain of deductions would then be in jeopardy.[9]

With this in mind, we may turn to what is thought to be the first extant fragment. Simplicius quotes B1 at *In Phys.* 162.24ff as Melissus' rejection of the generability of what-is, in order to parallel Parmenides' similar denial of generation at B8, 6–10.[10] What Simplicius does not make explicit, however, when quoting this fragment is where it occurred within Melissus' treatise.[11] Two surviving paraphrases of Melissus' treatise attest the placing of this fragment at or near its beginning. However, crucial differences between the two paraphrases necessitate close consideration. These discrepancies pose two challenges that must be tackled: (1) Did DK B1 open Melissus' treatise? and (2) Does the fragment reflect the whole of Melissus' argument against the generation of what-is?

Before we turn to a detailed study of the two paraphrases of Melissus' arguments, it is worth asking whether his treatise originally contained any prefatory material immediately following the title. We know, of course, that Melissus' 'Eleatic' predecessor Parmenides provided a 32-line proem to his poem. Should we imagine that Melissus' treatise contained something comparable? There is no trace of any such introductory material in our sources. Yet the unlikelihood of an extended preliminary section at the head of the work does not rule out the possibility of a brief introduction in which Melissus introduced himself and his subject matter.

---

[9] This is recognised by Aristotle at *Physics* 186a8–16. Melissus, according to Aristotle, makes unsound assumptions from which invalid arguments are raised. Aristotle's thinking seems to be that if he can demonstrate that Melissus makes an invalid move from 'no beginning in time' to 'no beginning in space' the whole of Melissus' treatise crumbles. See also *De Generatione et Corruptione* 325a13–23, where I take it, as I have discussed above, that Melissus is among those who are said to ignore perception and follow arguments which lead to absurd, even insane, conclusions. For a proper emphasis on the deductive nature of Melissus' treatise, see Sedley 1999: 125.

[10] Simplicius, in the lines that immediately follow, also attributes the principle that nothing comes-to-be from nothing to Anaxagoras, citing it as an ἀξίωμα.

[11] Simplicius quotes B1 in a wide-ranging discussion of coming-to-be along with the views of Parmenides and Anaxagoras. This is one possible reason why an indication of B1's place in Melissus' treatise is omitted.

35

A challenge one might raise to the possibility that Melissus' treatise contained prefatory remarks before B1 is that that fragment starts with an asyndeton. If there are no particles connecting back to a previous sentence, it might seem a reasonable assumption to make that B1 stood at the beginning of the treatise.[12] I will dissolve the pertinence of this objection in due course.

The inclusion of a *sphragis* naming or describing the author of the work is likely to have been a standard practice in the literature of the fifth-century Greek world in both poetry and prose.[13] For the former, we find evidence of *sphragides* in Hesiod's *Theogony* (22–34), the Theognidean corpus (18–22), and the Homeric *Hymn to Apollo* (165–72). In prose we may look to Hecataeus of Miletus, an Ionian prose writer as Melissus was, and a predecessor of Herodotus. Although his work survives only fragmentarily, we are fortunate enough to have what is likely to be the very beginning of his book:[14]

Ἑκαταῖος Μιλήσιος ὧδε μυθεῖται· τάδε γράφω, ὥς μοι δοκεῖ ἀληθέα εἶναι· οἱ γὰρ Ἑλλήνων λόγοι πολλοί τε καὶ γελοῖοι, ὡς ἐμοὶ φαίνονται, εἰσίν.[15]

Hecataeus of Miletus says as follows: I write these things as they seem to me to be true. For the stories of the Greeks are many and absurd, as they seem to me.

Besides naming himself, Hecataeus offers his audience both a claim of truth (ἀληθέα) for his work and a statement of his intention to supplant the stories circulating in the Greek world that he considers fanciful (γελοῖοι). What Hecataeus provides, then, is a short yet highly revealing indication of his literary and historical intentions.

Herodotus, whose prose is probably our closest extant linguistic parallel, temporally and geographically, for Melissus, closely follows Hecataeus' prefatory model. The extent of Herodotus' proem is the subject of some dispute. Several commentators, for example, have argued that the historian's prefatory remarks extend to as far

---

[12] Palmer (2009: 209 n.31) makes this point.
[13] See, in particular, Porciani 1997 and Fehling 1975: 61–75.
[14] Quite what Hecataeus is trying to achieve with this statement has been subject to considerable debate. However, the fact that it opened his work is widely accepted. For two recent interpretations, see Bertelli 2001: 80–4 and Fowler 2001: 101–3.
[15] I understand the preface to encompass the whole of the quoted material and not simply the first sentence. This is suggested by the content.

as the end of 1.5.[16] Precisely what Herodotus aims to achieve in his preface is less important for our purposes than the following two points of interest: (1) Whatever Herodotus' intentions for his proem were, it clearly plays *some* integral part in his work. (2) Whether the proem extends to the end of chapter 5 or merely consists of Herodotus' first sentence, the following sentence in each case is asyndetic.

> Herodotus' second sentence: Περσέων μέν νυν οἱ λόγιοι Φοίνικας αἰτίους φασὶ γενέσθαι τῆς διαφορῆς.
> The beginning of 1.6: Κροῖσος ἦν Λυδὸς μὲν γένος

Neither has a particle directly connecting it with the previous sentence. This as an indication that the asyndeton of B1 is no guarantee of its place at the very start of Melissus' treatise. I will soon argue that B1 is incomplete, i.e. that it originally stood as a part of a longer sentence in which a connecting particle *did* feature. My point here is only the narrow claim that the lack of a connecting particle is unhelpful for our purposes.

A final example of a *sphragis*, this time philosophical, comes from Alcmaeon:

> Ἀλκμαίων Κροτωνιήτης τάδε ἔλεξε Πειρίθου υἱὸς Βροτίνωι καὶ Λέοντι καὶ Βαθύλλωι· περὶ τῶν ἀφανέων, περὶ τῶν θνητῶν σαφήνειαν μὲν θεοὶ ἔχοντι, ὡς δὲ ἀνθρώποις τεκμαίρεσθαι

The text here is somewhat difficult to construe; however, the structure of the sentence, including the provision of the author's name and city coupled with a verb of saying, is very much in line with what we saw in the Hecataeus fragment.[17]

Let me review what I have thus far concluded. (1) Prefaces appear to be a standard feature of fifth-century Greek prose treatises. (2) The asyndeton of B1 is no obstacle to the possibility of

---

[16] First suggested in Jacoby 1913: 283–5. See also Węcowski 2004: 143–64.
[17] This should not be surprising if we remember that the distinctions we take for granted in intellectual life were certainly less fine-grained in the fifth century. Thomas (2000: 188–90) has argued persuasively that Herodotus' use of deductive reasoning, for example, would have seemed little different to his audience than similar types of reasoning found in Melissus and the medical writers. This claim serves to reinforce her more general thesis that a shared intellectual and cultural milieu encouraged a wide spectrum of enquiries that contemporaries saw as interconnected.

a preface in Melissus' treatise. For these reasons, I tentatively propose the following reconstruction:

<Μέλισσος Σάμιος τάδε λέγει περὶ φύσεως ἢ περὶ τοῦ ἐόντος.>

Melissus of Samos says the following about nature or what-is.

I follow the standard practice here of providing the name of the author and his city. I omit the name of Melissus' father, said by Diogenes Laertius to be Ithaegenes, because Alcmaeon's inclusion of his father's name may be atypical, to judge from the *sphragides* of Hecataeus and Herodotus.[18]

Paraphrases: Simplicius and the *MXG*

Determining the relative reliability of the two major extant paraphrases of Melissus' treatise has occupied scholars for over a century. Beginning at *In Phys.* 103.13ff, Simplicius provides a detailed sketch of Melissus' chain of deductions. These arguments are offered by the commentator as evidence for Aristotle's dismissive appraisal of Melissus as φορτικός (crude) at *Physics* 186a4–13. Simplicius' presentation of Melissus' thought is incomplete: for example, B9 on the bodilessness of what-is is absent. However, Simplicius makes no promise of completeness and specifically remarks at the conclusion of his sketch (104. 16–17) that he has supplied only enough of Melissus' treatise to illuminate Aristotle's remarks. What is striking is that, despite its admittedly selective nature, the paraphrase is itself unusually lengthy and detailed. Nowhere else in Simplicius' work do we find a parallel presentation of a Presocratic's treatise. It is true that we find extensive quotations from ancient philosophers there. For example, there is significant space devoted to the fragments of Parmenides, Anaxagoras, and Diogenes of Apollonia in Simplicius' works. However, the provision of a nearly complete paraphrase of a philosophical treatise is *not* a standard Simplician

---

[18] Cf. the beginning of Thucydides, where Athens is mentioned but not his father. See also Porciani (1997: 3–78) who argues that proems were ultimately epistolary in character and meant to foster long-distance intellectual communication at the expense of local concerns. If this is correct, there would be a good reason to omit biographical details relevant only to a local audience.

exegetical tool. We can do no more than speculate about the reasons that motivated Simplicius to provide such a unique treatment of Melissus' treatise. Yet adequately representing the intricate deductive structure of Melissus' work seems, at least speculatively, a likely motive. What makes Simplicius' paraphrase even more striking is that the commentator provides verbatim fragments from Melissus just a few pages later.

Indeed the paraphrase of Melissus' chain of deductions provided by Simplicius is so extraordinary in both length and detail that, until the pioneering work of Pabst in the late nineteenth century, it was thought not to be a paraphrase but rather a selection of verbatim quotations.[19] Pabst's study of Simplicius' paraphrase noted certain elements that appear to be interpretations rather than quotations.[20]

The scholarly estimation of the value of Simplicius' paraphrase has been in decline since Pabst's work with the notable exception of the paraphrase's first sentence.[21] Here Simplicius indicates that Melissus' initial starting-point (that something *is*) is demonstrated explicitly.[22] On this account B1 does *not* open Melissus' treatise. Let us look to the beginning of the paraphrase:

νῦν δὲ τὸν Μελίσσου λόγον ἴδωμεν, πρὸς ὃν πρότερον ὑπαντᾷ. τοῖς γὰρ τῶν φυσικῶν ἀξιώμασι χρησάμενος ὁ Μέλισσος περὶ γενέσεως καὶ φθορᾶς ἄρχεται τοῦ συγγράμματος οὕτως. '**Εἰ μὲν μηδὲν ἔστι, περὶ τούτου τί ἂν λέγοιτο ὡς ὄντος τινός;** εἰ δέ τι ἐστίν ...'

Let us now look at the argument of Melissus, which he [i.e. Aristotle] earlier opposed. For Melissus, using the axioms of the natural philosophers concerning coming to be and passing away, began his treatise thus: if it is nothing, what could be said about it as if it were something, but if it is something ...

Many interpreters have argued for the inclusion of the above sentence (in bold and henceforth referred to as **Q**)[23] in the

---

[19] See, for example, Gomperz 1906: 185–6. The paraphrase was generally numbered as the first five fragments.

[20] Pabst 1889.

[21] For the *communis opinio*, see Kirk, Raven, and Schofield 1983 (KRS): 392 n.1.

[22] Loenen (1959: 125–32) offers a sustained argument that 'something is' is Melissus' fundamental starting-point. See also Reale 1970: 24 n.97, and Merrill 1998: 29.

[23] Reale (1970) calls the sentence in bold Bo.

collection of verbatim quotations from Melissus.[24] It is certainly a very tempting hypothesis. If it is genuinely Melissan, we are left not with the mere assertion that something exists, but with something more robust. It does also, as Burnet notes, seem 'thoroughly Eleatic in character'.[25] In addition, we have Simplicius' suggestive claim that Melissus began his treatise (σύγγραμμα) on generation and destruction with the sentence in bold. It is highly plausible that Simplicius' quotations of Presocratic thinkers are taken from a set of texts (though not necessarily those in their original form) he had in his possession. We can be reasonably confident in this conclusion because reference to the location of a quotation within a thinker's text is a feature of Simplicius' commentaries. A look at his account of Anaxagoras' work bears this out. At *In Phys.* 155.26ff Simplicius refers not only to the first book of Anaxagoras' treatise but also to this book's very beginning: 'δηλοῖ διὰ τοῦ πρώτου τῶν Φυσικῶν λέγων ἀπ' ἀρχῆς ... κτλ'.[26] A reference to the place that a quotation originally occupied within an author's original text is the closest hallmark of authenticity that we are likely to encounter in an ancient commentator.[27]

If we are confident of Simplicius' scruples and of the fact that he had a reliable source in front of him, should we then embrace **Q** as genuine? Reale thinks that Simplicius' introduction (ἄρχεται τοῦ συγγράμματος οὕτως) is unmistakable proof of authenticity.[28] I agree that it is highly suggestive, but it is hardly unequivocal. We noticeably lack the presence of a verb of saying (λέγει, εἰπών, &c.) that typically features in Simplicius' introductions to verbatim quotations.[29] Also, if the first sentence is the *ipsissima verba* of

---

[24] See particularly Reale 1970):34–45 and, especially, 368. Also, Merrill 1998: 212 and Burnet 1930: 321 n.5. Barnes (1981: 78–9) suggests that, at the very least, **Q** is a reliable paraphrase.

[25] Burnet 1930: 321 n.5.

[26] Cf. *In Phys.* 164.14–22 (Anaxagoras B3) and *In Phys.* 151.30 (on Diogenes of Apollonia). See also Baltussen 2008: 65.

[27] We should note that this is not a feature unique to Simplicius. See the quotation of B1 of Heraclitus in Sextus Empiricus, *Adv. Math.* VII.132 and Aristotle, *Rhet.* 1407b16–17. Both preface Heraclitus' words with a reference to its location at the start of his treatise.

[28] Reale 1970: 368: 'Questo frammento doveva costituire l'inizio del libro di Melisso, come fanno fede le inequivocabili affermazioni di Simplicio.'

[29] See Long 1976: 648.

Melissus, why not also the second and the third? There is no obvious transition provided by Simplicius to indicate a change from verbatim quotation to paraphrase.

To see why **Q** is nevertheless likely to be authentic, let us look first to an illuminating passage from the Hippocratic treatise *De Arte* chapter 2:

δοκεῖ δή μοι τὸ μὲν σύμπαν τέχνη εἶναι οὐδεμία οὐκ ἐοῦσα· καὶ γὰρ ἄλογον τῶν ἐόντων τι ἡγεῖσθαι μὴ ἐόν· **ἐπεὶ τῶν γε μὴ ἐόντων τίνα ἄν τίς οὐσίην θεησάμενος ἀπαγγείλειεν ὡς ἔστιν;** εἰ γὰρ δὴ ἔστι γ᾽ ἰδεῖν τὰ μὴ ἐόντα, ὥσπερ τὰ ἐόντα, οὐκ οἶδ᾽ ὅπως ἄν τις αὐτὰ νομίσειε μὴ ἐόντα, ἅ γε εἴη καὶ ὀφθαλμοῖσιν ἰδεῖν καὶ γνώμῃ νοῆσαι ὡς ἔστιν· ἀλλ᾽ ὅπως μὴ οὐκ ᾖ τοῦτο τοιοῦτον· ἀλλὰ τὰ μὲν ἐόντα ἀεὶ ὁρᾶταί τε καὶ γινώσκεται, τὰ δὲ μὴ ἐόντα οὔτε ὁρᾶται οὔτε γινώσκεται.

It seems clear to me that, on the whole, there is no art that is not, since it is irrational to think that something is one of the things that are when it is not included in them. **For what being could anyone observe of the things-that-are-not and report that they are?** For if in fact it is possible to see the things-that-are-not, just as it is to see the things-that-are, I don't know how anyone could consider not-beings those things of which it was possible both to see with the eyes and to know with the mind that they are. I'm afraid that is not so, but that whereas the things-that-are always are in every case seen and known, the things-that-are-not are neither seen nor known.[30]

This passage has long been associated with Melissus. The connection has been supported by the very close overlap between the last sentence printed and a sentence from Melissus' B8:

ὥστε συμβαίνει μήτε ὁρᾶν μήτε τὰ ὄντα γινώσκειν.

Unfortunately, this sentence from B8 has been pronounced a gloss by Barnes.[31] I am not convinced this is correct, but even without its support a look at the relationship between the sentence printed above in bold (henceforth **R**) and **Q** should give us pause.

I take it that both Melissus and the Hippocratic author attempt to bring about the same end, that is to say, both ask what we could say about what-is-not. The question is no doubt of Parmenidean inspiration, but if we look to the language and structure of **Q** and **R**, it is very difficult to believe they were composed entirely

---

[30] The text is from Jones (1923). The translation is my own but owes something to Mann (2012).
[31] Barnes 1982: 298 n.3.

independently of each other. Both also employ the ἄν-plus-optative formula to convey the idea that a counterfactual is to be considered, something characteristic of Melissus.

Now it would be going too far to say that **Q** and **R** are identical in meaning. **R** includes in addition the notion of observation. This, however, is perfectly in keeping with the importance of sense perception for the author of *De Arte*. My proposal is that, despite the long association between Melissus and elements of the above passage, the previously undetected overlap between **Q** and **R** is suggestive of **Q**'s authenticity.

The second piece of evidence I call attention to is that the absence of an indication of something like **Q** in the pseudo-Aristotelian *MXG* (*De Melisso, Xenophane, Gorgia*) is less significant than is often thought. The paraphrase found in this pseudo-Aristotelian work is considered by many scholars to follow Melissus' treatise more closely than its Simplician counterpart. In broad terms I agree with the consensus. Yet a look at the beginning of the *MXG* account reveals that it in no way eliminates the possibility that **Q** is genuinely Melissan. It begins: ἀΐδιον εἶναί φησιν εἴ τί ἐστιν, εἴπερ μὴ ἐνδέχεται γενέσθαι μηδὲν ἐκ μηδενός ('He [Melissus] maintains that if anything is it must be eternal, given that it is impossible for anything to come to be from nothing'). All we learn here is that Melissus argued from the hypothesis that something is; we have no reason to think that this premise did not receive a prior statement of assent to this fact that the author of the *MXG* chooses to ignore. This would be all the more plausible if the suggestion that **Q** figured within a lost preface were accepted.

We can even go further and say that there is a good reason for thinking that the author would omit a prior defence of the premise that something is. All three parts of the *MXG* begin schematically. In the section on Xenophanes, we find: ἀδύνατόν φησιν εἶναι, εἴ τι ἔστι, γενέσθαι, τοῦτο λέγων ἐπὶ τοῦ θεοῦ. For Gorgias: οὐκ εἶναί φησιν οὐδέν· εἰ δ' ἔστιν, ἄγνωστον εἶναι· εἰ δὲ καὶ ἔστι καὶ γνωστόν, ἀλλ' οὐ δηλωτὸν ἄλλοις. A comparison of all three indicates that the author of the treatise consistently attributes the same conditional (if there is something) to all three philosophers. It is from this starting-point that the three paraphrases proceed. In such a case, it should be hardly surprising that a prior argument made by only one of the three would be omitted. My point, then, is simple but important. Despite scholarship's attachment to the reliability of the *MXG*, I maintain that its testimony should be invoked neither for denial nor for affirmation of **Q**'s authenticity.

Paraphrases on the Generation and Destruction of What-is

Let us now look at the second question I raised earlier about the beginning of Melissus' work. Bɪ is his argument against the possibility of the generation (and destruction) of what-is. Simplicius' paraphrase suggests that Melissus' original treatise contained a more complex argument than Bɪ provides.

That Simplicius would find it beneficial to include an extended paraphrase of Melissus' book is made clear if we consider the context for which it is adduced. Simplicius is commenting on *Physics* 186a4–13, where Aristotle makes two crucial points about Melissus. Firstly, both Parmenides and Melissus make unsound assumptions and argue unsoundly from them. Secondly, Melissus is the μᾶλλον . . . φορτικός of the two; this leads Aristotle to rehearse quickly his standard criticism that Melissus illicitly denies the antecedent, before retuning to Parmenides at 186a22. What we should take away from this is that Simplicius' provision of a paraphrase beginning at 103.15 is absolutely in keeping with his aim of making sense of Aristotle's criticism of the nature of Melissus' arguments. Adding Melissan material is clearly meant to add textual support to the criticism and to bolster Aristotle's claims.

Simplicius, *In Phys.* 103.15ff

Εἰ μὲν μηδὲν ἔστι, περὶ τούτου τί ἂν λέγοιτο ὡς ὄντος τινός; εἰ δέ τι ἐστίν, ἤτοι γινόμενόν ἐστιν ἢ ἀεὶ ὄν. ἀλλ᾽ εἰ γενόμενον, ἤτοι ἐξ ὄντος ἢ ἐξ οὐκ ὄντος· ἀλλ᾽ οὔτε ἐκ μὴ ὄντος οἷόν τε γενέσθαι τι (οὔτε ἄλλο μὲν οὐδὲν ὄν, πολλῷ δὲ μᾶλλον τὸ ἁπλῶς ὄν) οὔτε ἐκ τοῦ ὄντος. εἴη γὰρ ἂν οὕτως καὶ οὐ γίνοιτο. οὐκ ἄρα γινόμενόν ἐστι τὸ ὄν. ἀεὶ ὂν ἄρα ἐστίν, οὔτε φθαρήσεται τὸ ὄν. οὔτε γὰρ εἰς τὸ μὴ ὂν οἷόν τε τὸ ὂν μεταβάλλειν (συγχωρεῖται γὰρ καὶ τοῦτο ὑπὸ τῶν φυσικῶν) οὔτε εἰς ὄν. μένοι γὰρ ἂν πάλιν οὕτω γε καὶ οὐ φθείροιτο. οὔτε ἄρα γέγονε τὸ ὂν οὔτε φθαρήσεται· ἀεὶ ἄρα ἦν τε καὶ ἔσται.

(1) If it is nothing, what could be said about it as though it were something? (2) But if it is something, either it has come to be or it has always existed. But if it has

come to be,[32] it has done so either from what-is or from what is not. (2a) But nothing is able to come to be either from what is not (neither something else which is nothing, nor, more especially, what absolutely is) (2b) nor from what is. For in that way it would already exist and not come to be. Therefore what-is did not come to be. (3) Therefore it exists always. Nor will what-is be destroyed. For what-is can change neither into what is not (for this is agreed by the natural philosophers) nor into what-is. For in that case what-is will remain and would not be destroyed. Therefore what-is neither has come to be nor will be destroyed. Therefore it always was and will be.

The dilemmatic structure of the above account has been taken to suggest that a similar form was employed by Melissus at the beginning of his treatise. Reale has drawn attention to this point and adduced a number of ancient attributions of dilemmatic reasoning to Melissus.[33] Although Reale's basic thesis has been favourably received,[34] we should be cautious when attributing to Melissus a line of reasoning, unattested in his verbatim fragments. After all, B1 provides an argument for the thesis that what-is is not generated that is wholly non-dilemmatic. So, then, there is the possibility and, I will suggest, the likelihood, that the dilemmatic reasoning is a product of the later interpretative tradition.

We find in Philoponus' commentary on Aristotle's *Physics* a further paraphrase attributing dilemmatic argumentation to Melissus. Just as in the case of Simplicius considered above, the Philoponean material is provided as evidence to support Aristotle's criticisms of Melissus, beginning at *Physics* 186a4. Indeed Philoponus makes it clear that he intends to consider Melissus' arguments as fully as possible and then to examine how Aristotle's refutes them (50.27–9). So it is once again in the context of explicating Melissus' argument in the service of demonstrating the validity of Aristotle's criticisms that dilemmatic argumentation is attributed to Melissus:

---

[32] The verb changes from γινόμενον in line 16 to γενόμενον in line 17. I doubt the change of tense indicates any change of aspect because I doubt Diels' reading of γενόμενον in 17 is correct: γινόμενον has superior manuscript authority there. Also, we find γινόμενον in the conclusion to this point in line 20.

[33] Reale 1970: 35–45. Cf. ps. Alexander, *in Soph. Elen.* 49.20, Anon., *in Soph. Slen. Paraph.* 15.26, and Philoponus, *In Phys.* 16.51.20.

[34] Merrill 1998: 212 and Long 1976: 648. Note, however, the vociferous objection of Palmer (2009: 36 n.34).

Paraphrases on the Generation and Destruction of What-is

ὅτι μὲν γὰρ τὸ ὂν οὐ γέγονε, δείκνυσιν οὕτως. εἰ γὰρ γέγονε τὸ ὄν, ἢ ἐξ ὄντος γέγονεν ἢ ἐξ οὐκ ὄντος· εἰ μὲν οὖν ἐξ ὄντος, ἔσται τὸ ὂν πρὶν γενέσθαι (τὶ μὲν γὰρ ὂν ἐκ τινὸς ὄντος γίνεται, τὸ δὲ ἁπλῶς ὂν οὐκ ἂν ἐξ ὄντος γένοιτο· αὐτὸ γὰρ ἐξ αὐτοῦ γίνοιτο ἄν. ὥστε πρὶν γενέσθαι ἦν, ὅπερ ἄτοπον), εἰ δὲ ἐξ οὐκ ὄντος, ἀνάγκη ἐκ τοῦ μηδαμῇ μηδαμῶς ὄντος· τὸ γὰρ ἁπλῶς ὂν εἰ γίνεται, ἐκ τοῦ ἁπλῶς μὴ ὄντος γένοιτ' ἄν. ἀλλὰ τοῦτο κοινόν ἐστιν ὁμολόγημα πάντων τῶν φυσικῶν τὸ μηδὲν ἐκ τοῦ μηδαμῇ μηδαμῶς ὄντος γίνεσθαι.

He shows that what-is did not come into being as follows: if what-is came into being, it came either from what-is or what-is not. If it came from what-is, what-is will be there before it comes into being (for what is something comes from what is something, but being, *tout court*, could not come from being; it would be coming from itself, so that it was before it came into being, which is absurd). If it came about from what is not, it must be from what is not in any manner or form; for if what-is *tout court* comes into being, it would come into being from not-being *tout court*. But there is a consensus among all the natural philosophers, that nothing comes to be from what is in no way and in no respect is. (Philoponus, *In Phys.* 51.20–7, trans. C. Osborne, modified)

Philoponus makes no mention here of Melissus' hypothesis that something exists or of the possibility that he offered a counter-factual conditional in its support.[35] He, therefore, omits the deduction that Simplicius provides, from the claim that something exists to the dilemma opposing generation with sempiternal existence.

What Philoponus does provide is a strong suggestion that Melissus discounted the generation of what-is using a dilemmatic argument. It is true that Philoponus does miss out the governing dilemma presented in Simplicius' account (either it has come to be or it has always existed). Both accounts opposing generation *ex nihilo* and generation from that which is already existent present the dilemma in similar terms.

Simplicius: ἀλλ' εἰ γενόμενον, ἤτοι ἐξ ὄντος ἢ ἐξ οὐκ ὄντος
Philoponus: εἰ γὰρ γέγονε τὸ ὄν, ἢ ἐξ ὄντος γέγονεν ἢ ἐξ οὐκ ὄντος

Generation from what is already existent is ruled out, on Simplicius' presentation, because it is already existent and, therefore, cannot be generated. This may appear to differ from Philoponus' account, yet they amount to much the same argument. Philoponus merely extends his discussion to what the conditions would have to be to allow for this type of generation. On both

---

[35] This does not entail that Philoponus did not think that Melissus provided such a proof.

accounts, the fact that being already exists is sufficient to rule out the possibility of its generation.

The accounts offered by Simplicius and Philoponus of Melissus' denial of generation *ex nihilo* bear largely the same relation to each other as do their accounts of generation from something already existent. Philoponus' presentation appears more detailed, but on close analysis the discrepancies fade. Simplicius' paraphrase merely reports that it is not possible for something to come to be from what is not: 'ἀλλ' οὔτε ἐκ μὴ ὄντος οἷόν τε γενέσθαι τι' (*In Phys.* 103.17–18).

Therefore, the superficial differences are of no importance for recovering Melissus' thought; neither commentator assigns a significant argument targeting generation *ex nihilo* to Melissus. How then does Melissus resist generation *ex nihilo* on Philoponus' account? The commentator appeals to a claim that this assumption is the common opinion of natural philosophers. Philoponus brings in the common opinion of natural philosophers specifically within the context of Melissus' rejection of generation. Simplicius does not do so within his paraphrase but this does not imply that a mention of natural philosophy is absent from his account of Melissus. In fact, Simplicius emphasises Melissus' reliance on the axioms of previous natural philosophers from the very beginning of the paraphrase: 'τοῖς γὰρ τῶν φυσικῶν ἀξιώμασι χρησάμενος ὁ Μέλισσος περὶ γενέσεως καὶ φθορᾶς ἄρχεται τοῦ συγγράμματος οὕτως' (*In Phys.* 103.13–15). Further evidence of the importance of the axioms of natural philosophers for Melissus' argument against generation is also found in Simplicius' introduction of B1 at 162.23–4: 'καὶ Μέλισσος δὲ τὸ ἀγένητον τοῦ ὄντος ἔδειξε τῷ κοινῷ τούτῳ χρησάμενος ἀξιώματι'.[36]

The two paraphrases may suggest that dilemmatic argumentation played an inferential role for Melissus. One might suppose that the agreement of the testimonies is indicative of their value. We have different sources that provide us with a mutually consistent picture. However, this is, I argue, a mistaken conclusion. The mention of the opinions or axioms of natural philosophy suggests that the testimonies are *not* independent. It suggests

---

[36] Cf. [Alexander of Aphrodisias] Michael of Ephesus 49.26–8.

rather a *common* source, which is the product of a confused reading. Both strands common to the commentary tradition (dilemmatic reasoning and the invocation of natural philosophy) are, in my view, traceable back to Aristotle in the first book of the *Physics*. This should hardly be surprising given the fact that both works are commentaries on this first book.

Consider this passage from the *Physics*:

ζητοῦντες γὰρ οἱ κατὰ **φιλοσοφίαν πρῶτοι** τὴν ἀλήθειαν καὶ τὴν φύσιν τῶν ὄντων ἐξετράπησαν οἷον ὁδόν τινα ἄλλην ἀπωσθέντες ὑπὸ ἀπειρίας, **καὶ φασιν οὔτε** γίγνεσθαι τῶν ὄντων οὐδὲν οὔτε φθείρεσθαι διὰ τὸ ἀναγκαῖον μὲν εἶναι γίγνεσθαι τὸ γιγνόμενον ἢ ἐξ ὄντος ἢ ἐκ μὴ ὄντος, ἐκ δὲ τούτων ἀμφοτέρων ἀδύνατον εἶναι· οὔτε γὰρ τὸ ὂν γίγνεσθαι (εἶναι γὰρ ἤδη) ἔκ τε μὴ ὄντος οὐδὲν ἂν γενέσθαι· ὑποκεῖσθαι γάρ τι δεῖν. καὶ οὕτω δὴ τὸ ἐφεξῆς συμβαῖνον αὔξοντες οὐδ᾽ εἶναι πολλά φασιν ἀλλὰ μόνον αὐτὸ τὸ ὄν. (*Physics* 191a25–33)

The **first** of those who **studied philosophy** were misled in their search for truth and the nature of things by their inexperience, which as it were thrust them into another path. **So they say that none of the things that are either comes to be or passes out of existence, because what comes to be must do so either from what is or from what is not, both of which are impossible. For what is cannot come to be (because it is *already*), and from what is not nothing could have come to be (because something must be underlying).** So too they exaggerate the consequence of this, and go so far as to deny even the *existence* of a plurality of things, maintaining that only what is itself is. (Trans. R. P. Hardie and R. K. Gaye)

Aristotle does not specifically name the philosophers he is describing here in this passage. It has sometimes been suggested that the Eleatics are the relevant targets: the denial of plurality in *Physics* I is *only* associated with the Eleatics. The early physical monists are also a possible target here, at least up to the final sentence of the quoted text. Here, at the very end of the passage, it is impossible to include their number as among those Aristotle had in mind, as in *Physics* I.4 (187a15–16) they are explicitly said to arrive at a plurality, so long as it generated from a single underlying substance, through a process of condensation and rarefaction. This, however, does *not* suggest that they are irrelevant to the main, general point Aristotle makes early opinions about coming-to-be.

In fact, just a few sentences later in I.4, Aristotle confirms that the dogma 'nothing can come-to-be from what is not' is common to all early natural philosophers, including Anaxagoras:

ἔοικε δὲ Ἀναξαγόρας ἄπειρα οὕτως οἰηθῆναι διὰ τὸ ὑπολαμβάνειν **τὴν κοινὴν δόξαν τῶν φυσικῶν** εἶναι ἀληθῆ, ὡς οὐ γιγνομένου οὐδενὸς ἐκ τοῦ μὴ ὄντος. (187a26–9)[37]

What this suggests is that the connection and natural philosophy, a commitment to the impossibility of *ex nihilo* coming-to-be, and the analysis of such a claim using dilemmatical argumentation are recognisably Aristotelian in origin on the evidence of the first book of the *Physics*. As our paraphrases of Melissus' book arrive in the context of commentaries on that very work, it is hardly surprising that the structural elements of Aristotle's presentation of early philosophers make their way into the explication of Melissus in the commentary tradition.

Therefore, I maintain that the significant parallelism between Aristotle's remarks and the commentators' reports on Melissus' denial of generation is suggestive. We may notice a nearly identical opposition between generation from what-is and generation from what-is-not. Generation from what-is is denied because it is not proper generation. This closely aligns with Simplicius' report. Generation *ex nihilo* is denied because something would have to be pre-existing (compare Philoponus' account).

The suggestion is that this passage from *Physics* I.7, with the further support of I.4, is the source for a report upon which Simplicius and Philoponus depended. It is significant that the dilemmatic argumentation Aristotle discusses is directly attributed to those who 'first studied philosophy'. This mention suggests a connection with Simplicius' φυσικῶν ἀξιώμασι. The idea, then, is that an intermediary noticed that the thinking that Aristotle ascribes to Presocratic physicists (i.e. both the early monists and later thinkers like Anaxagoras) fitted Melissus particularly well and, therefore, he highlighted the axioms that Melissus shared with the earlier physicists. Once this connection had been made, the dilemmatic argumentation Aristotle ascribes to οἱ κατὰ

---

[37] Recall that Simplicius repeats this very point at *In Phys.* 162.26–8.

φιλοσοφίαν πρῶτοι would easily transfer to Melissus' treatise. I suggest that an explanation in these terms makes best sense of the parallelism between Aristotle's text and the dilemmatic arguments we have seen ascribed to Melissus by Simplicius and Philoponus.

We must consider the *MXG* as well. This pseudo-Aristotelian treatise also suggests that Melissus had a richer, dilemmatic argument against generation.

Anonymous, *MXG* 974a1–9

Ἀίδιον εἶναί φησιν εἴ τι ἔστιν, εἴπερ μὴ ἐνδέχεσθαι γενέσθαι μηδὲν ἐκ μηδενός· εἴτε γὰρ ἅπαντα γέγονεν εἴτε μὴ πάντα, ἀΐδια ἀμφοτέρως· ἐξ οὐδενὸς γὰρ γενέσθαι ἂν αὐτὰ γιγνόμενα. ἁπάντων τε γὰρ γιγνομένων οὐδὲν προϋπάρχειν· εἴτ' ὄντων τινῶν ἀεὶ ἕτερα προσγίγνοιτο, πλέον ἂν καὶ μεῖζον τὸ ὂν γεγονέναι· ᾧ δὲ πλέον καὶ μεῖζον, τοῦτο γενέσθαι ἂν ἐξ οὐδενός· <ἐν> τῷ γὰρ ἐλάττονι τὸ πλέον, οὐδ' ἐν τῷ μικροτέρῳ τὸ μεῖζον, οὐχ ὑπάρχειν. (Apelt)

Melissus holds that, if something is, it must be eternal, on account of the fact that it is not possible for something to come to be from nothing. For whether everything has come to be or only some things, in both cases they are eternal. If not, these things would have to come to be from nothing. On the one hand, if everything has come to be, then nothing was pre-existent. On the other hand, if some things existed always and others were added to them, it would have to become greater and larger. And this greater and the larger would have come to be from nothing. For the greater cannot exist in the lesser, nor can the larger be in the small.

Is this account a product of confused doxography as well? Possibly, but a fuller look at the treatise suggests a better explanation. Dilemmatic argumentation is not ascribed to Melissus alone, but appears in all *three* sections of the *MXG* with great frequency. This should not surprise us given our earlier look at the treatise. The author begins his section on Xenophanes as follows:

ἀδύνατόν φησιν εἶναι, εἴ τι ἔστι, γενέσθαι, τοῦτο λέγων ἐπὶ τοῦ θεοῦ· ἀνάγκη γὰρ ἤτοι ἐξ ὁμοίου ἢ ἐξ ἀνομοίου γενέσθαι τὸ γενόμενον· (977a14–16.)

Xenophanes says that, if anything exists, it cannot have become, and he applies his conclusions to God. For that which has come into existence must have arisen either from the like or from the unlike. (Trans. W. S. Hett)

Our fragments of Xenophanes perhaps show some evidence of an argument against God's coming-to-be (B14) but absolutely no

49

evidence of such an argument formed dilemmatically.[38] In the section on Gorgias, dilemmas abound.[39] What are we to make of this? In my view, dilemmatic formulations of the destructive sort found in this text do not represent the original versions of the arguments reported in the *MXG*, but rather are a matrix imposed by the author of the treatise. If this is correct, the evidence of the *MXG* is too compromised to serve as a reliable confirmation of original dilemmatic argumentation in Melissus' treatise. My conclusion, then, is that we need not accept that dilemmatic argumentation targeting generation and corruption is original to Melissus' treatise. That such argumentation is alien to Melissus' strategy of reductio will become apparent as we move along. Yet this does *not* damage the argument in favour of **Q**.

It is significant that **Q** figures *before* the dilemmatic argumentation targeting generation begins. This point, in addition to Simplicius' unambiguous presentation of **Q** as verbatim, tilts the balance of evidence in my favour. However, we should have another look at the text of the question as Simplicius provides it: 'εἰ μὲν μηδὲν ἔστι, περὶ τούτου τί ἂν λέγοιτο ὡς <ἐ>όντος τινός; εἰ δέ τι ἐστίν . . .'

If we agree that Simplicius' paraphrase is infected by a later tradition of indiscriminately attributed dilemmatic arguments, we must determine where the useful account of Melissus' treatise ends and the resort to doxography begins. The μέν in **Q** is informative. Though μέν is occasionally used for an emphatic purpose independently of a following adversative particle, this is not the case here.[40] We find directly following the question the expected, and absolutely standard, answering clause with δέ: εἰ δέ τι ἐστίν.

---

[38] Lesher (1992: 190) makes this point.

[39] Indeed it is a possibility that Gorgias' use of dilemmatic arguments, particularly for the claim that nothing exists, inspires the author of the *MXG* to interpret Melissus and Xenophanes using a similar framework. John Palmer (2009: 220–1) suggests something along these lines by taking the dichotomous classification of theses (everything is one, or many; what-is is generated, or ungenerated; what-is is changing, or at rest etc.) attributed to Gorgias in the *MXG* as the source for such dichotomous frameworks found in the likes of Aristotle (*Physics* 1.2, 184b15–22). On such an account, it is reasonable to assume that it is Gorgias who introduces a dilemmatic structure to 'Eleatic' arguments. The author of the *MXG* encourages such a thought by portraying Gorgias as someone who proceeded from 'Eleatic' arguments, specifically mentioning Melissus and Zeno (979a22).

[40] See Denniston 1959: 359–69.

This strongly suggests that the two clauses together form an antithesis.[41] It is rather surprising that both Reale and Vitali, each of whom wishes to adopt **Q** as genuine, fail to grasp this point. It is only after these closely connected clauses that the dilemmatic arguments targeting generation, which we have determined to be probably un-Melissan, begin. On the basis of this compelling evidence, we should accept the authenticity of εἰ δέ τι ἐστίν as well.

Let us review the text of Melissus' treatise thus far established:

Περὶ φύσεως ἢ περὶ τοῦ <ἐ>όντος:όντος

<Μέλισσος Σάμιος τάδε λέγει περὶ φύσεως ἢ περὶ τοῦ ἐόντος.>

εἰ μὲν μηδὲν ἔστι, περὶ τούτου τί ἂν λέγοιτο ὡς <ἐ>όντος τινός; εἰ δέ τι ἐστίν ...

---

[41] This is a sort of dilemma, but crucially it is of a different kind from what Simplicius and the author of the *MXG* attribute to Melissus. The dilemmatic arguments described in the presentations of Simplicius and the *MXG* are *destructive*. The argument I attribute to Melissus is *eliminative*; this is far more in line with Melissus' strategy of using *reductio*.

B1: WHAT-IS DID NOT COME TO BE

εἰ δέ τι ἐστίν . . .

We encounter here a highly Parmenidean interpretative crux. Parallel with Parmenides' B2, we must determine the force of ἔστι and find the subject of Melissus' conditional. There are a number of possible construals here and I do not intend to offer an exhaustive elimination of each one. Rather I will propose a reading that attributes what I take to be the clearest and most satisfying argument to Melissus. To this end, I offer the suggestion that the treatise's preface (as I have reconstructed it) provides us with a ready answer: it is nature or what-is that is the subject of **Q**. This follows on from the construal of the Greek, offered by KRS: 'If *it* is nothing, what could be said about this – as though it were something?'[1] Where I go further is by offering the thought that by 'it' we should understand nature or what-is.

Against this suggestion, one might think that μηδέν (nothing) is Melissus' subject in **Q**. Burnet takes it this way and translates as follows: 'If nothing is, what could be said of it as of something real.'[2] This makes some sense.[3] We seem to be encouraged, on such a translation, to interpret 'nothing is' as meaning that that which is nothing (perhaps like Melissus' concept of void in B7) exists. Where a difficulty emerges is in the conditional (εἰ δέ τι ἐστίν) that follows **Q**. The μέν . . . δέ construction implies that both halves share the same subject unless otherwise specified. In order to make sense of the change-of-subject option we would need to take τι as the subject of εἰ δέ τι ἐστίν. The antithesis would then be: if nothing is . . . but if something is . . . We cannot reject this reading outright. However, I discount its likelihood because it

---

[1] See Barnes 1982: xix for a similar translation.   [2] Burnet 1930: 321.
[3] Loenen (1959: 140) misunderstands the Greek here.

requires an awkward shift in the use of τινός/τι from attributive to subjective in only a few words.

A further option, more difficult to eliminate entirely, is to take εἰ μὲν μηδὲν ἔστι . . . as 'if there is nothing . . .'.[4] This might be taken along the lines of Burnet's translation discussed above or, intriguingly, as the hypothesis that there is nothing at all, i.e. the total absence of anything. Certainly, the latter is the sort of nihilist thesis that Gorgias argues for in *On What-is Not, or On Nature*.[5] The difficulty of adopting such a translation is that the strategy Melissus adopts to eliminate the hypothesis in the rhetorical second half of Q becomes unsatisfactory. Melissus, on any understanding of the subject of the sentence, intends the fact that we could not talk about this subject to eliminate our commitment to the original hypothesis and to establish its contrary (that it is something, on my translation). Yet this fact does no such thing. The proponent of the thesis that there is nothing at all might well *agree* that we could not talk about it; indeed the hypothesis itself might be thought to demand such a commitment.[6] Thus a translation that understands the hypothesis to deny that there is anything at all attributes an inapt argument to Melissus. What I will suggest below is that Melissus' strategy is dialectical, i.e. the intention is to expose a contradiction between the commitments of one holding such a hypothesis. This achieves its most satisfying construal if we take what-is or nature as Melissus' subject, as the above reconstruction of the prefatory material suggests.

First it is worth exploring how we ought to read the verb 'to be' in Q. ἔστι presents us with a serious challenge. Scholars have offered many interpretations of the use of ἔστιν and οὐκ ἔστιν in Parmenides' B2. The verb has been taken to be a verb of existence, predication, or perhaps even truth for Parmenides. Others have offered theories that combine these uses in a variety of ways. Does

---

[4] The phrase is commonly translated along these lines, though without much argument. See Graham 2010: 469 and Huby and Taylor 2011: 16.

[5] This is confirmed by both accounts of the work (*MXG* (979a14) and Sextus, *Adv Math* VII.65ff).

[6] Indeed Gorgias, in the third thesis in *On What-Is-Not, or On Nature*, maintains much the same point.

the ambiguity (or confusion) many have attributed to Parmenides also hold for Melissus?

We must consider whether ὡς <ἐ>όντος τινός functions as a genitive absolute. If this were correct, we might translate περὶ τούτου τί ἂν λέγοιτο ὡς <ἐ>όντος τινός as 'what could be said about this (what-is) as if there were something'. The genitive absolute construction entails that the subject of ὡς <ἐ>όντος τινός is different from the subject of the main clause, namely what-is. Although I cannot firmly rule out this reading, it is syntactically less natural than the reading I will soon propose and gives a less satisfying construal of Melissus' argument.

Rather it looks very much as if τινός functions predicatively following <ἐ>όντος. I translate 'περὶ τούτου τί ἂν λέγοιτο ὡς <ἐ>όντος τινός' as *what could be said about it as if it were something*. So construed, it raises the tantalising suggestion that, for Melissus, the verb 'to be' is strongly associated with predication. We might imagine that this shows that Melissus is improving on Parmenides by making it clear that 'to be' is explicitly predicative. This is not to say that the verb is never used by Melissus with existential force. Indeed in B8 we find such an example, though it is at odds with the frequent predicative use of verb elsewhere in the fragment:

εἰ γὰρ ἔστι γῆ καὶ ὕδωρ καὶ ἀὴρ καὶ πῦρ καὶ σίδηρος καὶ χρυσός . . .

For if there *is* earth, water, air, fire, iron and gold . . .

Plainly, Melissus intends to consider whether or not earth, water, air etc. exist. There can be little doubt on this point.[7] This might dissuade us from attributing a strongly predicative aspect of the verb 'to be' in **Q** to Melissus. Yet the point to take away here is not that the verb 'to be' is used consistently throughout the work or that a strongly predicative usage at the start commits Melissus to such consistenty. Rather what I suggest is that, at the crucial opening of the book, which roughly corresponds to Parmenides' B2, Melissus is earmarking the verb's predicative function and,

---

[7] Though it has been doubted without a convincing argument by some, e.g. Alexander Mourelatos 1965: 362–3.

thus, setting up the task of deducing the predicates of what-is that will constitute the bulk of the work.

Returning to **Q**, on the predicative reading the thought seems to be as follows. Melissus raises for consideration a statement of a version of nihilism (that what-is is nothing and not the more familiar nihilist thesis that nothing exists). This idea is not countered by appealing to the highly debatable notion that if what-is does not exist we cannot speak of it. Rather Melissus rhetorically asks what could be said about it ὡς <ἐ> ὄντος τινός. The point is that if you hold both that what-is is nothing and that you could say something about it ὡς <ἐ> ὄντος τινός, your position is self-contradictory. That is to say, the reason why you could not speak of that which is nothing is that to do so would be to predicate something of it, whereas its being nothing rules out its having predicates. The τινός is vitally important; the purported impossibility of speaking of what-is-not centres on its not being *something* (i.e. *anything at all*). On this understanding, Melissus is beginning his work on natural philosophy at its most fundamental level. He is asking what we could say about what-is if we could not attach any predicates (i.e. attributes) to it.

This reading of **Q** provides an early indication of the character of Melissus' response to Parmenides' poem. Melissus picks out the predicative nature of the Greek verb 'to be' as a part of a stratagem to gain his audience's assent that there is something and that we can talk about this something. The alternative, Melissus suggests, is to embrace nihilism. By 'pick out' I do not mean 'choose' or 'distinguish'; recent work on the verb 'to be' in Greek confirms that the traditional copula/existence dichotomy is unhelpful. Lesley Brown, for example, has argued that the complete/incomplete distinction onto which the copula/existence dichotomy is often grafted obscures the fact that a so-called 'complete' use of the verb can often take a complement.[8] Particularly germane is the ultimate conclusion Charles Kahn has reached in his work on the verb: the predicative function has a claim to some logical priority over other 'uses' one may identify (e.g. existential or veridical) insofar as it functions as syntactically fundamental. This does not mean that the

---

[8] Brown 1986: 52–4.

predicative functions *independently* of other uses, only that these uses are second order (and semantic) in character.[9] My suggestion is that Melissus is ultimately making Kahn's point by indicating that the acceptance of the fact that 'something is' follows from our agreement that we can talk about it: the priority of predication is being confirmed. Melissus, if this account is correct, is making an entirely characteristic improvement upon the ambiguity of Parmenides' poem, strikingly on just the point (the use of the verb 'to be' in his B2) where his murkiness is at its greatest.

Does the genuine material provided by Simplicius simply end with εἰ δέ τι ἐστίν? After all, this means that he shifts from quotation to paraphrase (or gloss) in the middle of a sentence. However, if we have a look at the remainder of the sentence, we see that the destructive dilemmatic framework begins precisely here and includes dilemmatic reformulations of argument we have in verbatim form: εἰ δέ τι ἐστίν, ἤτοι γινόμενόν ἐστιν ἢ ἀεὶ ὄν. If we accept the possibility that the dilemmatic argumentation attributed to Melissus is a product of the Aristotelian tradition (which I take to be more likely than not, though it must be admitted that it cannot be conclusively discarded), it makes sense to divide where I have recommended. My suggestion is that εἰ δέ τι ἐστίν originally introduced B1. Melissus has convinced us that what-is is something. Now he can begin his deductive account of its properties. It is plausible that it is at this point that the dilemmatic framework targeting generation would be inserted. One suggestion is that Simplicius had access to both a verbatim report of Melissus' opening and an account of the dilemmatic arguments he allegedly used against generation. The latter attributed to Melissus a much more substantial piece of reasoning. It is perfectly natural that the author would think that the longer, more detailed version was original even if he was not sure where to locate it in the full text.

ἀεὶ ἦν ὅ τι ἦν καὶ ἀεὶ ἔσται

This text, according to both Diels and Covotti, is universally attested by our Simplician manuscripts. The double mention of

[9] Kahn 2009: Essay Five.

Melissus' reliance on 'axioms' both at the start of the paraphrase at
103.14 and in the introduction to B1 at 162.23–4 also suggests the
latter stood near the beginning of his treatise, where editors usually
place it. Despite the unanimity, the text has been seriously challenged by Loenen, who emends the second ἦν to ἔστι.[10]

I translate the manuscript reading as follows: 'it always was
whatever it was and always will be'. Two arguments must be made
in favour of this translation. First one must accept that the second
ἦν can be thought to be a genuine past tense ('was'). Second,
I argue that ὅ τι is generalising in nature ('whatever') and need
not have a concretely determined referent.

Loenen offers a two-part argument for the conjecture. He claims
that the emendation to ἔστι is required to ensure logical consistency. This concern stems from his argument that the starting-point
of Melissus' chain of deductions is that 'something' exists (τι ἔστι)
and that he is not speaking about a far broader notion, the whole of
things (τὸ πᾶν)[11] or the all-encompassing Parmenidean being (τὸ
ἐόν). He reasons that if Melissus is making his deductions from the
hypothesis τι ἔστι it is difficult to make sense of the past tense in
ὅ τι ἦν. This, on Loenen's view, undermines the 'strict meaning' of
τι ἔστι that his thesis requires.[12] If τι ἔστι is so quickly and so
loosely converted into the past tense, we might think it played a far
less significant role for Melissus than both Loenen and I maintain.

Loenen marshals but then rejects what may seem a solution to
his worry.[13] The imperfect tense of ἦν could be taken to indicate
a fact that has been and continues to be the case. The paradigmatic
example for this usage is the Aristotelian formulation used to
describe a thing's essential nature, τὸ τί ἦν εἶναι.[14]

I hesitate to put too much weight on the Aristotelian usage as it
is very plainly a technical term quite outside of ordinary Greek.

---

[10] Loenen 1959: 144–7. This emendation is accepted by Barnes (1982: 184 n.13).
[11] See *Soph. Elen.* 167b13–16 and *Physics* 213b12–14.   [12] Loenen 1959: 144.
[13] Cf. Reale 1970: 59 n.60 and Vitali 1973: 16 n.1.
[14] This is called the philosophical imperfect by Reale. According to Smyth (1956: 426
(Sec. 1903)) this is not quite correct as this usage is used to refer to a topic previously
discussed, e.g. Plato, *Republic* 522a. Rather the Aristotelian formula seems to be
a product of an extension of a typical use of the imperfect to indicate a state that obtains
now and obtained in the past. Outside of this unique usage, one would expect the particle
ἄρα to accompany the verb 'to be' to indicate something that it is continuing to be
realised. See Denniston 1959: 36–7.

Yet Loenen also fails to notice that ὅ τι ἦν[15] is used *again* at B8.19, suggesting that this was a comfortable formula for Melissus, telling against the proposed emendation. Thus saving the manuscript reading becomes the more attractive option.

Loenen also marshals one version of B2 quoted by Simplicius: ὅτε τοίνυν οὐκ ἐγένετο, **ἔστι δέ**, ἀεὶ ἦν καὶ ἀεὶ ἔσται καὶ ἀρχὴν κτλ (*In Phys.* 109.20). He prefers this reading because it supposedly conforms best to the basic hypothesis τι ἔστιν. However, a different version, often taken as superior,[16] is provided earlier in Simplicius' commentary, at 29.22: ὅτε τοίνυν οὐκ ἐγένετο, ἔστι τε καὶ ἀεὶ ἦν καὶ ἀεὶ ἔσται καὶ ἀρχὴν κτλ. I find no persuasive reason to accept the preference for the text at 109.20–1. It is not obviously the *lectio difficilior* nor is it easy to account for a corruption from ἔστι δέ to ἔστι τε καὶ as merely 'the error of a copyist'.[17] A fuller discussion can be found later in the section on B2.

I take away two morals from the above. Loenen's emendation seems hasty and unnecessary. However, the retention of ἦν cannot be adequately justified on the grounds offered by Reale and Vitali that it is an imperfect in the Aristotelian manner. I maintain that the verb is just as it appears to be, *a genuine past*. It would be odd if ἦν were to change in meaning within the space of three words.

Although it has been occasionally captured correctly in translation, scholars have ignored the force of ὅ τι. KRS translate (correctly) ὅ τι ἦν as 'whatever it was',[18] DK as 'was da war'.[19] We ought to wonder though whether Melissus is making the specific claim that what-is is *exactly* as it was previously. Does what-is always share the same set of attributes? Certainly Melissus *does* want to come to this conclusion. His universe, after all, is completely unchanging and sempiternal. We ought to be cautious however. In B1 he is confined to the claim that what-is is ungenerated and imperishable. He is not yet entitled to the claim (argued in B7) that what-is is changeless.

---

[15] This construal is found elsewhere in the fifth century, only, to my knowledge, in the Hippocratic treatise *De Arte*. As I have suggested above, it is likely that the author of this treatise was familiar with Melissus' work. See Mann 2012: 24–6 and 92–3.

[16] E.g. by DK, Reale 1970, and Vitali 1973.   [17] Loenen 1959: 145.   [18] KRS: 393.

[19] DK 1951: 268.

Rather we should think that Melissus is making a weaker, but no less essential, point. His ὅ τι simply refers back to the hypothesis that what-is is *something*. If my account is correct, we have already assented to this notion before the start of B1. The idea is that what-is has never been nothing but has always borne at least one predicate, i.e. it has at all times been possible to say something truly about what-is in the present tense.

At the start of B2 (ὅτε τοίνυν οὐκ ἐγένετο, ἔστι τε καὶ ἀεὶ ἦν καὶ ἀεὶ ἔσται), the point made here is recast as the premise for the argument for spatial infinity. The use of the traditional 'eternity formula' (it was, it is, and it will be – though not necessarily in that order), used to describe something sempiternal, suggests the intriguing thought that B1 provides a philosophical argument to support an idea frequently assumed in the broader tradition, philosophical and otherwise.[20] As such, we can glimpse Melissus' place in the philosophical interpretation and development of traditional, poetical notions of the universe.

†εἰ τοίνυν μηδὲν ἦν, οὐδαμὰ ἂν γένοιτο οὐδὲν ἐκ μηδενός†

This last line of B1 presents us with the greatest textual difficulties of the fragment. In DK the line reads: εἰ τοίνυν μηδὲν ἦν, οὐδαμὰ ἂν γένοιτο οὐδὲν ἐκ μηδενός. Our manuscript readings for the beginning of this sentence are divided into two groups. The first group, DE, provides two, largely similar readings for the beginning of the sentence: εἰ τύχη νῦν D, εἰ τύχοι νῦν E. The ἂν of the apodosis confirms that the reading of E with the optative should be preferred. The second group of readings, aF, gives εἰ τοίνυν. In the former construal, EITYXOINYN, Diels claims, 'latere videtur ὅτε τοίνυν' of the beginning of B2 (*In Phys.* 109.20). This is an interesting but untenable suggestion. Melissus is offering up for consideration the hypothesis that what-is was nothing before it came to be. The conditional constructions given in the manuscripts are far more likely in this context. ὅτε τοίνυν is used to introduce a conclusion not a tentatively stated hypothesis.

---

[20] Examples of the 'eternity formula' include *Iliad* 1.70, *Theogony* 38, and Heraclitus B30. See Kirk 1962: 310 for a fuller list.

εἰ τύχοι νῦν might be the product of a corruption of εἰ τοίνυν. Yet we should not overlook the superior attestation in the manuscript tradition of the former reading. It also seems likely that εἰ τύχοι νῦν is the *lectio difficilior*, suggesting the corruption would rather proceed *from* this reading *to* εἰ τοίνυν. Yet even if we were to leave aside palaeographical concerns, there is good reason to reject Diels' preference for εἰ τοίνυν on philological and logical grounds.

Let us begin by pursuing an account of the meaning of the final sentence of BI if it were indeed to begin with the preferred reading of Diels.[21] Our task is to grasp the role of τοίνυν here. The most common usage of this particle in fifth-century literature is inferential. A look also at the uses of τοίνυν in Melissus' fragments suggests that he is firmly committed to this use of the particle. In fact, every use of τοίνυν elsewhere in the treatise is within a sentence that draws a conclusion from previously established premises. This is not to say that the logical force of τοίνυν is identical throughout the fragments, but rather that, given Melissus' rather frequent use of the particle implying at least some inferential or conclusive element, it would be surprising if it were used in the weakly connective manner often suggested here in BI. A look at B7 will be instructive.

εἰ τοίνυν πλέων ἐστίν, οὐ κινεῖται.

Therefore, if it is full, it does not move.

ἀνάγκη τοίνυν πλέων εἶναι, εἰ κενὸν μὴ ἔστιν.

Therefore, it must be full, if there is no such thing as empty.

Both examples are unambiguously inferential.[22]

It is worth noting here that translators have almost universally chosen to disregard Melissus' consistent inferential use of the particle elsewhere and understood a transitional use instead. For εἰ τοίνυν μηδὲν ἦν DK offers, for example, 'Wenn nun nichts war.' A further translation in the same vein includes 'now if it is

---

[21] The reading in DK is quite generally accepted, including by Reale and KRS.
[22] Further inferential uses of τοίνυν are found in B2 and B8.

nothing' advocated by McKirahan, Barnes, and KRS.[23] All, as we shall soon see, peg Melissus with an unnecessary weakening of his inferential vocabulary.

Melissus establishes that the generation of what-is requires that before it came into being it was nothing. It is then that, on the usually favoured manuscript reading, we get εἰ τοίνυν μηδὲν ἦν, οὐδαμὰ ἂν γένοιτο οὐδὲν ἐκ μηδενός. Melissus' standard usage of the particle strongly suggests that we should take this sentence as an inference stemming from the previous premise.

However, the prohibition of *ex nihilo* generation does *not* follow from Melissus' understanding of the generation of what-is as the coming to be of something from nothing. If Melissus were attempting to reason his way to this conclusion, he would need, at the very least, the additional thought that the concept of nothing that his definition of generation would require cannot obtain.

Rather – and this explains why translators have been hesitant to understand the logical, conclusive use of τοίνυν – the impossibility of *ex nihilo* generation seems not a conclusion or an inference but a *further premise*. A look back at the structure of the fragment makes this plain. It is easy to assume that an argument will begin with premises before working towards a conclusion. On this model, the last sentence of B1 would be Melissus' conclusion. However, Melissus' fragments are much more prone to begin with the desired conclusion before offering premises from which that conclusion is drawn. The arguments against motion in B7 and plurality in B8 are excellent examples. The conclusion in each case is provided near the beginning of the argument, and then the argument is made before a further restatement of the conclusion. B1 in combination with the first sentence of B2 conforms to this model. Therefore, I take it that the first sentence of B1 is the conclusion that Melissus is aiming to establish from a premise or premises that follow, and that the sentence currently under examination is among those premises.

τοίνυν in B1, then, is at odds with the remainder of Melissus' fragments and unlikely to be correct. It is easy to speculate on the

---

[23] Barnes 1982: 184, McKirahan 1994: 292, and KRS: 393. Sedley (1999: 26) also follows suit.

reasons why τοίνυν crept into the manuscript tradition. The use of the same particle in B2 to reiterate the results of B1 may have led to a dittography of a kind. Perhaps it is simply a matter of a scribe making the easy mistake of thinking that Melissus was using the common construction of the conditional with τοίνυν. Melissus uses this construction twice in B7 alone. Whatever the reason, we may now turn to the second family of manuscript readings.

The alternative reading, εἰ τύχοι νῦν, also faces a number of obstacles to its easy acceptance. The sentence is, for example, asyndetic, violating Melissus' standard practice.[24]

We are faced with a difficulty: εἰ τύχοι νῦν μηδὲν ἦν is not possible Greek. The bar to accepting this reading has been the incongruity of τύχοι with ἦν. Where we expect to find a participle to agree with τύχοι, we have ἦν. The straightforward emendation of ἦν to the participle ἐόν[25] gives a ready solution to our problem and, thereby, provides us with a working text that is credible Melissan Greek.[26] It is easy enough to imagine how ἐόν was replaced with ἦν in the manuscript tradition, especially when coupled with the presence of the double ἦν in the first sentence of the fragment. This would have yielded an ungrammatical sentence, then routinely normalised by the change of τύχοι to the reassuringly Melissan τοίνυν. It is, of course, likely that Melissus would have written ἐόν for ὄν as he does in B7. Accepting the emendation, I translate the clause εἰ τύχοι νῦν μηδὲν ἐόν as 'If it happened that it were now nothing.'

Two final areas are worth exploring. First I offer the translation of οὐδαμά as the temporal 'at no time' in place of the more commonly understood 'in no way' and its variants.[27] This is perfectly standard Greek and it is surprising that it has heretofore not been suggested. LSJ, in fact, give 'never' as their first definition of οὐδαμά. The use of the word in the poem(s) of Empedocles provides further support for the temporal translation. All three uses of οὐδαμά in Empedocles are clearly intended to mean 'never'.[28]

---

[24] Vitali (1973: 163–8), the only commentator I know of who takes up this second reading, fails to address this issue.

[25] Huby and Taylor (2011: 69 n.58) consider but reject this emendation. See also Ritter and Preller (1888) who suggest εἰ τοίνυν τύχοι μηδὲν ἐόν.

[26] Vitali (1973) emends ἦν to εἶναι. I doubt this is possible Greek.

[27] KRS: 393) has 'in no way'. Vitali (1973: 131) has the similar 'in nessun modo'.

[28] B17.15, B17.21, and B26.13.

†εἰ τοίνυν μηδὲν ἦν, οὐδαμά ἂν γένοιτο οὐδὲν ἐκ μηδενός†

We are left then with two wrinkles to iron out. Eliminating the possibility of reading τοίνυν leaves us with a decidedly un-Melissan, asyndetic sentence. We might simply leave it as such. However, the absence of any parallels in the other fragments tells against leaving it asyndetic. Rather I prefer to make the simple addition of δέ to normalise the sentence.

Finally, we need to work out the correct reading of the first sentence of B2, which likely follows directly on from B1. This is important because the sentence acts as a restatement of the conclusion reached in B1.[29] This has been well recognised by Sedley,[30] who suggests re-punctuating the sentence to make proper sense of the division between Melissus' argument for temporal infinity and his second argument, to which the bulk of B2 is devoted, for spatial infinity. I follow Sedley's suggestion below.

However, we still face the problem of which reading of the sentence to accept.

(a) ὅτε τοίνυν οὐκ ἐγένετο, **ἔστι δέ**, ἀεὶ ἦν καὶ ἀεὶ ἔσται
    Therefore, since it did not come to be, but *is*, it always was and always will be.

(b) ὅτε τοίνυν οὐκ ἐγένετο, **ἔστι τε** καὶ ἀεὶ ἦν καὶ ἀεὶ ἔσται
    Therefore, since it did not come to be, it is, always was and always will be.

The conclusive nature of the sentence tilts the balance in favour of (b). All that is needed is a restatement of the conclusion reached in B1. This is what we find in (b). In (a) we do not find a simple restatement of a conclusion but also a restatement of τι ἔστιν, the fundamental premise of B1. This is extraneous to Melissus' argument; therefore, I favour (b).

Text

Περὶ φύσεως ἢ περὶ τοῦ <ἐ>όντος

<Μέλισσος Σάμιος τάδε λέγει περὶ φύσεως ἢ περὶ τοῦ ἐόντος.> εἰ μὲν μηδὲν ἔστι, περὶ τούτου τί ἂν λέγοιτο ὡς <ἐ>όντος τινός; εἰ δέ τι ἐστίν, ἀεὶ ἦν ὅ τι ἦν καὶ ἀεὶ ἔσται. εἰ γὰρ ἐγένετο, ἀναγκαῖόν ἐστι

---

[29] First suggested by Verdenius (1948: 9).   [30] Sedley 1999: 125–6.

πρὶν γενέσθαι εἶναι μηδέν. εἰ <δὲ> τύχοι νῦν μηδὲν ἐόν, οὐδαμὰ ἂν γένοιτο οὐδὲν ἐκ μηδενός. ὅτε τοίνυν οὐκ ἐγένετο, ἔστι τε καὶ ἀεὶ ἦν καὶ ἀεὶ ἔσται.

Translation

On Nature or What There Is

Melissus the Samian says the following concerning nature or what is. If it is nothing, what could be said about it as if it were something? But if it is something, it always was whatever it was and always will be. For if it came to be, it is necessary that prior to coming to be it was nothing. But if it happened that it were *now* nothing, at no time would anything come to be from (that) nothing. Since, therefore, it did not come to be, it both is and always was and always will be.

B2 AND B3: SPATIAL INFINITY

ὅτε τοίνυν οὐκ ἐγένετο, ἔστι τε καὶ ἀεὶ ἦν καὶ ἀεὶ ἔσται καὶ ἀρχὴν οὐκ ἔχει
οὐδὲ τελευτήν, ἀλλ' ἄπειρόν ἐστιν. εἰ μὲν γὰρ ἐγένετο, ἀρχὴν ἂν εἶχεν (ἤρξατο
γὰρ ἄν ποτε γενόμενον) καὶ τελευτήν (ἐτελεύτησε γὰρ ἄν ποτε γενόμενον)·
ὅτε δὲ μήτε ἤρξατο μήτε ἐτελεύτησεν, ἀεί τε ἦν καὶ ἀεὶ ἔσται <καὶ> οὐκ ἔχει
ἀρχὴν οὐδὲ τελευτήν· οὐ γὰρ ἀεὶ εἶναι ἀνυστόν, ὅ τι μὴ πᾶν ἔστι.

(DK30B2)

ἀλλ' ὥσπερ ἔστιν ἀεί, οὕτω καὶ τὸ μέγεθος ἄπειρον ἀεὶ χρὴ εἶναι.

(DK30B3)

Introduction

Printed above is the text of B2 and B3 as it appears in DK. Below
a text with an accompanying translation that reflects several modifications is offered. I will defend each change in turn. However,
before we come to this, it is worth quickly exploring the range of
interpretations B2 has received. As we shall see, the fragment has
played an outsized role in the history of the criticism of Melissus'
argumentation since Aristotle. We shall also see how Melissus
engages with a highly controversial theme in early Greek thinking:
the nature of body and bodiliness, and the level of abstraction
evident on the road towards a concept of 'matter'. Melissus, I will
argue, stands at the centre-point of this process of conceptual
development.

It is well known that Aristotle did not think much of Melissus'
philosophy. What is perhaps less familiar is that Aristotle's low
opinion did not amount to complete disregard. Aristotle deemed
Melissus too valuable an example to be dismissed outright or
ignored. Rather Melissus proved a useful fool; he was so

65

obviously guilty of logical blunders that he provided a textbook demonstration of an argument gone awry.[1]

Aristotle's use of Melissus as a negative example is fairly standardised.[2] In the *Sophistici Elenchi* (*SE*), Aristotle's compendium of fallacious arguments, the same objection to Melissus is repeated three times in similar terms. The first instance, at 167b12–20, is the fullest:

ὁμοίως δὲ καὶ ἐν τοῖς συλλογιστικοῖς, οἷον ὁ Μελίσσου λόγος ὅτι ἄπειρον τὸ ἅπαν, λαβὼν τὸ μὲν ἅπαν ἀγένητον (ἐκ γὰρ μὴ ὄντος οὐδὲν ἂν γενέσθαι), τὸ δὲ γενόμενον ἐξ ἀρχῆς γενέσθαι· εἰ μὴ οὖν γέγονεν, ἀρχὴν οὐκ ἔχει τὸ πᾶν, ὥστ' ἄπειρον. οὐκ ἀνάγκη δὲ τοῦτο συμβαίνειν· οὐ γὰρ εἰ τὸ γενόμενον ἅπαν ἀρχὴν ἔχει, καὶ εἴτι ἀρχὴν ἔχει, γέγονεν, ὥσπερ οὐδ' εἰ ὁ πυρέττων θερμός, καὶτὸν θερμὸν ἀνάγκη πυρέττειν.

The same happens in syllogistic reasoning too, such as in Melissus' argument, that the universe is infinite. It takes it as a premise that the universe has not come into being (for nothing could come to be from what is not) and that that which has come to be has come from a beginning. Therefore, he says, if the universe has not come to be, it has no beginning and, therefore, is infinite. But this does not necessarily follow; for if everything that has come to be has a beginning, it does not follow also that anything that has a beginning has come to be, any more than, if a man who has a fever must be hot, it follows that a man who is hot must necessarily have a fever.

There are a number of notable features to be found in this passage. It is significant that Aristotle thinks it is τὸ ἅπαν (the universe) that is Melissus' subject. In the previous section, we determined that this misses the force of Melissus' strict deductive method: it is not 'the universe' but rather 'what-is' or 'nature' that is the subject of his treatise. Most striking, however, is Aristotle's underdetermined use of ἄπειρον. This is especially puzzling. The argument to which Aristotle refers in the quoted passage is found in fragment B2, the very place where Melissus seems to proceed from temporal to spatial infinity.[3] Whether Melissus did make such a shift from the established premise of sempiternity to

---

[1] See Brémond (2016: 47–8) for the claim that Aristotle's interest in Melissus is twofold: (1) Melissus is a prime example of a second-rate thinker, and (2) Melissus is the chief representative of Eleaticism.

[2] This point is made by Bostock (2006: 105).

[3] That this shift occurs in B2 is frequently denied. See, for example, Merrill 1998: 377–8. In any case, in B3 and B4 it is clear that, at least by then, Melissus thinks he is entitled to the claim that what-is is spatially infinite.

a claim of spatial infinity (in all directions) in B2 has been a matter of some scholarly controversy and we might think that it is rather unfortunate that Aristotle is not of more help in the matter here. I believe that it is clear that Melissus does make such a move and this will become evident as we go along. My suggestion here is that, in the context of the *SE*, Aristotle had no need to specify whether he thought Melissus had temporal or spatial infinity in mind.[4] Aristotle is only interested in demonstrating that Melissus fell victim to shoddy logic and, thus, seeking out a specific understanding of ἄπειρον would be a superfluous exercise and perhaps serve only to distract from his point.

A look at the end of the quoted passage will help make my point. The mention of the feverish man is suggestive. Aristotle is charging Melissus with the fallacy of denying the antecedent. The use of ἀνάγκη (necessity) in the final line emphasises this point. Aristotle takes it that we can agree that a man who has a fever is hot,[5] just as we can agree that anything that has come into being has a beginning. The converse, however, does not follow of necessity, i.e. the negation of its antecedent does not entail the negation of its consequent. Someone who feels hot may have a fever; we might even agree that this person is more likely to have a fever than a person who feels neither hot nor cold. It is, however, not necessary that such a person has a fever.

We find the same structure in the argument that in Aristotle's account purports to be Melissan. If the universe came to be, it has a beginning. Therefore, if the universe did not come to be, it has no beginning. If A, then B, but not-A; therefore not-B. Of course, much of what we will soon explore is whether Aristotle fairly represented Melissus' argument. The point to take away here is that, in the *SE*, Aristotle does exactly what we would expect of him. He finds an example of what he takes to be faulty logic and exploits it for its didactic value.

The *Rezeptionsgeschichte* of B2 has been dominated by Aristotle's criticism in the *Sophistici Elenchi* and the similar but

---

[4] Bostock (2006: 105) is right to note that spatial infinity seems a likely candidate because it is what is at stake between Aristotle and Melissus.

[5] I.e. hot to the touch of an external observer. Anybody who has had a fever will remember that they probably felt cold despite their abnormally elevated internal temperature.

somewhat more complex treatment in the *Physics*. As one might expect, the response to Aristotle's claim that Melissus made the logical blunder of falsely drawing a conclusion from a denial of the antecedent of a conditional has largely divided into two camps. There are those who are sympathetic to Aristotle's complaint and thus find Melissus' argument wanting.[6] Others have attempted (with mixed results) to extricate Melissus from Aristotle's scrapheap. Two prominent efforts of the latter are those of Burnet and Cherniss/Verdenius.[7]

Burnet holds that Aristotle's criticism would be fair if it were clear that Melissus inferred that what-is is spatially infinite from the premise that what-is lacks a beginning or end in time. However, Burnet denies that B2 makes a claim that what-is is without limit in space. On this account, B2 is little more than a recapitulation of what is found in B1. Burnet seems mistaken in this regard. Even if we were to agree that B2 does not make such a claim, B3 and B4 certainly do. All Burnet's reading succeeds in achieving is to delay Melissus' blunder until those latter fragments, unless we are to think that these are the product of a lost bit of reasoning, originally situated between B2 and B3.

Cherniss, with a clarification added by Verdenius, offers us a much more creditable effort.[8] The latter provides the following translation and schematisation of B2 (square brackets are my own):

Since, then, it (i.e. Being) was not the result of a process,[9]

1) It is and always was and always will be[10]
    a) And has no beginning or end but is infinite [both temporally and spatially speaking]. For, had it been the result of a process, it would have a [temporal and spatial] beginning (because it would at some time have been at the commencement of the process) and a [temporal and spatial] end (for it would at some time have been at the end of the process)[11]

---

[6] The level of Melissus' culpability according to this group varies quite considerably from outright damnation (Gomperz 1906: 186–7) to affectionate, but condescending, sympathy (Barnes 1982: 196). See Reale (1970: 66–104) for a full account.

[7] Burnet 1930: 325, Cherniss 1935: 67–71, and Verdenius 1948: 8–10.

[8] It is worth noting that Reale (1970) largely accepts their solution.

[9] This is the conclusion Cherniss takes from B1.   [10] ἔστι τε καὶ ἀεὶ ἦν καὶ ἀεὶ ἔσται.

[11] εἰ μὲν γὰρ ἐγένετο, ἀρχὴν ἂν εἶχεν (ἤρξατο γὰρ ἂν ποτε γινόμενον) καὶ.
    τελευτήν (ἐτελεύτησε γὰρ ἂν ποτε γινόμενον), accepting γινόμενον for γενόμενον.

b) But since it neither began nor stopped and always was and always will be, it has no [temporal or spatial] beginning or end),

c) For it is impossible for that to be always which is not everything.[12]

Verdenius' contribution to this schema is to (rightly) clarify that (1) is not a conclusion reached in B2 but rather a reiteration of the conclusion reached in B1, recapitulated to serve as a premise in B2. Also he offers the suggestion that (c) is not a bridge between (a) and (b) but rather a statement of the conclusion, in negative form, that that which is not infinite could not be eternal.

Does this reading prove Aristotle was off the mark in his criticism of Melissus? Well, yes and no. The benefit of the proposed interpretation is that B2 does nothing more than flesh out what Cherniss and Verdenius take Melissus to understand by 'generation'. Verdenius confirms this by offering a syllogistic rendering of his improved interpretation:

'(A) Being is eternal,

(B) What is eternal has no [temporal or spatial] beginning or end,

(C) Consequently, Being has no beginning or end.'

What this amounts to is simply the claim that generation, by definition, is a process with a beginning and end in both time and space. ἀρχή has, then, the dual senses of 'spatial starting-point' and 'temporal beginning' and is used interchangeably with τελευτή.[13] Therefore, originative processes have (spatial) beginnings and (spatial) ends. Since what-is (or Being as Cherniss and Verdenius have it) is not generated, it is not a process, and, thus, it has no spatial ἀρχαί.

On the face of it, this understanding gives us some reason to think that Aristotle's criticisms are unfair. On the Cherniss/Verdenius reading, we might object that Melissus simply did not accept that generation could be instantaneous, on a non-growing model. This does not absolve Melissus of getting simple generation wrong (at least as Aristotle understands it), but it does give us a plausible reason for why he did so.

What about Aristotle's insistence that Melissus improperly drew a conclusion by denying the antecedent of a conditional?

---

[12] οὐ γὰρ ἀεὶ εἶναι ἀνυστόν, ὅ τι μὴ πᾶν ἔστι.   [13] Cherniss 1935: 69–70.

I fail to see how the Cherniss/Verdenius reading ultimately provides a sufficient defence of Melissus. In order for their proposal to be palatable, we need more than the dual claims that generation is not the result of a process and that a process is something with both a temporal and spatial end and beginning. We also need the further claim that *only* those things which are the result of a growing, originative process have spatial ends and beginnings.[14] Let us call their reading with this extra needed premise the *improved* Cherniss/Verdenius reading. With such a modification, we can perhaps escape the claws of logical fallacy. However, it is difficult not to think that Cherniss and Verdenius are guilty of attributing the fault of *petitio principii* to Melissus. If we take the premise 'What-is is eternal' to be understood as already entailing that what-is is spatially infinite, we run the risk of denying any kind of argument (good or bad) to Melissus. The end result of the Cherniss/Verdenius reading risks collapsing in circularity. We also face the problem that the understanding of generation attributed to Melissus is implausible. Not only must generation be a growing process, it must also be the only means of giving what-is spatial limits.

My proposal is to re-examine B2 and determine the premises of the argument. Aristotle suggests that Melissus thought he was entitled to two premises that led to the conclusion of spatial infinity: (a) what-is is sempiternal and (b) what is sempiternal has neither an ἀρχή nor a τελευτή. Notice that Aristotle's criticism hinges on the acceptance by Melissus not only of these premises but also of the claim that they alone necessarily entail the conclusion of spatial infinity. If we could establish that Melissus had in mind a more sophisticated argument, my suggestion is that Aristotle's criticism will appear less apt and more misleadingly reductivist. Ultimately, I will argue that Melissus is committed to the view that generation entails both a temporal and a spatial beginning and end in B2. In this respect, I am indebted to Cherniss and Verdenius. Where I differ is that I deny that Melissus commits himself to this entailment as anything like

---

[14] Natorp (1890: 147–51) seems to suggest such an idea. This is recognised by Cherniss, but he fails to incorporate the suggestion adequately into his own interpretation.

a definition of generation. Rather I suggest that Melissus draws an exclusive connection between generation and spatial beginnings and ends only as a product of hypothetical charity. The idea is that if there were a spatial beginning and end of what-is, Melissus can only rationally conceive of such a state of affairs as the product of generation. This, I maintain, is quite an important caveat to the Cherniss/Verdenius reading and helps us to conform better to the substance of Melissus' argument.

B2: Text and Translation

(a) ὅτε τοίνυν οὐκ ἐγένετο, ἔστι τε καὶ ἀεὶ ἦν καὶ ἀεὶ ἔσται. (b) καὶ ἀρχὴν οὐκ ἔχει οὐδὲ τελευτήν, ἀλλ᾽ ἄπειρόν ἐστιν. εἰ μὲν γὰρ ἐγένετο, ἀρχὴν ἂν εἶχεν (ἤρξατο γὰρ ἄν ποτε γινόμενον) καὶ τελευτήν (ἐτελεύτησε γὰρ ἄν ποτε γινόμενον)· ὅτε δὲ μήτε ἤρξατο μήτε ἐτελεύτησεν, ἀεί τε ἦν καὶ ἀεὶ ἔσται,[15] οὐκ ἔχει ἀρχὴν οὐδὲ τελευτήν· (c) οὐ γὰρ ἀεὶ εἶναι ἀνυστόν, ὅ τι μὴ πᾶν ἐστι.

(a) Therefore, since it did not come to be, it both is and always was and always will be. (b) And it has no beginning or end, but is infinite. For if it had come to be it would have a beginning (for it would have begun coming-to-be at some time) and end (for it would have ended coming-to-be at some time). But since it neither began nor ended, and it always was and always will be, it has no beginning or end. (c) For whatever is not entire cannot be always.

The above text and translation reflect two points established in the previous section. In (a) the text found earlier in Simplicius' commentary at 29.22, ἔστι τε καί, is preferable to the reading ἔστι δέ, found at 109.20. This is because I take it that (a) functions as a recapitulation of the conclusion of B1, not a restatement of the premises that underpinned that conclusion. If we accept ἔστι δέ, it is just such an unnecessary restatement of the premise that what-is *is* that we find Melissus offering. My preferred reading merely provides the absolutely expected recapitulation of the conclusion that what-is is sempiternal, reiterated to act as premise in the coming argument for spatial infinity. I submit that this preference better conforms to Melissus' deductive method, as we can confirm by looking elsewhere, e.g. at the start of B7. The second point to note is that I place a full stop after ἔσται, following David Sedley's

---

[15] <καί> is inserted here by many editors, including DK. Sedley (1999: 132) rightly acknowledges that there is no need for it as taking τε as 'and' is all we need here.

suggestion. This follows naturally once we accept that (a) is simply the conclusion Melissus established in B1.[16] On this basis, we can further say that it is evident that B2 immediately followed B1 in the original arrangement of Melissus' treatise. While Simplicius does not make this explicit (though he says nothing to exclude it), the highly Melissan restatement of a conclusion previously established virtually guarantees B2 is continuous with B1.

A further change to the standard DK text is also printed above. I accept γινόμενον for γενόμενον in both instances in (b). This change is widely accepted,[17] conforms better to the manuscript tradition, and is needed to make best sense of the argument. If we were to accept γενόμενον, we would find that the parenthetical explanations merely restate the points they are trying to prove, i.e. that something that has come to be has a temporal beginning and end. The acceptance of γινόμενον saves the text from needless repetition and gives it some sense.[18] This is because we are able to construe γινόμενον, a present participle – but not γενόμενον – as working in tandem with ἤρξατο. Translating γενόμενον yields the unhelpful '... have a beginning (for having come into being, it would have begun at some time', while reading γινόμενον makes the important claim that generation is process, i.e non-instantaneous.

The heart of B2 is the argument contained within (b). Its structure is resolutely Melissan. The conclusion to be demonstrated is first announced, followed by a piece of reasoning that closely parallels the argumentative method we observed in B1. Melissus once again makes use of a conditional statement that offers a counterfactual for consideration. What is entailed by provisionally accepting the counterfactual is next stated. The argument is concluded by demonstrating that the consequent raised in the conditional cannot hold true. A look at the argument against motion in B7 confirms how thoroughly typical this pattern of argumentation is for Melissus.

---

[16] Sedley 1999: 132. Verdenius (1948) is the first, to my knowledge, to offer this understanding of the logic of the argument.

[17] E.g. by Barnes (1982: 195–6), Reale, and, of course, Cherniss and Verdenius. See Vitali (1973: 169–75) for an interesting, though unpersuasive, argument for γενόμενον.

[18] Barnes (1982: 196) forcefully makes this point.

What is Melissus' argument in **(b)**? Well it should be uncontroversial to say that Melissus understands that if what-is has not come to be it has neither an ἀρχή nor a τελευτή. Our look at Aristotle's criticism of Melissus in the *SE* did not make it clear that he thought Melissus had spatial, as opposed to temporal, ἀρχαί and τελευταί in mind. However, we shall soon see that in the *Physics* such a spatial reading is unambiguously adopted. Some scholars (e.g. Burnet) have criticised Aristotle's interpretation as misleading, but it is clear that the evidence firmly supports a spatial reading. Fragment B3, which Simplicius discusses immediately following B2, strongly suggests that Melissus did hold that what-is is spatially unlimited. The language of that fragment is unambiguous: 'ἀλλ' ὥσπερ ἔστιν ἀεί, οὕτω καὶ τὸ μέγεθος ἄπειρον ἀεὶ χρὴ εἶναι'. Perhaps one might object that this only *suggests* that B2 argues for a thesis of spatial infinity, it does not *prove* it. After all, it is conceivable that Simplicius misses out a bit of reasoning that Melissus originally supplied between B2 and B3. However, Kirk, Raven, and Schofield rightly point out that B2 is far too complex an argument to be simply aimed at proving temporal infinity, something B1 has already accomplished![19] On the internal evidence of the treatise and the external confirmation of Aristotle, it seems safe to accept that Melissus aims at a conclusion of spatial infinity in B2.

Melissus proceeds by considering what would be entailed were we to accept that what-is came to be. What comes to be for Melissus, on the improved Cherniss/Verdenius reading, has a spatial beginning and end. This is because, as we learn in the parenthetical explanations, what comes to be must begin coming-to-be some time and end coming-to-be at some time.[20] Our acceptance of γινόμενον for γενόμενον confirms that Melissus conceives of coming-to-be as a *process*. What does this mean? Well, the two instances of ποτέ indicate that generation is not instantaneous for Melissus but necessarily occurs within temporal bounds. At one time generation starts, it continues for a time, and then it finishes at a time later than it began. Generation, then, is

---

[19] KRS: 394.
[20] Simplicius supports this reading by emphasising the chronological sense (χρονικόν) of ποτέ at *In Phys.* 109.25.

best understood on Melissus' account as something like a process of growth on a biological model. Just as the sapling begins growing at one point in time and space and finishes its growth at another, so does the generation of what-is. One could take issue with this understanding of generation, as I will suggest Aristotle does in the *Physics* passage discussed below. However, we ought to follow Aristotle's cue and consider Melissus' argument not only in terms of the veracity of his premises, but also in respect of the quality of his argument.

Let us, then, provisionally accept that generation is a process of growth that begins at one time and ends at another. Yet, however we understand generation for Melissus, Aristotle's criticism in the *SE* still seems to hold true. Melissus argues: if (p) (what-is is generated), then it began to be generated at some time and it ended being generated at some time and thus (q) (it has spatial ἀρχαί); but not (p), therefore not (q). Must we accept that Melissus is guilty of fallaciously arguing from a denial of the antecedent? Unless we plump for the improved version of the Cherniss/ Verdenius reading, according to which he simply holds that what is not the product of a generative process, by definition, does not have a spatial ἀρχή or τελευτή, Melissus' argument seems vulnerable to Aristotle's criticism. In addition, as we shall see, even such a solution leaves Melissus open to the charge that he grossly misconstrues the nature of generation.

Yet we might give Melissus a more sympathetic reading if we consider what he takes to be entailed by understanding generation as a process. As I have noted, this seems to amount to the claim that generation is not instantaneous but begins and ends at different times.[21] However, it is clear that Melissus has a richer notion in mind. If we think that what-is came to be at one time and did not finish coming to be at that same time, clearly one *part* of it came to be first. It is this thought that brings us from a consideration of what-is in time to what-is in space. Generation, construed as a growing process, seems to entail spatial ἀρχή and τελευτή for Melissus. It is how we understand this entailment that will help put Aristotle's objection in context and, hopefully, dissolve it. Yet,

---

[21] This is confirmed, in a round-about way, by Simplicius, at *In Phys.* 109.24ff.

prima facie, Aristotle's criticism still has bite. Even accepting that generation is a process and that that process produces spatial beginnings and ends, we are still left thinking that Melissus fails to consider that what-is might not be generated yet have a spatial ἀρχή and τελευτή (understood as spatial limits). Indeed, one might reasonably think, Aristotle himself argues that this is indeed true of the universe.

If this analysis is correct, the criticism levelled at Melissus by Aristotle and subsequent critics turns on the failure to confront the possibility that what-is is ungenerated yet spatially limited. It is perhaps surprising, from a historical perspective, that Melissus' detractors have been so ready to ground their disparagement on this point. Whatever we make of the details of Melissus' relationship with Parmenides, it is uncontroversial to think that he builds upon Parmenidean arguments, using novel arguments to defend the earlier Eleatic's positions, while differing, at least superficially, in places. One such area of disagreement is the nature of the limits of what-is (τὸ ἐόν, as Parmenides has it). Indeed, on one natural reading of Parmenides' B8.42–4, Being or what-is is presented as spherical and thus has bounds (πείρατα). For Parmenides, then, Being is ungenerated (ἀγένητον at B8.3) yet limited. Of course, many commentators have argued that Parmenides' comparison of Being to the mass of a well-rounded ball (εὐκύκλου σφαίρης ... ὄγκῳ) is intended not as a physical description but as an analogy used to emphasise the perfection of Being. This is one possible, and arguably charitable, reading of the text. However, there is every reason to think that Melissus understood Parmenides' point spatially. The evidence of the ancient reception of Parmenides suggests that he was universally understood to have held that Being is spherical.[22] This is clear, for example, from the argument raised by the Eleatic Stranger in Plato's *Sophist*, beginning at 244e1, in which B8 is marshalled to demonstrate that Parmenides unwittingly commits himself to divisibility and, therefore, the existence of parts.[23] Indeed there is no hint in ancient sources that Parmenides was taken to have metaphorical limits in mind. I submit that, with

---

[22] This is not always properly recognised, but see Barnes 1982: 201–4.
[23] Aristotle, at *Physics* 186b12–14, also seems to think that Parmenides was committed to the thought that what-is is extended in magnitude.

this thought in place, we should be especially wary of thinking that Melissus failed to take account adequately of the possibility that what-is is not generated yet has spatial ἀρχαί.

Therefore, there is every reason to think that Melissus believed he had successfully eliminated a spatial ἀρχή and τελευτή from his picture of what-is in his B2. This can only be because he is committed to the thought (in B2 at least) that a spatial beginning and end, understood as spatial limits, could only come about from a process of generation. So far, we have, in the main, reached the improved Cherniss/Verdenius understanding. As I have intimated, this construal goes some way towards dismissing Aristotle's criticism that Melissus fallaciously denies the antecedent. However, Melissus is still left with what seems to be an indefensible understanding of generation. I do not go so far as to claim that we can cleanly extract the hook from Melissus' mouth, but let us see if we can determine why he takes the bait so enthusiastically.

First it is worth taking into account a connection David Sedley has drawn between B2 and a testimonium that comes down to us from Pseudo-Plutarch on the doctrine of Democritus.[24]

Δημόκριτος ὁ Ἀβδηρίτης ὑπεστήσατο τὸ πᾶν ἄπειρον διὰ τὸ μηδαμῶς ὑπό τινος αὐτὸ δεδημιουργῆσθαι. (DK68A39)

Democritus of Abdera maintained that the universe is infinite because it has in no way been crafted by anyone.

Sedley takes this to be a 'version' of Melissus' argument. The vexed problem of determining the relative dates of Democritus and Melissus means that we can say nothing with certainty about who originated the argument. However, that is not important for our immediate purposes. The explanation of the universe's spatial infinity attributed to Democritus suggests that he, like Melissus, was committed to the idea that spatial limits could only come about as the product of a process of generation.

It is true that Democritus' motivation for adducing this sort of argument is likely to have been very different from what we can discern in Melissus. While it would be unwise to attribute to Democritus the theological implications of the later version of

---

[24] Sedley 2007: 136 n.6.

atomism propounded by Epicurus and his followers, it is clear enough that developing a theory where atoms are self-organising without the need for an intelligent force is evident in early atomism. One might recall here the remark found in Diogenes Laertius 9.34–5 (DK68B5), where Democritus is said to have criticised Anaxagoras because of his views on cosmic ordering and *nous*. We might conjecture that Democrtius is particularly hostile to demiurgic creation because it poses a direct threat to the explanatory economy that is the hallmark of atomism. We might think, as well, that it is just this emphasis on economy that motivates the criticism of the role of *nous* or an intelligent organising force in cosmic ordering that Anaxagoras adopts.

It is also crucial, as David Sedley points out, that the universe be infinite if the rather modest self-organising properties of Democritean atoms are to be taken to be sufficient to explain the complex phenomena of life in our world.[25] If there are infinitely many atoms in infinitely many worlds, then every possible arrangement of atoms is in place somewhere in the whole of what there is.[26] On such a model, the fact that life has flourished in our world is no longer surprising. Indeed, if it had not happened to us, it would have happened somewhere else.

Both the growing model of generation Melissus seems to adopt and the craftsman analogy of Democritus turn on spatial beginnings and ends. Just as a tree begins growing in one spot and finishes in another, the potter begins moulding the clay on the wheel at one point and finishes it at another. The thinking seems to be, as Sedley suggests, that both Democritus and Melissus are proceeding from the default assumption, common in Ionian natural philosophy, that the universe is infinite.[27] For both, it seems that the only good reason to reject this default assumption and think that the universe has a spatial ἀρχή and τελευτή and therefore spatial limits would be to accept that the universe is the product of a generative process. As both deny this, they maintain that the universe is infinite.[28]

---

[25] Sedley 2007: 136.   [26] See Cicero, *Academica* II.55.

[27] Sedley 2007: 136–7. Anaximander and Anaxagoras are prime examples.

[28] That both Democrtius and Melissus use a similar argument to establish infinity provides an interesting clue to the nature of the Eleatic influence on atomism. It is, of course, very often assumed that it is in response to the Eleatics that Leucippus and Democritus

Does this dissolve Aristotle's criticism? I think we can begin to see why Melissus would want to argue for a thesis of spatial infinity, but we still lack any convincing argument why spatial limits can *only* be said to come about on account of the universe's generation. However, Sedley's point that Melissus worked within the tradition of Ionian natural philosophy and its assumption of an infinite universe is important and points towards a solution.

I suggest that, using recognisably Melissan materials, we can construct an argument which eliminates spatial beginnings and ends, escapes Aristotle's criticism of fallaciously denying the antecedent and, importantly, does not necessarily attribute a grossly mistaken understanding of generation. Let us review first what premises we have discerned in Melissus' argument thus far in B2.

(a) What-is is not generated.
(b) Generation is a growing process that entails an ἀρχή and τελευτή of a spatial nature (generation begins at one point in space and ends at a different point in space)
(c) If what-is is (see Melissus' preface), it is infinite unless there is a reason to think otherwise.

This last premise perhaps seems outrageously question-begging. We can hardly say that Melissus thinks that what-is is infinite because he is working from a shared cultural assumption that it is infinite. However, what I suggest is that (c) is less feeble than we might think at first sight and that it points towards a very serious objection to the thought that what-is is ungenerated yet spatially bound. Melissus is, in effect, demanding an explanation for spatial bounds. Borrowing from Melissus' favoured model of counter-factual argumentation, assume that what-is is spatially limited. If what-is is spatially limited, there must be a reason why this is the case. Going further we might demand a reason why the limits occur at one place rather than another. It is here that one of the

formulating their atomism, most strikingly by turning the Eleatic denial of what-is-not on its head by adopting its Melissan association with void and accepting it as a central piece of their physics. That Democrtius shares the argument with Melissus furthers the view that it is *this* Eleatic in particular who is the most relevant figure for atomism. See KRS: 408–9 for a reading of *De Generatione et Corruptione* 325a2ff that maintains that, for Aristotle at least, it is a near certainty that it is Melissus who had the greatest impact on Leucippus.

great advantages of this line of reasoning may be observed. Melissus is offering not only an *ou mallon* argument but one that strikes at the very heart of Parmenides' commitment to a spherical universe. We might think that Melissus provides here something of a companion argument to Archytas' famous rebuttal to the notion of a finite universe: he wonders whether, if he stood at the edge of the universe, he could not extend his hand or cane outside it.[29] Melissus is asking why the edge on which Archytas stands should be in one place rather than another. Ultimately, this suggests that Melissus is demanding an answer as to why Parmenides' universe should have one radius rather than another.

Melissus, on this construal, is objecting to the arbitrary nature of assuming that what-is is ungenerated yet has a spatial beginning or end. Perhaps an opponent would raise the objection that assuming that what-is does not have spatial limits is equally objectionable. No doubt they might. Yet Melissus would have recourse to the intuitively plausible notion that it is more reasonable to question the existence of something than its non-existence. The detective reasonably may ask why a man was near the scene of a crime; it is less sensible to ask why he was not.

On my construal, I submit that Melissus need not be understood to maintain that spatial limits are necessarily the product of generation, but rather that the only good explanation for their existence in the case of what-is (i.e. an explanation that overcomes the default assumption of infinity) is that they are the product of generation. My suggestion then is that B2 avoids the objection that Melissus assumes an implausible understanding of generation if we think that it rests on something like indifference reasoning.[30]

By indifference reasoning, I mean nothing more than that Melissus is committed to a confident epistemological position. If one characteristic of Melissus derived from his treatise is abundantly apparent, it is that he thinks deductive argument is sufficient to produce an understanding of the universe. This belief in

---

[29] DK47A24

[30] See Makin 1993: particularly 33–41. Makin finds the clearest instance of indifference reasoning in Melissus at B7.2. I use 'indifference reasoning' and not the 'Principle of Sufficient Reason' here because I understand Melissus to be committed to an epistemological and not necessarily a metaphysical position.

reason's valence is vividly contrasted with the instability of sense perception in B8. Yet there is no hint in Melissus that he embraced any form of the scepticism about the limitations of human access to knowledge that we find in Xenophanes' fragments (particularly B34 and B38).

If this is correct, Melissus is committed to the thought that the existence of features of the universe is subject to demands for explanation. We have already observed this in action. Why does Melissus think there is something and not nothing? He raises the question of how we could speak about nothing as though it were something. This is, of course, not a *proof* of the claim that there is something, but, by offering us the choice between 'what-is is nothing' or 'what-is is something', Melissus is content to indicate that should the former be the case, his treatise would already be at an end.

Why is it that what-is is not generated? *Ex nihilo nihil fit.* How then does indifference reasoning work for Melissus? A default assumption of infinite spatial extension (in all directions) encourages one to demand reasons if the assumption is to be abandoned. The idea, then, is that the nexus of questions plausibly asked about the existence of spatial limits (Why here rather than there? Why this part rather than another? etc.) can only be answered by Melissus through an assumption of a process of generation.

Surely though there could be found an indefinite number of reasons for the existence of spatial limits and why they are at a particular place without thinking that they are the product of a generative process? What about Parmenides' πείρατα in B8? It is worth considering why Parmenides' adopts his spherical language. If we look to B8.42–3, we learn that there is a strong connection between limits and Being's completeness:

αὐτὰρ ἐπεὶ πεῖρας πύματον, τετελεσμένον ἐστί
πάντοθεν

But since there is a furthest limit, it is perfected
From every angle

The point we seem to be encouraged to take away is that for Parmenides the existence of πείρατα confirms that τὸ ἐόν is all-embracing in the sense that it leaves nothing out, i.e. limits establish wholeness. Melissus makes just the opposite assumption. If we look at his argument establishing numerical monism in B6, infinite spatial extension proves that there can be only one thing. Two three-dimensional entities cannot both be infinite because they would limit each other and no longer be infinite. Why? Well it is clear that Melissus understands the infinite not as a line or an extension beginning from a point, but as something unlimited. Therefore, the different assumptions of Parmenides and Melissus about the infinity of the universe are made plain. Both want to establish that what-is embraces the whole of reality: for Parmenides this necessitates limits, for Melissus infinity.

This reading of the infinite for Melissus is confirmed by the last sentence of B2(c): οὐ γὰρ ἀεὶ εἶναι ἀνυστόν, ὅ τι μὴ πᾶν ἔστι. I translate as: 'For whatever is not entire cannot be always.' The sentence has not received the attention it deserves and this is unfortunate because it is not clear, at least on first inspection, what role it plays within Melissus' argument for spatial infinity. Indeed, the aim of the argument seems to switch directions here. Temporal infinity has led to spatial infinity in B2, but one might think (c) seems to indicate that it is spatial infinity that secures its temporal counterpart. What I will suggest is that Melissus does not actually reverse his argument here, but rather is interested in spelling out why coming-to-be is a threat to sempiternity.

Let us make our way through (c). I take ὅ τι in the same way as I do in B1, as generalising in nature, i.e. as simply designating whatever satisfies the predicate in the sentence without further specification. What sort of completeness does Melissus have in mind here? The fact that a process of coming-to-be is described in the previous sentence suggests that it is the incompleteness entailed by this process that is most relevant to the point. So it is not just that a process of coming-to-be acts to establish spatial boundaries at the points it begins and ends, but also that the occurrence of the process itself makes its subject's eternal existence impossible.

Why should this be? On its surface, it does not seem impossible that something might come-to-be and thereafter enjoy an everlasting existence. Of course, the origin stories of many divinities (e.g. Dionysus and Aphrodite) reflect the idea that something's coming-to-be need not have destruction as its corollary.

One approach might be to think that the connection Melissus (and Parmenides) makes between coming-to-be and destruction is significant. Melissus, like Parmenides, takes it that an argument that targets coming-to-be is so easily recast to target destruction that neither provides such a complementary proof, though both proceed as if the issue had been settled.[31] If coming-to-be is eliminated, destruction is thought impossible as well, with the corollary that allowing for the former countenances the latter. With this in mind, it might not seem surprising that Melissus would take the incompleteness of a subject undergoing a process of coming-to-be to imply the possibility, indeed in the whole of time the necessity, of the contrary process. The thought, then, is that the incompleteness involved in a process of coming-to-be intolerably raises the possibility of its subject's destruction.

Consider two related arguments Melissus raises in B7:

(i) εἰ γὰρ ἑτεροιοῦται, ἀνάγκη τὸ ἐὸν μὴ ὁμοῖον εἶναι, ἀλλὰ ἀπόλλυσθαι τὸ πρόσθεν ἐόν, τὸ δὲ οὐκ ἐὸν γίνεσθαι. εἰ τοίνυν τριχὶ μιῆι μυρίοις ἔτεσιν ἑτεροῖον γίνοιτο, ὀλεῖται πᾶν ἐν τῶι παντὶ χρόνωι.

For if it is being qualitatively altered, it is necessary that what-is is not qualitatively alike, but what was previously is being destroyed and what is not is coming to be. Therefore, if it were to undergo qualitative alteration by a single hair in 10,000 years, in the whole of time it all would perish.

(ii) οὐδὲ ἀλγεῖ· οὐ γὰρ ἂν πᾶν εἴη ἀλγέον·
οὐ γὰρ ἂν δύναιτο ἀεὶ εἶναι χρῆμα ἀλγέον.

Nor does it suffer pain. For it would not be entire if it were in pain, for a thing in pain could not be always.

In (ii) we can discern a parallel to what we find in (c), thus suggesting that Melissus was committed to a general principle. What is in pain cannot be entire (πᾶν): therefore, what is in pain cannot be always (ἀεί). The implication that what is not entire cannot be always is identical with what we find in (c). Let us call this principle the Completeness Assumption (CA).

---

[31] See, for example, Parmenides at B8.40.

The precise motivation for the details of Melissus' argument is quite obscure.[32] Why what-is should be explicitly argued not to suffer pain is mysterious and unexpected. Perhaps, as has sometimes been suggested, Melissus proceeded from an assumption that what-is is a living thing. If so, such an argument might seem apposite. More minimally, Melissus could simply be using a model of life to structure his arguments. What one would want to deny for a life understood as complete one might assume is reasonable to deny for reality, understood as something ungenerated, sempiternal, infinite, unique, and homogeneous, i.e. something that shares many of the traditional features ascribed to the perfect life, i.e something divine. In any case, the point I wish to make clear is that CA has some intuitive, or naïve, appeal, at least in a sempiternal universe.

CA gains in attraction if we consider the first argument (i) I have printed above. Here we find the most prominent instance of indifference reasoning in Melissus.[33] We learn that what undergirds CA is the thought that alteration of any kind leaves what-is vulnerable to destruction: if what-is alters, in time it is necessary that it will be destroyed. Why should anyone believe this? One might think of revolution or qualitative change. Both are alterations of a kind but neither seems to imply that their underlying subject must, in time, perish.

Melissus' argument relies on indifference reasoning because he generalises from a single alteration to the possibility of all alterations, including perishing. If one alteration is possible, he seems to think that there is no reason why what-is should not alter in every other respect. The *possibility*, then, of every alteration is put on the table because of the hypothesised instance of a single one.[34]

With the exception of Makin, the explicitly modal nature of Melissus' argument has not been given its sufficient due. Melissus is evidently concerned about eternally unrealised

---

[32] KRS: 397.   [33] See Makin 1993: 37–41 for this suggestion and an excellent analysis.
[34] An alternative reading one might pose is that indifference reasoning is not what is relevant here but rather a strong notion of identity. Such a reading accounts for the notion that were what-is to change, it would have first to be destroyed before coming into being again as the altered subject. Any change means A becomes not-A. However, I fail to see how this understanding would account for the final sentence beginning εἰ τοίνυν.

potentialities.[35] Melissus nips the problem in the bud by denying *any* alternation, and thus he denies the possibility of *every* alteration. However, we may go further than Makin by looking at the vocabulary Melissus adopts. We have seen in (i) the use of ἀνάγκη and in (ii) we find δύναιτο. This suggests that Melissus is indeed concerned with the notions of possibility and necessity and not in a more modest, non-modal argument.

Let us return to (c). It is striking, though hardly unexpected given our previous discussion, that Melissus uses the unambiguously modal ἀνυστόν. This word, connoting possibility, has a strong Presocratic pedigree. It is found in Parmenides, Anaxagoras, and Diogenes of Apollonia, each time in the sense of something possible (or, with a sign of negation, impossible).[36] We learn, then, not only that what-is, understood as all-embracing (πᾶν), *is* infinite, but that it *must* (οὐ ... ἀνυστόν) be so in order to be eternal. Here we find an early indication of the kind of indifference reasoning we discussed above, as found in B7.

An alternative reading of (c) is also worth exploring. One might think that Melissus' point is, in fact, far simpler than what I have sketched above, as it is merely a logical or definitional claim about what it means to be ἀεί. On such an account, the idea is that one cannot call something ἀεί if it is incomplete either now or at any point, in the past or future. If we take 'incomplete' here as what Melissus thinks the process of coming-to-be to entail, something that underwent that process is, by definition, not ἀεί because it has not always been what it is now. This, of course, means taking ἀεί not merely as eternal but as sempiternal.

I take it that on either one of the two above accounts, the role of (c) becomes clearer. We do not have a reversal of B2's argument which changes the inferential priority of the argument. Rather we

---

[35] Did Melissus think that everything that can happen will happen? Maybe, but Makin's suggestion that we take the more restricted view concerning only temporally unlimited possibilities is more plausible (considering the nature of Melissus' universe) as well as more charitable. The idea, then, is not the trivial thought that every possibility, including things like my winning the lottery, must be actualised, but the more significant notion that a possibility that remains temporally open must, in the whole of time, be actualised. The example of a change by a hair in B7 confirms this interpretation.

[36] DK28B2, DK59B5, and DK64B3.

have further confirmation of why the spatial completeness of what-is must follow necessarily from its sempiternity.

The Confirmation of Aristotle

The upshot then is that, for Melissus, what-is is all-embracing, understood as infinitely extended, and it must be so to maintain its sempiternity. A further look at Aristotle reinforces my interpretation.

ὅτι μὲν οὖν παραλογίζεται Μέλισσος, δῆλον· (a) οἴεται γὰρ εἰληφέναι, εἰ τὸ γενόμενον ἔχει ἀρχὴν ἅπαν, ὅτι καὶ τὸ μὴ γενόμενον οὐκ ἔχει. (b) εἶτα καὶ τοῦτο ἄτοπον, τὸ παντὸς εἶναι ἀρχήν, τοῦ πράγματος καὶ μὴ τοῦ χρόνου, (c) καὶ γενέσεως μὴ τῆς ἁπλῆς ἀλλὰ καὶ ἀλλοιώσεως, ὥσπερ οὐκ ἀθρόας γιγνομένης μεταβολῆς. (*Physics* 186a10–16)

It is clear that Melissus reasons fallaciously. (a) For, he thinks he has it as a premise that if everything that comes into being has a starting-point, that which has not come into being does not have one. (b) Secondly, this too is absurd, that everything <that comes into being> has a starting-point – of the thing, not of the time – (c) and that there is a starting- point not <only> of absolute coming to be but also of alteration, as if change-all-over does not occur.

This passage has been subject to some scrutiny, and it has yielded some positive results, but no single account that fully captures Aristotle's argument. Let us examine the passage and, building on several previous accounts, try to offer something more comprehensive. What seems clear enough is that (a) is performing a different function from (b).[37] In (a) we simply have a repetition of the criticism in the *SE* that Melissus is guilty of fallacious reasoning: if p then q; so if not-p then not-q. The improved Cherniss/Verdenius reading dissolves this objection. In (b) we find something new and rather unexpected: Aristotle denies the truth of Melissus' premise, i.e. that what has come to be must have a spatial starting-point and end. Interestingly, this contrasts with the treatment of Melissus in the *SE*, where there is tacit acceptance of the premise of the argument.[38] The obvious explanation for Aristotle's shift is that, in the context of the *SE*, a criticism of Melissus' premise was neither necessary nor appropriate to his

[37] This is emphasised by Bostock (2006: 105).   [38] Gershenson and Greenberg 1961: 5.

project. All Aristotle needed was an unambiguous example of the logical fallacy of denying the antecedent. In the *Physics*, a work devoted to natural philosophy, Aristotle had a much greater incentive to criticise the perceived wrong-headedness of Melissus' assumptions and not simply his poor reasoning. And we are fortunate in this because Aristotle gives us greater access to his reading of Melissus' argument.

A further point of difference between the *SE* criticism and the one we find in the *Physics* is that, in the former, Aristotle is careful to specify τὸ ἅπαν (the universe) as the subject of Melissus' fallacious inference. In the *Physics*, we find that in (a) Aristotle merely recapitulates what he understands to be Melissus' premise. I take it that this suggests Aristotle is less interested here in exemplifying a kind of fallacious deduction than in attacking the assumption Melissus made in raising his argument. Once again, this reflects how Aristotle's aim is different in the *Physics* from that in the *SE*.

One point of concern the passage under consideration has provoked is the nature of the transition from (a) to (b). The εἶτα construction, however, strongly suggests that Aristotle is making an additional point. We can then safely set aside the implausible suggestion that it is the view of Melissus and not Aristotle that is reported in (b) and (c), up to 186a15, as Gershenson and Greenberg suggest.[39] Fortunately, commentators and translators have largely ignored this interpretation.

However, the most pressing puzzle we face in interpreting the passage is that Melissus does *not* hold the view Aristotle ascribes to him in (b) that *everything* has a starting-point. After all, Melissus could hardly be earnestly made to say just what he argued against, namely that the universe has a starting-point. Are we to think that Melissus said something in direct contrast with his known (from B2) position?[40] Ross offers the thought that Melissus might have provided what is found in (b) not as his concerted position but as a statement of what is entailed should one, incorrectly, think that generation/change does take place.[41] There is something to be said

---

[39] See Gershenson and Greenberg 1961: 7–9.
[40] This seems to be the position of Prantl (1854: 474 n.11).   [41] Ross 1936: 471.

in favour of Ross' point; Melissus' argument against motion in B7 shares a similar interest in developing arguments from impossible premises.[42] Just as Melissus posits void *per impossibile* as a precondition of motion, we might think he is exploring what is entailed should one think that generation occurs.

Ross' suggestion, though I think helpful, is not entirely satisfactory. The run of the passage is still quite obscure. In (a), as we have established, Aristotle is merely rehearsing his standard objection to Melissus' logic, though now Aristotle generalises the premise to concern ἅπαν (everything) and not just the universe (τὸ ἅπαν). In (b) we find something new, not because Aristotle is adding additional Melissan material not found in the *SE*, but rather because he is responding to Melissus' claim on a different level. The introduction to the passage (ὅτι μὲν οὖν παραλογίζεται Μέλισσος, δῆλον) is sufficient to remind his readers that Melissus' argument is indefensible on logical grounds. I suggest that in (b) Aristotle is moving beyond his standard criticism of the form of Melissus' argument to an examination of its content.

How does this work? The problem of the unwarranted ascription of the claim that everything has a starting-point to Melissus is dissolved if we assume, with Bostock, that we are meant to understand that (b) is restricted to only those things that have come to be.[43] This should be evident from the translation I have provided, where I follow the lead of Pierre Pellegrin.[44] On the question of whether some of Aristotle's Greek has fallen out of place here, I adopt a conservative position and remain agnostic. I merely recommend, with Bostock and Pellegrin, that the reader supply the restriction. This has the virtue of making good sense of the text without any messy emendation or addition.

Aristotle is telling us that Melissus' premise (everything that comes to be has a starting-point) itself is absurd. Why does Aristotle think this? A clue is to be found in the qualification made in (b): τοῦ πράγματος καὶ μὴ τοῦ χρόνου. What is absurd

---

[42] My reading of B1 in the previous chapter also lends some weight to the typicality of this model for Melissus.

[43] Bostock 2006: 105–6. I am greatly indebted in this section to his subtle exposition of Aristotle's criticism of Melissus.

[44] See Pellegrin 1999: 82. He provides, in angle brackets, 'qui a été engendrée'.

is that each thing itself (πρᾶγμα) should have an ἀρχή if it has been generated. I take it that μὴ τοῦ χρόνου is simply intended to eliminate any discussion of a temporal ἀρχή from the current context. If this is right, Aristotle understands Melissus' argument to imply that if one accepts the generation of something, one also accepts that its generation began from a spatial ἀρχή.

My point, then, is that (b) does not follow as a consequence of (a), but rather is a new criticism; the εἶτα suggests such a transition. Support for my interpretation is found if we consider Aristotle's criticism of Parmenides and Melissus found immediately prior to the passage under consideration (186a6–9):

ἀμφότεροι γὰρ ἐριστικῶς συλλογίζονται, καὶ Μέλισσος καὶ Παρμενίδης· καὶ γὰρ **ψευδῆ λαμβάνουσι** καὶ **ἀσυλλόγιστοί** εἰσιν αὐτῶν οἱ λόγοι· μᾶλλον δ᾽ ὁ Μελίσσου φορτικός.[45]

For both Parmenides and Melissus argue sophistically, as they **accept false premises and their arguments are invalid**. But Melissus is the cruder of the two.

Here we learn that not only do the Eleatics accept false premises (ψευδῆ λαμβάνουσι), they *also* reason unsoundly (ἀσυλλόγιστοι). After Aristotle enumerates these two criticisms, we read that Melissus is cruder than Parmenides. This segues nicely into the discussion of Melissus we have been examining. First Aristotle, in (a), reiterates for his readers the diagnosis found in the *SE* that Melissus committed the fallacy of denying the antecedent, before moving on in (b) to the falsity of Melissus' premise. My suggestion then is that Aristotle dutifully fulfils his promise to examine and criticise Melissus' argument in two different respects, i.e. for arguing unsoundly and accepting false premises.

With this in mind, we can begin to understand why Aristotle drops the definite article before ἅπαν in the *Physics* (186a10–16) passage. Aristotle is merely offering a generalised criticism of Melissus' poor reasoning. We might say as well that the

---

[45] A near identical version of this passage is also found at 185a7–12. On the difficult puzzle of the proper place of the passage, if we are to think that it is not original to both locations, I doubt that any uncontroversial solution is possible. The manuscripts have the passage in both locations and the ancient commentators are not in agreement. The suggestions of both Ross in his commentary and Wicksteed/Cornford in the Loeb are too speculative to be comfortably accepted.

elimination of the article goes some way towards strengthening the claim that Melissus is φορτικός (crude) and perhaps suggests something of an exaggeration of Melissus' fallacious argumentation on Aristotle's part.

Should we accept this reading, we are still left with a looming question. Why should Aristotle take issue with a rather academic notion of what the universe's generation entails when, like Melissus, he is committed to its sempiternity? The solution, I propose, it to be found not in what (b) suggests about generation, but rather in what is implied about spatial limits.

The thought is that Aristotle understood Melissus to have said that if the universe does not have a spatial ἀρχή, it is infinite in extent (in every direction). We can see why this argument would worry Aristotle. He might have thought that this conclusion simply does not follow. One might raise the quite reasonable objection that from a spatial ἀρχή, conceived to be something like a point, the universe could be extended infinitely in every direction. However, (c) suggests that Melissus' argument hit closer to home for Aristotle.

In (c) Aristotle shifts from a discussion of simple generation (γενέσεως) to a consideration of alteration (ἀλλοιώσεως). Bostock suggests that Aristotle's move indicates that he thought Melissus' premise is even more absurd when applied to alteration.[46] Perhaps, but we need not think that a consideration of alteration makes Melissus' premise *more* absurd. It could simply be the case, as I shall suggest, that exploring alteration provides a vivid example to reinforce Aristotle's criticism in (b).

The passage makes better sense if we think that (c) is epexegetical. I take it that a consideration of alteration is intended to explain further why it is absurd to think that what comes to be must have a spatial beginning and end. Alteration, then, is intended to be understood as *analogous* to simple generation. Both alteration and simple generation are kinds of coming-to-be. If it can be shown that spatial ends and beginnings are not entailed by alteration, one may infer that they are not, as a general rule, a function of coming to be. How does this work? The word 'ἀθρόα'

---

[46] Bostock 2006: 106.

in connection with change is rare in Aristotle and several scholars have helpfully suggested that we look to a relevant parallel, at *Physics* 8 (253b23–6).[47]

ὁμοίως δὲ καὶ ἐπ' ἀλλοιώσεως ὁποιασοῦν. οὐ γὰρ εἰ μεριστὸν εἰς ἄπειρα τὸ ἀλλοιούμενον, διὰ τοῦτο καὶ ἡ ἀλλοίωσις, ἀλλ' **ἀθρόα γίγνεται** πολλάκις, ὥσπερ ἡ πῆξις.

It is similar in the case of any kind of alteration as well. For it is not the case that, if the thing altered is infinitely divisible into parts, the same is for this reason true of alteration too, for often the alteration **occurs all at once**,[48] as in the case of freezing.

Aristotle offers here a rather curious, though eminently plausible, account of simultaneous alteration, i.e. simultaneous in the sense that the whole of the subject of change is altered at the same time.[49] The idea is that there need not be any starting (or finishing) spatial point of a case of alteration. This means that we could not pick out the spot(s) where the alteration began and ended. What we can say, however, is that the absence of spatial ἀρχαί in no way implies that the alteration has not occurred.

The example of freezing is interesting. It is easy to imagine the experience of seeing a pond at the end of the day untouched by ice and, then, waking up and noticing that the entire surface of the pond has frozen. It would be foolish, according to Aristotle, to try and identify the spot where the freezing had begun or ended because the water turned to ice all over the pond at the same time.[50]

---

[47] For example, Bostock 2006: 106 and Ross 1936: 471. NB that Bostock is mistaken to claim that the phrase 'ἀθρόα μεταβολή' is used at 253b25; rather it is ἀθρόα γίγνεται that is found. See *Politics* 1307b34–5 for an interesting discussion, using very similar language, of the imperceptibility of expenses that accrue slowly, yet steadily, raised in comparison with those that occur 'all at once'. See also *De Sensu* 443a1–3 for a further parallel.

[48] I take it, with Graham (1999: 68), that Aristotle is referring to an instantaneous change all over the subject of alteration.

[49] How this account is meant to square with *Physics* 6.4 is unclear. See Bostock 1991: 200. One point to consider is whether such a distinction between the subject of a change and the change itself might have contributed to Aristotle's refutation of Zeno's paradoxes of motion.

[50] It is unclear to me whether ἀθρόα is meant to imply that the freezing occurs all over a body of water at the same time or, more specifically, all over a body of water in an instant as opposed to a period of time as Graham (1999: 68) suggests. It is strictly irrelevant for my purposes as either reading captures the lack of a spatial beginning or end. I will say, however, that taking freezing as something that occurs instantly goes

What does this tell us about Aristotle's criticism of Melissus? What I would like to offer for consideration is the thought that the example of freezing goes a long way towards clarifying why Aristotle thinks that being generated need not entail having an originative spatial ἀρχή or τελευτή (i.e. points where something began to come-to-be) as Melissus' inference seems to assume. Freezing is the change of an extended, though normally finite, body from one qualitative state of matter into another. While certainly an alteration, it is dramatic enough to provide a vivid example of what Aristotle wants us to think simple generation might look like. Yet the example of the pond demonstrates (on a finite scale) that alteration can extend in space though lacking an originative spatial beginning or end. The point I take Aristotle to be making in this context, if we generalise from the example of alteration, is that there is nothing *prima facie* inconceivable about the simple generation of something without originative spatial limits.

Aristotle's example of alteration further strengthens his diagnosis of Melissus' logical blunder. In roughly distilled form, Melissus' error is to think that a spatial ἀρχή or τελευτή is exclusively the product of generation. If something has been generated, it has a spatial ἀρχή the thinking seems to go. The thrust of Aristotle's criticism, then, is that Melissus assumes, without warrant, that generation is a growing process and thus cannot occur simultaneously all over. Melissus seems to think that, as a growing process, generation must be temporally limited, thus the subject of generation would be spatially limited as something infinite could not be produced in a finite amount of time. For Aristotle, the size of the subject need not be correlated to the duration of its generative process because any magnitude, independent of its size, can undergo change in all its parts at the same time. This is the conclusion we are able to draw about simple generation from the analogous example of the frozen pond. Therefore, we may say that the *Physics* builds upon the three passages in the *SE* to target not only fallacious inferences but also improper assumptions about the nature of generation.

some way to support Aristotle's point that empirical evidence tells against the thought that all change is infinitely divisible. However, such a reading makes it hard to construe the example which follows of health taking a period of time to come about.

We have confirmation, then, that Melissus moved from sempiternity to spatial infinity. We learn too that Aristotle confirms that Melissus understood the infinite as something all-embracing. Let us consider his discussion of Parmenides and Melissus at *Physics* 3.6, 207a15–31:

διὸ βέλτιον οἰητέον Παρμενίδην Μελίσσου εἰρηκέναι· ὁ μὲν γὰρ τὸ ἄπειρον ὅλον φησίν, ὁ δὲ τὸ ὅλον πεπεράνθαι, "μεσσόθεν ἰσοπαλές". οὐ γὰρ λίνον λίνῳ συνάπτειν ἐστὶν τῷ ἅπαντι καὶ ὅλῳ τὸ ἄπειρον, ἐπεὶ ἐντεῦθέν γε λαμβάνουσι τὴν σεμνότητα κατὰ τοῦ ἀπείρου, τὸ πάντα περιέχειν καὶ τὸ πᾶν ἐν ἑαυτῷ ἔχειν, διὰ τὸ ἔχειν τινὰ ὁμοιότητα τῷ ὅλῳ. ἔστι γὰρ τὸ ἄπειρον τῆς τοῦ μεγέθους τελειότητος ὕλη καὶ τὸ δυνάμει ὅλον, ἐντελεχείᾳ δ᾽ οὔ, διαιρετὸν δ᾽ ἐπί τε τὴν καθαίρεσιν καὶ τὴν ἀντεστραμμένην πρόσθεσιν, ὅλον δὲ καὶ πεπερασμένον οὐ καθ᾽ αὑτὸ ἀλλὰ κατ᾽ ἄλλο· καὶ οὐ περιέχει ἀλλὰ περιέχεται, ᾗ ἄπειρον. διὸ καὶ ἄγνωστον ᾗ ἄπειρον· εἶδος γὰρ οὐκ ἔχει ἡ ὕλη. ὥστε φανερὸν ὅτι μᾶλλον ἐν μορίου λόγῳ τὸ ἄπειρον ἢ ἐν ὅλου· μόριον γὰρ ἡ ὕλη τοῦ ὅλου ὥσπερ ὁ χαλκὸς τοῦ χαλκοῦ ἀνδριάντος, ἐπεὶ εἴ γε περιέχει ἐν τοῖς αἰσθητοῖς, καὶ ἐν τοῖς νοητοῖς τὸ μέγα καὶ τὸ μικρὸν ἔδει περιέχειν τὰ νοητά. ἄτοπον δὲ καὶ ἀδύνατον τὸ ἄγνωστον καὶ ἀόριστον περιέχειν καὶ ὁρίζειν.

So one must judge Parmenides to have spoken better than Melissus: the latter says that the infinite is whole, the former that the whole is finite, 'evenly balanced from the middle'. For the *infinite* is a different kettle of fish from the *universe* or *whole* – yet it is from this that people derive the dignity attributed to the infinite, that it surrounds everything and contains everything in itself, because it has some similarity to the whole. In fact, the infinite is the material of the completeness of magnitude, and is that which is potentially but not actually whole, being divisible by a process of reduction and by the inversely corresponding addition, but being whole and finite not in itself but in respect of something else. Nor does it surround, *qua* infinite, but is surrounded, and for this reason is unknowable, *qua* infinite; for the material cause has no form. Hence it is manifest that the infinite is to be reckoned rather as a portion than as a whole; for the material cause is a portion of the whole, as the bronze is of a bronze statue. (If it surrounds in the perceptible world, in the intelligible world too the large and small ought to surround the intelligibles.) For it is absurd and impossible that the unknowable and indefinite should surround and define. (Trans. E. Hussey, emphases original)

Here Aristotle makes the critical distinction between the infinite (ἄπειρον) and the whole (τὸ ὅλον). He chalks up Melissus' conflation of these separate notions to 'a certain resemblance' (τινὰ ὁμοιότητα) between the two. The point he makes there is that the infinite is the material from which a magnitude is created and, thus, being formless it would be unknowable (ἄγνωστον). The infinite is, then, best understood beneath the umbrella of the whole but not identical to it, that is to say as its material constituent on the model of the bronze in a bronze statue. If the infinite were understood using the traditional conception of it as something all-embracing, we would face the intolerable situation that the unknowable (ἄγνωστον) and undefined (ἀόριστον) embraces and defines something knowable and defined.

What does this criticism amount to? It is a quite radical attack on the traditional notion of the infinite as a whole in which everything is contained. Aristotle raises two closely related points in his discussion: one before and one after his mention of Parmenides and Melissus in *Physics* 3.6. The first, as we have seen, is that Aristotle maintains that the infinite is inherently unknowable on the basis of an analogy between the infinite and matter. The conclusion he draws is that, just as matter exists only potentially and is thus *qua* matter unknowable, the infinite, being literally 'without bounds', is similarly indeterminate and unknowable.[51] A second argument is discernible at 206b33–207a8:

συμβαίνει δὲ τοὐναντίον εἶναι ἄπειρον ἢ ὡς λέγουσιν. οὐ γὰρ οὗ μηδὲν ἔξω, ἀλλ' οὗ ἀεί τι ἔξω ἐστί, τοῦτο ἄπειρόν ἐστιν ... ἄπειρον μὲν οὖν ἐστιν οὗ κατὰ τὸ ποσὸν λαμβάνουσιν ἀεί τι λαμβάνειν ἔστιν ἔξω.

It follows that what is infinite is just the opposite of what it is said to be. For it is not that beyond which there is nothing, but that which there is always something beyond, that is infinite ... Infinite then is that of which, taking it quantitatively, it is always possible to take something outside what has already been taken.

Aristotle's thought, then, that the infinite is unknowable is founded upon a departure from its traditional conception. For Melissus the infinite is all-embracing; for Aristotle the infinite is precisely the opposite. Aristotle believed he had very good reasons to hold that the universe is spatially finite. Beginning in *De Caelo* 1.5, Aristotle goes to great length to deny that a spatially infinite body could exist, a position he attributes to most of the older philosophers (οἱ πλεῖστοι τῶν ἀρχαίων φιλοσόφων) at 271b3, though the character of the arguments brought to bear makes it unlikely that Melissus is specifically targeted. Aristotle's arguments turn on the impossibility of an infinitely extended body

---

[51] This point is well made by Lear (1988: 71–3).

completing a revolution in a finite time. If a body is infinitely extended, the distance between radii would themselves be infinite – making it impossible for any completed motion, from point to point, to occur. Continuing in chapters 6 and 7, Aristotle takes up the issues of place, weight and lightness, and movement in relation to an unlimited body, concluding in 7 that the universe is not unlimited. In 1.9 we learn that, since the universe contains everything that is and each thing has its natural place within, there cannot be anything, including void and place, beyond the circumference of the heavens.

It makes perfect sense, then, that Aristotle is more sympathetic to Parmenides than to Melissus at *Physics* 207a15: διὸ βέλτιον οἰητέον Παρμενίδην Μελίσσου εἰρηκέναι. While Aristotle and Parmenides understand limits to ensure completeness, Melissus thinks limits imply just the opposite. Finally, we can discern what is at the heart of Aristotle' criticism of Melissus. It is not merely faulty reasoning, as we have seen that, with a little clarification, B2 can stand up to scrutiny. It is also divergent notions of how we are to think of the universe as everything that is or can be.

Our look at Aristotle's criticisms in the *Physics* has served at least two functions. First, I take it that our examination has established Aristotle's confirmation that Melissus is committed to a spatial thesis in B2 and that he understands the infinite as something all-embracing, following the traditional Ionian model. The second point is that the richer argument for spatial infinity I have attributed to Melissus can stand up better to Aristotle's criticism, because I have argued that Melissus need not be seen to be committed, as a general rule, to the thought that generation entails a spatial beginning and end. Rather, I have suggested, Melissus held no more than the weaker notion that the only rational explanation for hypothetical spatial limits would be a process of generation. If such a reading of Melissus' B2 is correct, Aristotle's insistence that Melissus misunderstood the nature of generation somewhat misses the mark.

B3: Text and Translation

Finally, so far as infinity is concerned, we may turn to B3: ἀλλ' ὥσπερ ἔστιν ἀεί, οὕτω καὶ τὸ μέγεθος ἄπειρον ἀεὶ χρὴ εἶναι.

I translate: 'But just as it is always, so too must it be always infinite in magnitude.' The fragment is usually placed immediately after B2 and this is no doubt correct. However, it should be appreciated that B3 is not simply the next fragment in the deductive structure, but the conclusion to the argument offered in B2. Therefore, B2 and B3 are of a piece. How can we know this for sure? The first clue is that B3 is marshalled by Simplicius to support his under-standing that Melissus is talking about 'substance' (οὐσία) when considering coming-to-be in B2:

ὅτι δὲ ὥσπερ τὸ 'ποτὲ γενόμενον' πεπερασμένον τῇ οὐσίᾳ φησίν, οὕτω καὶ τὸ ἀεὶ ὂν ἄπειρον λέγει τῇ οὐσίᾳ, σαφὲς πεποίηκεν εἰπών 'ἀλλ' ὥσπερ ἔστιν ἀεί, οὕτω καὶ τὸ μέγεθος ἄπειρον ἀεὶ χρὴ εἶναι'. (*In Phys.* 109.29–32)

And that just as he says that what 'came to be at some time' is limited in substance, in the same way he also says that what always is is infinite in substance, he has made clear by saying . . . (B3).

Of course, we can set aside the details of Simplicius' interpreta-tion, including the anachronistic and highly Neoplatonic introduc-tion of the Aristotelian notion of substance. However, it is surely significant that Simplicius treats B2 and B3 together in relation to the same interpretative point. It follows naturally, then, that Simplicius understood B3 to cap off B2.

We must grant, however, that Simplicius is quite happy to jump around Melissus' treatise and quote according to his own agenda. It would be a mistake to assume that Simplicius made any parti-cular effort to quote Melissus' fragments while adhering to the running order of his treatise. This does not negate the point made above as it does not directly turn on merely the order of Simplicius' presentation of the fragments, but it does suggest that the argument is not sufficient.

Fortunately, the nature of B3 itself, without reference to its Simplician context, confirms its place immediately following B2, as it is abundantly clear that B3 summarises the argument and conclusion of B2. The way in which it conforms to the typical Melissan argumentative structure of stating the premise (often a conclusion previously established), thesis to be established, argument, and then conclusion, makes B3 exceptionally attractive as the final element of the argument begun in B2. A further piece of evidence bolstering my claim is the relationship between part (c) of B2 and B3. The reader will remember that I offered an interpretation of (c) that construed it as a supplementary argument in support of spatial infinity. The argument worked by extending the previous thesis that what-is had no opportunity to establish spatial limits to a stronger claim of their impossibility. Such an impossibility, I submitted, was predicated on the thought that a spatial beginning or end limited what-is for Melissus, in contrast to Parmenides. Using the indifference reasoning evident in B7, if one limitation is possible, in the whole of time every limitation is possible, compromising the integrity of what-is. Thus what-is must have no spatial beginning or end, understood as limits, on pain of its eventual destruction.

The notion of necessity found in B3, established by the introduction of χρή, directly connects the talk of impossibility in (c) with the latter fragment. Therefore, attaching B3 to the end of the argument in B2 attributes to Melissus the orderly run of demonstration evident from his other extant fragments. We may say, then, that something of a pattern has emerged in Simplicius' quotation of Melissus' fragments and this is fortunate for our task of reconstruction. Just as the first sentence of B2 confirms its immediate place following B1, as it is both the conclusion to B1 and the fundamental premise of B2, so too B3 serves the same two functions. It is both the conclusion to the argument found in B2 and, as we shall see in the next section, restated for the sake of announcing a premise for the next, adjacent piece of reasoning. Let us first, however, restate the text of Melissus' treatise as it has thus far been established:

Περὶ φύσεως ἢ περὶ τοῦ <ἐ>όντος

<Μέλισσος Σάμιος τάδε λέγει περὶ φύσεως ἢ περὶ τοῦ ἐόντος.> εἰ μὲν μηδὲν ἔστι, περὶ τούτου τί ἂν λέγοιτο ὡς <ἐ>όντος τινός; εἰ δέ τι ἐστίν, ἀεὶ ἦν ὅ τι ἦν καὶ ἀεὶ ἔσται. εἰ γὰρ ἐγένετο, ἀναγκαῖόν ἐστι πρὶν γενέσθαι εἶναι μηδέν. εἰ <δὲ> τύχοι νῦν μηδὲν ἐόν, οὐδαμὰ ἂν γένοιτο οὐδὲν ἐκ μηδενός. ὅτε τοίνυν οὐκ ἐγένετο, ἔστι τε καὶ ἀεὶ ἦν καὶ ἀεὶ ἔσται. καὶ ἀρχὴν οὐκ ἔχει οὐδὲ τελευτήν, ἀλλ' ἄπειρόν ἐστιν. εἰ μὲν γὰρ ἐγένετο, ἀρχὴν ἂν εἶχεν (ἤρξατο γὰρ ἄν ποτε γινόμενον) καὶ τελευτήν (ἐτελεύτησε γὰρ ἄν ποτε γινόμενον)· ὅτε δὲ μήτε ἤρξατο μήτε ἐτελεύτησεν, ἀεὶ τε ἦν καὶ ἀεὶ ἔσται, οὐκ ἔχει ἀρχὴν οὐδὲ τελευτήν· οὐ γὰρ ἀεὶ εἶναι ἀνυστόν, ὅ τι μὴ πᾶν ἔστι. ἀλλ' ὥσπερ ἔστιν ἀεί, οὕτω καὶ τὸ μέγεθος ἄπειρον ἀεὶ χρὴ εἶναι.

B4, B5, B6: WHAT-IS IS ONE

ἀρχήν τε καὶ τέλος ἔχον οὐδὲν οὔτε ἀίδιον οὔτε ἄπειρόν ἐστιν.

(DK30B4)

εἰ μὴ ἓν εἴη, περανεῖ πρὸς ἄλλο.

(DK30B5)

εἰ γὰρ <ἄπειρον> εἴη, ἓν εἴη ἄν· εἰ γὰρ δύο εἴη, οὐκ ἂν δύναιτο ἄπειρα
εἶναι, ἀλλ᾽ ἔχοι ἂν πείρατα πρὸς ἄλληλα.

(DK30B6)

Introduction

B4, B5, and B6 are not usually grouped together by commentators.
B5, for example, is omitted by KRS and elsewhere taken to repeat
merely, in compacted form, what is argued in B6.[1] Pilo Albertelli
even goes so far as to argue that B5 should be considered
a 'pseudo-fragment' on the basis of his reading of the paraphrase
found in the *MXG*.[2] Reale persuasively refutes Albertelli's argument and there is every reason, as we shall see, to accept its
authenticity.[3] B4 is something of an orphan: it is naturally associated with the argument in B2, but its exact function within
Melissus' treatise has never been adequately explained. B6, meanwhile, is of particular importance as it is the clearest extant
exposition of Eleatic monism.[4] Many have wondered whether
Melissus is here advocating a Parmenidean position or advancing

---

[1] See, for example, McKirahan 1994: 298.
[2] Albertelli 1939: 234 n.1. See also Barnes (1982: 205 n.8), who thinks that B5 is
a paraphrase of B6.
[3] Reale 1970: 380–1.
[4] 'Monism' is a hotly contested word in the context of the Eleatics. I do not mean here
anything particularly conceptually sophisticated, but take 'monism', at least for
Melissus, as simply the thesis that *only* one thing exists, or that what-is is singular and

97

something novel. In short, all three fragments pose challenges that must be met.

The upshot of our look at Q, B1, and B2 was the provision of a robust understanding of the typical formulation of Melissus' argumentation. We have witnessed how he adopts an exceptionally neat and formulaic mode of demonstration. This should help us to reconstruct the argument for monism. In both B1 and B2, Melissus establishes a pattern. First he states the conclusion to be demonstrated, followed by the heart of the proof incorporating counterfactual conditionals. Once the counterfactuals have been proposed, Melissus draws what he takes to be the obvious and natural conclusion, supporting his initial thesis statement. Each step is well marked and easily identifiable. Though each attribute of what-is is discretely established, once demonstrated a conclusion serves as a premise for the next piece of reasoning. Obviously, this argumentative form puts editors in an extremely fortunate position as reconstructing Melissus' treatise is ultimately a matter of accurately establishing the run of his argument and then arranging the fragments accordingly. I shall argue that B4, B5, and B6 constitute such a piece of reasoning, following on from the argument for spatial infinity in B2 and B3.

It should be sufficiently clear that the argument for monism begins from the conclusion established in the previous section, i.e. from B3. This, of course, follows the standard formula and is in line with previous interpretations. Melissus' next step, which I contend he must have made, is to state the monistic conclusion he is to demonstrate in B4, B5, and B6. This move does not survive in the fragments but there is every reason to think that it originally featured in the treatise and has simply been lost. Not only have we seen a parallel introductory component in both B1 and B2, such a method is also abundantly apparent in B7.[5] For dispositive confirmation we may also look to the paraphrase found in the *MXG*:

---

unique. Sometimes this understanding is termed 'numerical monism': see Curd 1998: 64–94 for a discussion.

[5] Cf. (2) καὶ οὔτ' ἂν ἀπόλοιτο οὔτε μεῖζον γίνοιτο οὔτε μετακοσμέοιτο οὔτε ἀλγεῖ οὔτε ἀνιᾶται, and (7) οὐδὲ κενεόν ἐστιν οὐδέν· τὸ γὰρ κενεόν οὐδέν ἐστιν· οὐκ ἂν οὖν εἴη τό γε μηδέν. οὐδὲ κινεῖται· ὑποχωρῆσαι γὰρ οὐκ ἔχει οὐδαμῇ, ἀλλὰ πλέων ἐστίν.

ἄπειρον δ' ὄν ἓν εἶναι·[6] εἰ γὰρ δύο ἢ πλείω εἴη, περαίνειν ἂν ταῦτα πρὸς ἄλληλα. (974a11–12)

Also, being infinite it is one. For if it were two or more, these would terminate in each other.

The text of the above passage is far from sound and I hesitate to draw too strong a conclusion. However, the exact construal of the disputed first sentence is not what is at stake for our purposes. Rather, the fact that the paraphrase preserves a statement of what is to be proved prior to a conditional (presumably deriving from B5 and B6) and which is entirely unlike B4 adds significant support to the argument that Melissus originally offered more than what survives in the preserved fragments. Therefore, it makes good sense to accept the minimal addition, in angle brackets, of an introductory sentence following along the lines of the sentence from the *MXG*, though, of course, in Melissus' Ionic: ἄπειρον δ' ἐὸν ἓν ἐστίν.[7] We should assume that some such sentence immediately followed B3. Although this is a speculative proposal, it is entirely in line with Melissus' method and the evidence of the *MXG*.

It is how we are to proceed next that is more opaque. The natural temptation, I suppose, would be to take up B4 first, in conformity with nearly every other reconstruction thus far offered.[8] It is clear enough that B4 simply states what B1 and B2 have already demonstrated. However, I advise caution. Simplicius provides no hint that he thought B4 followed B3 in the way he made clear that B3 capped the argument in B2. In fact, B4 is marshalled following his quotation of B9, which addresses the bodilessness of what-is. Simplicius does, however, seem to suggest that B4 figured within the argument for monism: this implies that the fragment does play some role in the argument we are reconstructing, but not necessarily one directly adjacent to B3.

---

[6] I follow the reading of Apelt here (1888: 166). Daniel Graham (2010: 466) offers πᾶν δὲ καὶ ἄπειρον ὄν <ἓν> εἶναι, εἰ γὰρ δύο ἢ πλέω εἴη, πέρατ' ἂν εἶναι ταῦτα πρὸς ἄλληλα. The differences are several but the sense is largely identical.

[7] I suppose that the indicative mood is most appropriate here. Melissus typically (cf. B2 and B3) uses the indicative when stating a conclusion deduced from premises he takes to be true and the optative when the inference proceeds from something counterfactual. B6 proves, however, that this is not a universal rule.

[8] The only exception is the improbable interpretation of Vitali (1973).

How, then, should we proceed? I suggest that B4 is not presented by Simplicius in tandem with B3 because, in fact, B5 should be given priority. As I have intimated, B5 has usually been thought to hold a precarious place in Melissus' treatise. While it is true that B4 is quoted before B5 by Simplicius, a look at the text confirms that this does not imply that he understood the latter to follow the former:

καὶ ἐφεξῆς δὲ τῷ ἀιδίῳ τὸ ἄπειρον κατὰ τὴν οὐσίαν συνέταξεν εἰπών "ἀρχήν τε καὶ τέλος ἔχον οὐδὲν οὔτε ἀίδιον οὔτε ἄπειρόν ἐστιν" ὥστε τὸ μὴ ἔχον ἄπειρόν ἐστιν.[9] ἀπὸ δὲ τοῦ ἀπείρου τὸ ἓν συνελογίσατο ἐκ τοῦ "εἰ μὴ ἓν εἴη, περανεῖ πρὸς ἄλλο".

And also, following eternity,[10] he added infinity in respect of substance by saying '[B4]', so that what does not have them [i.e. a beginning and an end] is infinite. From infinity he argued to unity on the basis that '[B5]'.

All Simplicius commits himself to in this passage is that B5 is argued on the basis of the infinity of what-is. As Melissus establishes infinity in B2 and B3 and not in B4, there is no reason to think that Simplicius' order of quotation must significantly guide our reconstruction.

Therefore, there is the possibility that B5 originally *preceded* B4 and, as we shall see, this makes good sense. We may begin with the introduction I have suggested above. This leads naturally, following the standard Melissan formula, into a counterfactual conditional. While both B5 and B6 contain such a conditional, there are attractive reasons to think that the former is the relevant fragment. Importantly, B6 poses a contrary (what-is is two) but not the desired contradictory thesis (what-is is not one). A further point, to be made below, is that use of modal language in B6 also suggests that this fragment figured later in Melissus' argument. For these reasons, it is more plausible to take B5 first.

---

[9] It is occasionally suggested (e.g. by Diels as well as Huby and Taylor (2011: 22 n.58)) that B4 extended to the end of this sentence. I doubt it as inferential ὥστε clauses are not evident in Melissus outside an exceptionally controversial (and perhaps inauthentic) sentence in B8, and it appears that Simplicius is bringing in the (correct) results of his previous analysis of B2.

[10] ἐφεξῆς I take to imply, at most, coming after B3 and *not* B9, quoted immediately prior, which Simplicius merely marshals to explicate what τὸ μέγεθος implies in B3.

B5: Text and Translation

How are we to interpret B5? I provisionally translate it as: 'For if it were not to be one, it will border another.' I speculatively add γάρ to resolve the sentence's asyndeton, which we have observed is atypical for Melissus. That such an addition is appropriate is supported by the context of the fragment's quotation in Simplicius: ἀπὸ δὲ τοῦ ἀπείρου τὸ ἓν συνελογίσατο ἐκ τοῦ: 'B5'. The fragment figures within the grammatical structure of Simplicius' sentence and, in such a case, it would make sense for him to eliminate a connective particle. Indeed for Simplicius' sentence to be grammatically correct he *had* to omit the original connecting particle. We may usefully compare the quotation of B5 with that of B10 in which the particle γάρ *is* reported: αὐτὸς γὰρ ἀδιαίρετον τὸ ὂν δείκνυσιν· 'εἰ **γὰρ** διῄρηται'. Here we see that Simplicius carefully sets up an introduction to his quotation of B10; thus the colon printed by Diels before the quoted words is entirely appropriate. B5 is not nearly so cleanly marked off from Simplicius' own exegesis and sentence structure.

The conditional in B5 is in a rather strange form for Melissus. In the protasis he adopts the optative mood of the verb just as he does in conditionals in B1 (on my reading), B6, B7, B8, B9, and B10. However, it is surprising that he does not follow suit in the apodosis along with the particle ἄν, a standard formula found in similar Melissan counterfactual conditionals.[11] Instead we find an optative in the protasis and a future tense (περανεῖ) in the apodosis.[12]

The future tense is somewhat out of character but nothing significant need be made of the variation. It is quite clear that the future tense here is best construed as an *inferential future*; this is supported by the mixed conditional form. The *inferential future* is used to indicate what can be inferred from previous discussion or from more general principles (without specific reference to the

---

[11] Melissus does also use the imperfect indicative (cf. B2 and B7) for unfulfilled conditionals, though, of course, without explicit reference to the future. It is not clear whether Melissus makes a systematic distinction between the forms of conditionals for any peculiarly philosophical reasons.

[12] This is not always appreciated, cf., for example, Barnes 1982: 201 n.8, Huby and Taylor 2011: 22, and Burnet 1930: 322.

temporal aspect). Therefore, we may say that the inferential future, while initially unusual, ultimately functions much as a simple present or an optative with ἄν would and we need not make much of Melissus' departure from his standard practice.

B4: Text and Translation

I take B4 after B5. This is an unprecedented suggestion, but it has the virtue of construing the fragment as an integral piece of Melissus' argument and not simply an unnecessary restatement of theses already established. KRS translate: 'Nothing that has both a beginning and an end is eternal or infinite.'[13] Such a translation requires taking τε καὶ as the corresponsive 'both . . . and'. While this is perfectly normal Greek, there are three worries that such a construal raises. First, on the face of it, we are obliged to take τε as operating as a connective between sentences, unless we are to think that the sentence is asyndetic or only partially quoted from an original, longer sentence. This has not been appreciated heretofore and tells against translations in the vein of what KRS provide. It is worth noting as well that Simplicius' manner of quotation suggests that he does *not* omit a connecting particle (καὶ ἐφεξῆς δὲ τῷ ἀιδίῳ τὸ ἄπειρον κατὰ τὴν οὐσίαν συνέταξεν εἰπών: 'B4'): this makes it difficult to accept the corresponsive reading. Second, Melissus elsewhere uses τε never as a sentence connective, but only as a word connective as in B2, and also, rather redundantly, in B8.[14] A third worry is that the corresponsive reading forces Melissus into a more emphatic claim (nothing with *both a beginning and an end* can be either eternal or infinite) than he needs for his argument to go through.

Such concerns should give us some pause. Fortunately, there is a straightforward remedy. There is an alternative manuscript reading of δέ for τε (aE), whose adoption nicely addresses the worries I have raised. This particle is a standard sentence connective for Melissus (see B8 in particular) and its acceptance frees us to understand the weaker, but more probable, claim that nothing that has a beginning and/or an end is either sempiternal or infinite.

---

[13] This is a fairly standard translation, cf. McKirahan 1994: 293.
[14] The redundant use of τε is common, see Denniston 1959: 512–13.

Obviously, Melissus has already covered this ground in B1 and B2. Why, then, does he seem to move backwards? I take the generalising nature of the fragment to be significant. Melissus is stating the non-subject-specific (οὐδέν rather than the negation of ἐόν or τὸ ἐόν) claim that anything with a beginning or end is not eternal or infinite. This should give us good reason to be sceptical about the standard ordering of the fragments.[15] B3 is incontestably conclusive in purpose; if so, why would a fragment like B4, which announces a general premise/conclusion, directly follow? Certainly, Melissus is accustomed to restate conclusions to serve as premises for following arguments. But B4 is *not* the conclusion previously established (cf. the beginning of B2 and B3) as it does not specifically refer to what-is.

The standard reading of B4, as we have seen, takes it in tandem with B3. Those who wish to deny that B2 establishes spatial infinity (in all directions) take B4 to do so as the inferential product of B3.[16] This assumption, easily giving rise to claims of fallacious reasoning, has undoubtedly contributed to the negative reputation of Melissus' argument for spatial infinity. Barnes correctly points out that B4 is not derived from B3, but parallel to it.[17] If we add, as well, the absence of what-is as the fragment's specific subject, we are left with the conclusion that B4 is particularly awkward in its traditional location. On the standard ordering of editors, therefore, B4 is inadequately accounted for.

It makes better sense to construe B4 as Melissus' objection to the counterfactual conditional raised in B5. Melissus reasons that if there were any two things they would border each other. Why does he think this? Two things could extend infinitely in different directions or in parallel and not share a border. Obviously, the objection that two discrete entities could be separated by something like void would not meet with Melissus' sympathy as he denies void's existence. However, he has yet to make that particular point. I have stressed that what-is is *not* Melissus' subject in B4; yet it is worth asking what he means by οὐδέν here. I have translated the word as 'nothing' but let us recast the sentence with

---

[15] Even those, like Richard McKirahan, who wisely move B9 and B10 before B7 keep B4 directly following B3.
[16] See, for example, Gomperz 1906: 186.   [17] Barnes 1982: 200.

'not anything' which, on the strongly predicative model I have attributed to Melissus in **Q**, I take to be its logical equivalent. We have then: 'Anything that does not have a beginning and/or end is eternal and infinite.' This is, of course, the upshot of B1 and B2. That seems to suggest that Melissus is not talking about anything specific but is rather assuming a subject that conforms to what he has demonstrated previously about what-is. This is important because it signals what Melissus is aiming to achieve in B4, B5, and B6.

So it seems that in B4 Melissus is not taking what-is as his subject yet he is still assuming what he has proven in B1, B2, and B3. This suggests that in the argument we are reconstructing he is aiming to demonstrate uniqueness and not unity. Unity I take to be the thesis that what-is is one and not two (or more). This, I contend, is adequately accounted for in the now lost, but certainly original, argument for homogeneity, which is to be considered in the next section. If what-is is all alike, how could it be two or more, except by having gaps of what-is-not? Uniqueness, on the other hand, is the claim that what-is is the only thing that there is. It is easy to see how the non-subject-specific, generalising nature of B4 encourages the latter thought, but why does Melissus assume, then, the attributes of what-is he has established? It is because he is committed to the thought that anything that is must be as he describes what-is in B1, B2, and B3, i.e. sempiternal and spatially infinite. This is suggested by the modal language we examined in B2. Therefore, the claim targeted in B4 is that there could be two things that share the demonstrated predicates of what-is. In short, he is challenging the notion that what-is could be multiply instantiated.

Let us step back for a moment and determine what roles ἀρχή and τέλος play here. If we were to take the fragment with B3, these would naturally refer back to the hypothetical spatial beginning and end of what-is countered in B2. Just as sempiternity and spatial infinity made spatial ἀρχαί and τέλη impossible, those entities which had these latter could not be sempiternal or infinite. My proposal is rather to understand the ἀρχή and τέλος in reference to the border described in B5. The idea, then, is that if there were two, the border between them would constitute an ἀρχή and a τέλος. It is for this reason that I weakly translate the καί following δέ and connecting ἀρχή and τέλος as 'and/or'. After all, a border is the beginning of one object or entity and the end of another. So Melissus need not be taken to emphasise that *both a beginning and an end* are needed as if they were in some way independent. If Melissus is taken to have meant 'nothing having *both* a beginning and an end' we would be implicitly encouraged to understand that a logical space has been opened up for something that has one of these but not the other. This would allow for the putative possibility that something could lack either a beginning or an end and still be considered infinite. Yet, as we saw in our discussion of B1 and B2, it is just such an implication that Melissus is keen to avoid. In B1 he takes it as sufficient to demonstrate that a temporal beginning of what-is is impossible and leave us to construct a parallel argument against a temporal end. As for spatial ends, in B2 it is clear that Melissus is committed to the concept of infinity understood as all-embracing. This eliminates the possibility of a body extending infinitely from a point. Therefore, it would be a mistake to think that Melissus emphasised *both* a beginning and an end here.

So far Melissus' assumptions appear sound enough. B4, using the results of arguments he has already made, provides the means to establish the impossibility of a plurality. If there were two, there would be an end and a beginning and they would be neither sempiternal (ἀίδιον) nor infinite (ἄπειρον). The soundness of Melissus' argument perhaps appears to fade here. It is easy to think, as Barnes recognises, that the old ascription of the fallacy of denying the antecedent to Melissus is again relevant.[18] In B2, Melissus concludes that what-is is spatially infinite because it lacks ἀρχαί, understood as the exclusive products of an originative process. Here in B4 we seem to find the possibly fallacious converse of this argument: 'if not-p, then q' becomes 'if p, then not-q'.

I say 'possibly fallacious' because if, as in the previous section, we construe having ἀρχαί and τέλη as true and exclusive contradictories of spatial infinity, the argument is made valid.

---

[18] Barnes 1982: 201.

On the question of spatial infinity, there is no difficulty. Any end or beginning is sufficient to eliminate the infinite, understood as something all-embracing. On the temporal beginnings and ends of generation, B4 may appear question-begging, but, as we have determined, we may acquit Melissus of such a charge. He is committed to a stronger thesis than simply that (hypothetical) generation entails spatial ἀρχαί. More robustly, Melissus held that spatial ἀρχαί could reasonably come about only as the result of a (hypothetical) generative process. If this is the case, anything with spatial ἀρχαί can be rationally understood only to be *both* generated and spatially limited. If my interpretation is correct, the worry one might pose that simply having ἀρχαί and τέλη is not sufficient to eliminate the possibility of sempiternity is dissolved.

Does this conclude Melissus' argument for uniqueness? It is worth here drawing out an assumption that Melissus tacitly makes which is crucial to its success. It is only if it is taken to be impossible that entities might overlap and occupy the same place at the same time that the argument appealing to spatial infinity and borders will go through. If the hypothesised plural entities could overlap without forming a border, i.e. co-locate, it would be perfectly possible to attribute spatial infinity to each of their number. Such an assumption of co-location's impossibility is not surprising; it is made again in the argument against motion in B7, which relies on the thought that being full dismisses something's ability to serve as the target location of movement, and is exceptionally common throughout accounts of motion and place in the history of philosophy and physics.[19]

With this tacit assumption added, all the pieces needed to refute plurality are in place, but Melissus is not yet satisfied that he has sufficiently demonstrated monism. It is here, on the proposed account, that B6 fits in.

---

[19] In early modern philosophy, for example, Descartes, Locke, and Leibniz engaged in a dispute about solidity and the possibility that bodies could interpenetrate. Barnes (1982: 223–6) brings in this debate in relation to Melissus. Sorabji (1988: chapter 5) takes up the issue in Anaxagoras and Aristotle.

B6: Text and Translation

It is perhaps obvious by now why many commentators have thought that B5 and B6 overlap to such an extent that both could not be accepted as verbatim quotations. I have attempted, in this chapter, to resist such a conclusion. The strongest argument in my favour, as I have suggested, is that B5 is unambiguously presented as a direct quotation by Simplicius. My second argument is the upshot of the reconstruction we are undertaking: if I can locate a persuasive place for B5 within Melissus' argument, I shall take this to be confirmation of Simplicius' testimony. The burden of proof is firmly on those who wish to see B5 as a paraphrase and not as a quotation.

B6 is remarkable for the context of its quotation. We still have Simplicius to thank for its preservation, but the fragment is found in the commentary on Aristotle's *De Caelo* not the more usual *Physics* commentary.[20] Is this significant for our purposes? Well, one might suppose that the different locations of quotation support those who conclude that B5 and B6 cannot both be fragments, but instead reflect a single piece of Melissan reasoning. Simplicius, on such an account, simply phrases the argument differently each time. This would be hardly unusual for Simplicius' treatment of Melissus. He quotes two versions of the first line of B2, and B9 is presented twice in rather different terms. I want to suggest that something similar is *not* the case for the argument for monism because, as I will endeavour to demonstrate, B5 and B6 are sufficiently different to favour keeping them as two separate pieces of reasoning.

I translate B6, as it is presented in DK, as follows: 'For if it were <infinite>, it would be one. For if it were two, they would not be able to be infinite, but would have boundaries against each other.' Our immediate task is to examine the suitability of the addition, first proposed by Burnet, of 'infinite' in angle brackets in the first sentence of the fragment.[21]

Simplicius introduces the quotation as evidence for the claim that Aristotle censures Melissus and Parmenides for thinking that

---

[20] The only other Melissan fragment preserved in the commentary on the *De Caelo* is B8.
[21] Burnet 1930: 322 n.2.

there is nothing else in reality apart from the substance of perceptible things, which, because they are one, exhaust what there is:

ἐκεῖνοι γάρ, φησίν, οὐδὲν μὲν ἄλλο παρὰ τὴν τῶν αἰσθητῶν οὐσίαν ὑπολαμβάνοντες
ἐν ὑποτάσει εἶναι ... τοῦ γὰρ αἰσθητοῦ ἐναργῶς εἶναι δοκοῦντος, εἰ ἓν τὸ ὄν ἐστιν,
οὐκ ἂν εἴη ἄλλο παρὰ τοῦτο. (*In De Caelo* 557.2–3)

The quotations, then, are marshalled to illustrate the commitment
to monism that both Parmenides and Melissus are said to share.
As such, there is no reason to think that Simplicius modifies his
quotations to fit his exegetical point, i.e. omitting ἄπειρον, if
indeed it were in his source text, would seem to contribute nothing
to his aim in the passage. It is clear that he thinks all he has to
demonstrate to prove his point is that both Melissus and
Parmenides are committed to the thesis that being (or what-is) is
one – that perceptible things exist is taken as read.

The addition has been nearly universally adopted, with only two
minor instances of dissent, both of which are founded on flawed
arguments. J. H. M. M. Loenen supports the thesis that Melissus
understood the verb 'to be' *sensu stricto* and that, thus, monism
can be derived from the fact that what-is is, not peculiarly from the
premise that it is infinite. This ignores the evidence of the *MXG*
and Simplicius, but we shall have a chance to examine further
Loenen's view below. Renzo Vitali, on the other hand, prefers to
add ὅμοιον rather than ἄπειρον. His reconstruction is dependent on
the bold but wholly implausible move of fragments B4, B5, and
B6 to the very end of Melissus' treatise, after B7 and B8.[22]

Burnet argues that the modification is justified by what we learn
from the paraphrase in the *MXG*. As we noticed above, at
974a11–12 (ἄπειρον δ' ὄν ἓν εἶναι. εἰ γὰρ δύο ἢ πλείω εἴη,
περαίνειν ἂν ταῦτα πρὸς ἄλληλα), Anonymous unambiguously
indicates that Melissus moves from infinity (both spatial and
temporal) to monism. This is confirmed by Simplicius in our
other paraphrase of Melissus' treatise at *In Phys.* 103.28 (εἰ δὲ
ἄπειρον, ἕν) and in his introductory words to his quotation of B5 at
110.5 (ἀπὸ δὲ τοῦ ἀπείρου τὸ ἓν συνελογίσατο ἐκ τοῦ: B5).
Therefore, unlike the two dissenting voices, we cannot reasonably

---

[22] Cf. Loenen 1959: 154–5 and Vitali 1973: 241–50.

claim that Melissus' argument for the infinite plays little or no role in his demonstration of monism.

However, we might proceed along a different line and ask if the addition of ἄπειρον is strictly necessary to reconcile B6 with the testimony of the paraphrasts. One may wonder if *any* addition to the text, as it is found in the commentary on *De Caelo*, must be made. There is no hint in the manuscript tradition that anything has been lost from the quotation and, significantly, it does not grammatically require any such modification. In defence of textual conservatism, Loenen has suggested that the beginning of the manuscript reading of B6 ought to be interpreted in light of the beginning of B9:

εἰ μὲν οὖν[23] εἴη, δεῖ αὐτὸ ἓν εἶναι· **(110.1–2)(B9)**

εἰ γὰρ εἴη, ἓν εἴη ἄν· **(B6)**

The similarity is certainly striking. Both sentences suggest that Melissus deduced monism from his fundamental hypothesis that what-is is. This, of course, supports Loenen's general reading of Melissus' argument. However, Loenen (and others) have misunderstood the place of εἰ μὲν οὖν εἴη, δεῖ αὐτὸ ἓν εἶναι in Melissus' treatise. It is not only the introduction to the argument that what-is lacks a body, but also, like B3, the restatement of a proof already demonstrated, namely that of monism. This suggests that B6 and the quoted element from B9 must be taken together. We shall see below what this amounts to.

Where does this leave us? The suggestion that B9 may provide confirmation for the wisdom of adhering to the manuscript reading of B6, i.e. without the addition of ἄπειρον, should be abandoned, as we shall see. One may object that we do not strictly need the testimony of B9 to reject ἄπειρον. Yet, without such support, we are left little to justify ignoring the witness of the *MXG* and Simplicius. I suggest that we must accept that Melissus argued from infinity to monism and not simply from the premise that what-is is. Such a view perhaps seems to demand that some change be made to the manuscript reading. However, our reconstruction

---

[23] ὄν is given by Diels in his edition of Simplicius' commentary, but not in DK. It is now usually acknowledged that ὄν is a corruption of οὖν: see Palmer 2003: 6 n.13.

of Melissus' argument thus far in B4 and B5 suggests a solution that has the virtue of requiring *no* manuscript emendation or addition.

My proposal that B4 bridges the gap between B5 and B6 suggests an alternative to the addition of ἄπειρον. If we take B4 to precede B6 immediately, the text would run as follows:

ἀλλ' ἀρχὴν δὲ καὶ τέλος ἔχον οὐδὲν οὔτε ἀίδιον οὔτε ἄπειρόν ἐστιν· εἰ γὰρ εἴη, ἓν εἴη ἄν· εἰ γὰρ δύο εἴη, οὐκ ἂν δύναιτο ἄπειρα εἶναι, ἀλλ' ἔχοι ἂν πείρατα πρὸς ἄλληλα.

This construal allows us to read ἄπειρον naturally as constituting the complement of εἴη in B6 but, crucially, *without* demanding that any additions be made to the text. Thus we may translate εἰ γὰρ εἴη as 'For if it were [i.e. sempiternal and/or spatially infinite]'. The addition in parentheses merely fleshes out a natural reading of the Greek. Such an understanding provides us with a simple solution to the apparent inconformity between the text and the witness of the paraphrasts, while also adhering to sound textual conservatism.

Now that the textual worries have been addressed, let us determine how B6 fits into Melissus' argument for uniqueness. We may schematise his demonstration as follows:

(a) Since what-is is infinite, it is one (*addidi*). For
(b) plurality entails borders (B5); but
(c) borders are ἀρχαί and τέλη (B4); and
(d) anything with ἀρχαί and τέλη is neither spatially infinite not sempiternal (B4)
(e) for if it were two <or more> these could not be ἄπειρα, since they would border each other, <and thus have ἀρχαί and τέλη>.

What does B6 add to the argument? It seems to rehearse largely the same argument we saw developed in B4 and B5. If this is the case, the scholarly consensus that B5 and B6 preserve the same bit of Melissan reasoning might seem sound. However, I would like to call attention to the point I raised earlier about the difference between the contrary and contradictory of the claim that what-is is one. I maintained that B5 is best understood as the contradictory of such a claim while B6 need only be understood as a contrary statement. This points towards a crucial difference between the respective roles of B5 and B6 in Melissus' argument.

The proposal is that we should read B6 as a supplementary argument akin to Melissus' appeal to the example of a change by a hair in B7. In that fragment (to be considered fully at a later point), Melissus introduces the putative alteration of the most minute kind to dismiss firmly the possibility of alteration. The argument does not do the heavy lifting of eliminating alteration; that is accomplished by appealing to the violation alteration poses to the previously established elimination of both coming-to-be, heterogeneity, and plurality. Yet by considering an absolutely minimal example of its kind, Melissus is able to dismiss alteration from his picture of the universe.

B6, on my account, works very much in line with the example of a change by a hair considered in B7. B4 and B5 are sufficient to prove uniqueness. What B6 adds is a consideration of an absolutely minimal instance of plurality, namely that what-is is two. The idea then is that *even* if what-is were *only* two, it would still have boundaries and no longer be ἄπειρον. Uniqueness, like changelessness, is resolutely established.

However, B6 raises a puzzle that, unanswered, seems to pose a difficulty for my suggestion of the mental addition of ἄπειρον as the only complement of the verb 'to be' in the fragment. If B4 immediately precedes B6 as I have suggested, should we not also include ἀίδιον as a second complement to be read mentally alongside ἄπειρον in B6? However, there is good reason to think that it is spatial infinity that is most relevant for Melissus as the fragment proceeds, because he adopts narrowly spatial language in the latter half of the fragment. He talks of his hypothetical two (δύο) as ἄπειρα, a word strongly associated with spatial infinity in B2. Temporal infinity, the reader will recall, is usually referred to by ἀίδιον and ἀεί in Melissus (B1 and B4).[24] In addition, it is hard not to think that πείρατα in B6 refer, at least in the first instance, to spatial boundaries.

The language of B6 is undoubtedly spatial: we are invited to consider the impossibility of there being two entities, both conforming to a notion of spatial infinity understood as something all-encompassing. Obviously this cannot be the case because such

---

[24] This point is rightly made by KRS: 394.

all-encompassing entities would inevitably come to meet each other at a spatial border, thus violating their spatial infinity. Yet by including both ἄπειρον and ἀίδιον in B4, we might think that Melissus is leaving room for an isomorphic argument for sempiternity without running through such an argument himself.

We can easily construct such a parallel temporal argument. If what-is is sempiternal, it is one. If it were two, a succession of iterations of what-is would be implied: one what-is would end and another would begin, forming a border, and the first would thus be no longer sempiternal. That Melissus would leave his audience with an argument to construct parallel to one explicitly provided is entirely in line with Eleatic method. The reader will remember that Melissus adopted the same procedure in B1, where an explicit argument is provided for the impossibility of *ex nihilo* generation but the audience is left to work out the isomorphic argument against destruction into nothing.[25] Thus I suggest the mental supplement of ἄπειρον in B6 but with the further thought that the argument will equally apply to eliminating plural temporal entities.

The virtue of the reconstruction thus far is that all relevant fragments have been given roles within the larger argument for uniqueness. However, there is still another feature of B6 to confirm further the attraction of the proposed construal.

In the previous chapter, I marked out the adoption of modal language at the end of B2 (ἀνυστόν) as significant. I would like to offer the thought that such a move at the conclusion of an argument is a highly Melissan move and further supports my placement of B6.

The final two sentences of B7:

ἀνάγκη τοίνυν πλέων εἶναι, εἰ κενεὸν[26] μὴ ἔστιν. εἰ τοίνυν πλέων ἐστίν, οὐ κινεῖται.

So it is **necessary** that it is full, if there is no empty. Therefore, if it is full, it does not move.

The final sentence of B8:

---

[25] It is worth noting as well that Parmenides, though explicitly naming Being as ἀνώλεθρον in B8.3, also does not provide any explicit argument for the predicate.

[26] I print κενεὸν for the manuscript κενὸν.

οὕτως οὖν, εἰ πολλὰ εἴη, τοιαῦτα **χρὴ** εἶναι, οἷόν περ τὸ ἕν.

So then, if there were many, it is **necessary** that they be just as the one.

In both fragments, Melissus concludes by stating what, at a minimum, must be concluded from his argument. This does differ from B2 as Melissus is concerned in that fragment with impossibility and in B7 and B8 with necessity. Nevertheless, the modalisation of the conclusion is common to all three. It is surely significant that such a move is shared by the three most extensive extant fragments. As Melissus has a strong tendency to adopt standardised argumentative formulas, it would be implausible to dismiss such a coincidence of modal notions within concluding statements as mere happenstance.

It is true, however, that the modal language of impossibility and necessity is not, within Melissus' fragments, limited to conclusive statements. We find such ideas expressed elsewhere in B7 and, of course, in B1. In B6, however, οὐκ ἂν δύναιτο should be understood as nearly identical to οὐ ... ἀνυστόν,[27] found, as we have seen, in the conclusion to B2. Such a statement of impossibility or necessity is *not* apparent in B5 and thus gives us strong cause to reject the oft-made claim that B5 and B6 express the same notion. If, then, we accept that there is a strong overlap between the conclusions to Melissan pieces of reasoning and the adoption of modal language, there is good reason to believe both that B5 and B6 featured separately in the same original argument, and that B6 figured after B5.

Does B6 conclude the argument for monism? Yes and no. The adoption of modal language suggests it did figure within the conclusion of the argument. Yet, as we saw in the case of the demonstration of spatial infinity, Melissus typically follows an argument with a reaffirmation of the predicate demonstrated. In that case, B3 restates the conclusion and sets up the next proof. While it has not been appreciated by previous commentators, there is strong evidence that the proof of monism follows suit. Consider the element of the quotation of B9 by Simplicius we considered above: **εἰ μὲν οὖν εἴη, δεῖ αὐτὸ ἓν εἶναι·** ἓν δὲ ὂν δεῖ αὐτὸ σῶμα μὴ ἔχειν. It is plain, if we examine it without prejudice, that

---

[27] The LSJ entry on ἀνυστόν has 'ὡς ἀνυστόν [ἐστι], like ὡς δυνατόν'.

the first half of the quotation reiterates the conclusion of uniqueness and thus serves a similar function to that we have attributed to B3. This strongly suggests that B9 is continuous with B6.

However, what are we to make of the fact that Melissus appears to deduce uniqueness from his foundational hypothesis that what-is is and not from sempiternity or infinity as in my reading of B6? The break from the typical deductive structure is striking. We have, then, the witness of the paraphrasts that uniqueness is deduced from sempiternity and infinity but also the evidence of B9 that suggests uniqueness follows from the hypothesis that what-is is.

The similarity between the beginnings of B6 and B9 strongly tells in favour of mentally supplying the predicate of spatial infinity as the complement in both instances. As we have seen, this is not merely an effort on Melissus' part to save words but an attempt at philosophical economy. By only running through the argument against spatial infinity and leaving us to construct an isomorphic one for sempiternity, Melissus avoids having to run through, perhaps rather awkwardly, two largely similar arguments. Such a suggestion also fits in well with the correlation of modal language with conclusions in Melissus' extant fragments. In B6 we find the modal claim that what is one of two *cannot* be infinite. Certainly this incorporates the modal notion of impossibility; yet it is merely repeating what is said to be impossible in B2. In B9 we find Melissus moving on to state the necessity that what-is is one, the aim of the entirety of the demonstration we have been considering. In addition, the οὖν in the fragment firmly suggests, in keeping with Melissus' general tendency, that the conditional is conclusive in nature.[28] Therefore, εἰ μὲν οὖν εἴη, δεῖ αὐτὸ ἓν εἶναι is ideally situated following B6.

Eudemus' Criticism

Before we end this chapter with a recapitulation of the text I have argued for, it is worth briefly taking up a criticism paraphrased by Simplicius. After he quotes B5, he marshals a criticism of its argument made by Eudemus, Aristotle's pupil. This criticism, we are told, turns on Melissus' imprecise statement of his assertion of monism.

---

[28] οὖν is certainly conclusive, if not inferential, for Melissus. See the final sentence of B8.

τοῦτο δὲ αἰτιᾶται Εὔδημος ὡς ἀδιορίστως λεγόμενον γράφων οὕτως· "εἰ δὲ δὴ συγχωρήσειέ τις ἄπειρον εἶναι τὸ ὄν, διὰ τί καὶ ἓν ἔσται; οὐ γὰρ δὴ διότι πλείονα[29] περανεῖ πη πρὸς ἄλληλα. δοκεῖ γὰρ καὶ ὁ παρεληλυθὼς χρόνος ἄπειρος εἶναι περαίνων πρὸς τὸν παρόντα. πάντῃ μὲν οὖν ἄπειρα τὰ πλείω τάχα οὐκ ἂν εἴη, ἐπὶ θάτερα δὲ φανεῖται ἐνδέχεσθαι. χρὴ οὖν διορίσαι, πῶς ἄπειρα οὐκ ἂν εἴη, εἰ πλείω.

But Eudemus criticises this [B5] as being stated imprecisely, when he writes:
'If someone were to agree that what-is is infinite, why will it also be one? For it is not because a plurality will come to border each other in certain places. For past time is thought to be infinite too, despite bordering on the present. So perhaps plural things could not be infinite in every direction, but it will appear that they could be infinite in the other direction. One must then define in what sense they would not be infinite, if they were plural.'

I believe scholars have largely missed the impact of Eudemus' assessment. Most take the force of the criticism to be simply that infinity does not necessarily entail monism.[30] Eudemus, we are meant to think, offers the example of infinite past time bounded by the present as a genuine rebuke and, thus, we are invited to test its applicability to Melissus' argument. Presumably, we would go about applying the temporal model by rehearsing the truism that a line extended infinitely from a point in one direction is bounded at its source. However, this interpretation wholly misconstrues what Eudemus is, in fact, complaining about in Melissus' treatise.

Both Simplicius' introduction to the quotation and the final sentence of Eudemus' criticism make it perfectly clear that it is Melissus' allegedly *imprecise use* of the term 'infinite' (ἄπειρον) that is in question. Thus we are not to take the example of past time as analogous to B5 but rather as an instance in which we call something infinite and yet also are happy to think it is bounded. Consider the following sentence:

πάντῃ μὲν οὖν ἄπειρα τὰ πλείω τάχα οὐκ ἂν εἴη, ἐπὶ θάτερα δὲ φανεῖται ἐνδέχεσθαι.

So perhaps plural things could not be infinite in every direction, but it will appear that they could be infinite in the other direction.

---

[29] I delete the comma placed here by Diels.
[30] See, for example, Barnes 1982: 205 and Merrill 1998: 381. Kirk and Raven (1957: 300) seem to try and side-step what they take to be Eudemus' criticism by implausibly claiming 'He argues for the unity of the One, in other words, from its infinity. *But that his real object was rather to prove its infinity from its unity is obvious enough*' (my emphasis).

Eudemus here concedes that plural entities would *not* be infinite in *every* direction, but insists that, at least in one way, they may be considered infinite. Yet it is presumably just the way in which Eudemus grants plural entities may not be infinite that is relevant for Melissus, i.e. when the infinite is understood as all-embracing. Therefore, Eudemus' complaint is ultimately the familiar Aristotelian trope that things may be said in different ways and that making the relevant distinctions is essential.

So on my interpretation, Eudemus leaves room for the possibility that Melissus' argument from infinity to monism is valid. Does he, though, have a point in objecting that Melissus fails to clarify what aspect of infinity he has in mind? Well, we might grant that Melissus could not make the same distinctions between senses of 'infinite' that Aristotle does in the *Physics*. Yet such a concession is unnecessary because, as we noticed in our look at B2, it is clear after a moment's thought what notion Melissus must have had in mind and this is confirmed by Aristotle himself. Therefore, Eudemus' complaint is irrelevant not because he thinks it is impossible for Melissus to move validly from the infinite to monism, but because he fails to understand that Melissus has made it rather plain and precise what he thinks the infinite is.

We may now conclude with a look at the text of the argument, as I have suggested it might be reconstructed:

< ἄπειρον δ' ἐὸν ἓν ἐστιν> εἰ <γὰρ> μὴ ἓν εἴη, περανεῖ πρὸς ἄλλο, ἀρχήν δὲ καὶ τέλος ἔχον οὐδὲν οὔτε ἀίδιον οὔτε ἄπειρόν ἐστιν· **<εἰ τοίνυν μὴ ἓν εἴη, οὔτ' ἀίδιον οὔτ' ἄπειρόν ἂν εἴη.>**[31] εἰ γὰρ εἴη, ἓν εἴη ἄν· εἰ γὰρ δύο εἴη, οὐκ ἂν δύναιτο ἄπειρα εἶναι, ἀλλ' ἔχοι ἂν πείρατα πρὸς ἄλληλα. εἰ μὲν οὖν εἴη, δεῖ αὐτὸ ἓν εἶναι.

<And being infinite [i.e. spatially infinite], it is one. For> if it turns out not to be one, it will come to border another; but nothing that has a beginning and/or an end is eternal or infinite; <therefore, if it were not one, it would not be eternal and spatially infinite.> For if it were <spatially infinite>, it would be one. For if there were two, they would not be able to be infinite, but would have boundaries against each other. Therefore, if it were <spatially infinite>, it is necessary that it be one.

---

[31] I add this sentence merely to provide a smoother transition between the sentences. The sense of the text is unaffected.

B9 AND B10: BODILESSNESS AND INDIVISIBILITY

εἰ μὲν οὖν εἴη, δεῖ αὐτὸ ἓν εἶναι· ἓν δ᾽ ἐὸν δεῖ αὐτὸ σῶμα μὴ ἔχειν. εἰ δὲ ἔχοι πάχος, ἔχοι ἂν μόρια, καὶ οὐκέτι ἓν εἴη.

(B9)

εἰ γὰρ διῄρηται, φησί, τὸ ἐόν, κινεῖται· κινούμενον δὲ οὐκ ἂν εἴη.

(B10)

Introduction

Melissus' B9, which purports to demonstrate that what-is has no σῶμα, has typically posed one of the greatest challenges for commentators. The puzzle is often said to be generated by the inconsistency between Melissus' claim in B9 that what-is lacks body and his assertion in B2 and B3 that it is infinite in extension (e.g. τὸ μέγεθος ἄπειρον, B3). This certainly appears irreconcilable *prima facie*, although the atomists, of course, were happy to think that void lacked body yet had extension.[1] Perhaps more apposite, and even more troubling, is Melissus' claim in B7 that what-is is completely solid and unmoving yet according to B9, curiously lacking in body (σῶμα) and thickness (πάχος). This mystifying contradiction in Melissus' fragments has drawn a great many suggested solutions. A brief survey may suffice to demonstrate the range of scholarly attempts to reconcile the apparent contradiction.[2]

(1) Early proposals in the modern era of scholarship focused on questioning the authenticity of B9.[3] This approach has also more

---

[1] See, for example, Aristotle's remarks on Leucippus and Democritus in *Metaphysics* 985b4–10, where void is explicitly contrasted with σῶμα.

[2] A full survey of previous proposals can be found by consulting Palmer 2003, Reale 1970: 193–225, and Curd 1993: 14–19. My schema largely follows from Curd's presentation.

[3] See Apelt 1886: 751–2, Tannery 1930: 406–10, and Albertelli 1939: 241–2.

recently received some sympathy, though no outright commitment, in KRS.[4]

(2) Others have approached the ostensible contradiction between B3 and B9 from the opposite end and argued that it is our understanding of infinite extension in B3 that must be modified. This proposal has its origin in Simplicius' comment *In Phys.* 109.33 that τὸ μέγεθος ἄπειρον should not be understood as describing spatial extension: 'μέγεθος δὲ οὐ τὸ διαστατόν φησιν.'[5] Gregory Vlastos has suggested that we ought to take the infinity referred to in B3 temporally and not spatially.[6]

(3) A proposal with wide support in various forms asserts that B9 does not play a role in Melissus' positive attempt to describe rigorously the features of what-is; rather, it has its place in a putative polemical section of his work. Melissus' alleged opponents range from the Pythagoreans[7] to pluralists more generally.[8]

(4) A fourth approach accepts the authenticity of both B3 and B9 and straightforwardly reads B3 as asserting some kind of spatial extension and B9 as an endorsement of the bodiless nature of what-is. The alleged inconsistency between the two fragments is tackled by drawing a distinction between μέγεθος and σῶμα. On this proposal what-is can fully take up space and yet have no body. This approach supposedly may indicate a certain naïveté on Melissus' part as he was pioneering but not yet mastering abstract concepts, as Raven claims.[9] A more sympathetic development of this proposal is offered by David Furley. He offers a reading of B9 that renders the infinite extension of what-is as neither physical nor geometrical space but rather as a substructure of the universe in the manner of the obscure ὑποδοχή of Plato's *Timaeus*.[10] On this proposal the substructure of the universe may extend infinitely while still allowing for its understanding as incorporeal.

The ingenuity of many of these approaches to our fragment is, if nothing more, evidence of its difficulty. However, none of these four classes of interpretation is ultimately persuasive. It is often mentioned that option (1) is supported by the absence of any

---

[4] KRS: 401.   [5] See also *In Phys.* 109.18–19.

[6] Vlastos 1953: 34–5. Cf. Loenen 1959: 149 n.41 and 155 n.55.

[7] Burnet 1930: 327 and Ross 1924: notes on 986b20, p. 153.

[8] Booth 1958: 62 and Barnes 1982: 228. Barnes, though, does not find the suggestion 'delicious'.

[9] Raven 1948: 87–92. Although he seems to be heading in this direction, he does accuse Melissus of lacking the conceptual tools necessary to articulate adequately the properly incorporeal. See also Raven's comments in Kirk and Raven 1957: esp. 304.

[10] Furley 1989: 119–22.

mention of the bodiless nature of what-is in the pseudo-Aristotelian *MXG* which provides a (generally reliable) paraphrase of Melissus' arguments. B9 is also mysteriously absent from the paraphrase of Melissus' deductions given by Simplicius, beginning at *In Phys.* 103.13. Both absences are easily overcome. The *MXG* has been poorly transmitted; and, in any case, we need not assume that it contains all of Melissus' arguments.[11] Simplicius does leave out B9 from his paraphrase; however, he twice quotes elements of the 'fragment' elsewhere using words of introduction that strongly suggest he believed it to be something Melissus actually wrote.[12] Our option (2) fares no better. Melissus had already argued for sempiternity in B1, thereby making another deduction in B3, unambiguously claimed by Simplicius to follow the proof of spatial infinity in B2, superfluous. Also, translating μέγεθος as something other than spatial extension is tortuous and leaves Melissus with an unnecessarily messy argument.[13] Option (3) is merely conjecture and, even so, has a fatal flaw. Surely Melissus was not so careless as to adopt a dialectical position to counter an opponent's argument that would also have teeth to attack his own positive account![14]

Option (4) is more promising; its proponents admirably attempt to make sense of Melissus without resorting to the chopping block or to positing phantom opponents. However, it is uncharitable (and I shall argue outright unfair) to claim that Melissus had a muddled or naïve concept of σῶμα as Raven and Gomperz assert.[15] In addition, Furley's reading, although quite ingenious, is not sufficiently supported by the evidence.

---

[11] See Mansfeld 1990: 200–37 for the reliability of the *MXG*. I agree with Curd (1993: 15 n.54) that even if we accept the *MXG* as representing authentic Melissan arguments, this does not imply that it contained the whole of Melissus' work.

[12] *In Phys.* 87.5.7 and 109.34–110.2

[13] This criticism is frequently made. See Guthrie 1965: 110 n.2 and Reale 1970: 197–8.

[14] Curd 1993: 16 n.60 *contra* Booth 1959: 62.

[15] Gomperz 1932: 158–9. Gomperz advocates understanding Melissus' claim that what-is lacks a body as meaning something like relatively unsolid. This works in conjunction with his reading of πάχος as indicating a lack of density rather than of thickness. Neither construal is tenable. Melissus makes it very clear in B7 that what-is *is* dense and completely solid without any admixture of void.

σῶμα

I propose to re-examine B9 and offer an interpretation that makes it not only fully consistent with the evidence of the other fragments but also an important element of Melissus' deductive inferential structure. To this end, I will not be completely discarding the approaches previously advocated. The motivation to overcome the ostensible contradiction between the fragments maintained in option (4) is wholly reasonable and I share its fundamental contention that we ought to try to save our fragments of Melissus from the cutting room floor.

In order to overcome the inconsistency between B3, B7, and B9, we must first attempt to define in what sense Melissus employed the term σῶμα. Commentators have tended to understand Melissus' term as quite conceptually sophisticated and capable of denoting a wide range of physical extensions. The assumption seems to be that σῶμα was used in the Greek of Melissus' era in parallel with the English use of 'body' as denoting both the figure of a person/animal and, more widely, something extended in space, e.g. a body of water.[16] On this understanding, 'body' comes very close to meaning something merely three-dimensional. The contradiction between the infinite extension of B3, the solidity apparent in B7, and the statement of bodilessness in B9 is strongest if we understand Melissus' use of σῶμα in this wide sense. The question then runs: how can something infinitely extended in all directions not be three-dimensional?[17] It is undoubtedly in answer to a question of this kind that commentators have posited some of the speculative conclusions we have surveyed above.

However, we might more fruitfully ask whether or not Melissus' σῶμα is capable of stretching as widely as the English 'body'. On this point Robert Renehan has published an important article denying that we have any evidence indicating that σῶμα had such a wide usage in the Greek of the fifth century

---

[16] We might also think of phrases like 'body of work' or 'body of evidence' which indicate a great deal of abstraction.

[17] It seems in answer to this question that Raven and Gomperz propose that Melissus was caught up in semantic confusion as σῶμα was moving towards increased conceptual sophistication.

BCE.[18] By the fourth century, the use of the term σῶμα appears to have broadened and could indicate something generally material and not narrowly anatomical.[19] However, when Melissus was writing in the fifth century, Renehan claims, 'σῶμα still meant primarily what it had always meant, namely the body of an organic being, living or dead.'[20]

Along with John Palmer, I find Renehan's conclusion persuasive.[21] However, the argument that σῶμα had not yet achieved conceptual sophistication in the fifth century is necessarily an argument from silence. Our evidence from the fourth century that σῶμα did, in fact, become a broader term also suggests caution.[22] We may, however, lend support to the notion that Melissus' σῶμα was anatomical (at least primarily so) by inquiring into what this move achieves for him in the argument. The denial that what-is possesses a bodily form bears a strong resemblance to the criticisms of anthropomorphic conceptions that we find in Xenophanes.[23] We have two fragments from Xenophanes that

---

[18] Renehan 1980: 118. Renehan persuasively rejects every early example of the word ἀσώματος and the attendant concept of bodilessness provided by Gomperz (1932). Cf. Guthrie 1965: 111 n.2.

[19] See Plato, *Timaeus* 31b where σωματοειδές is a general term for something visible and tangible.

[20] Renehan 1980: 118.

[21] Brooke Holmes (2010: 104) takes it that both Palmer, and Owen (1960: at 100–1), attempt to solve B9's apparent contradiction by denying that σῶμα should be taken to imply an abstract conception of space. She questions the assumption that we need make a distinction between a philosophically rich notion that such an abstract notion would imply and an 'ordinary' sense of σῶμα as either a physical solid (Owen) or 'an anatomic body' (Palmer). Her approach is to think that σῶμα is rather to be taken as 'a composite object formed from more durable stuffs and dynamically embedded within reconceived networks of power' and that it is 'mixture and dissolution' (105) that is the threat Melissus is militating against. So it is 'becoming' and not limited spatial extension that is at stake if Melissus were to say that what-is had a body. Part of her argument relies on using evidence from Plato that I take to be of limited value for interpreting Melissus, and I suggest that such a reading fails to explain why it is that πάχος and its implication of the loss of unity are obviously relevant for Melissus. I submit, then, that Owen is correct insofar as it is in light of *divisibility* that we should understand πάχος and μόρια. This will emerge more clearly below.

[22] Palmer 2003: 4. I am sympathetic to Palmer's exhortation to be careful when trying to discern the exact transition point in semantic shifts and, indeed, I will suggest that Melissus' use cannot be easily attributed to either camp.

[23] Palmer (2003: 4) sees Melissus' denial of an anthropomorphic conception of what-is (cf. Sedley 1999: 129–30) as a natural development of Xenophanes' critical theological fragments.

criticise understanding the gods as possessing bodies in any way like those of humans.

ἀλλ' οἱ βροτοὶ δοκέουσι γεννᾶσθαι θεούς,
τὴν σφετέρην δ' ἐσθῆτα ἔχειν φωνήν τε δέμας τε.   (21B14)

Mortals believe that the gods are born
And have human clothing, voice and form.   (Trans. R. D. McKirahan)

εἷς θεός, ἔν τε θεοῖσι καὶ ἀνθρώποισι μέγιστος,
οὔτι δέμας θνητοῖσιν ὁμοίιος οὐδὲ νόημα.   (21B23)

One god is greatest among gods and men,
not at all like mortals in body or in thought.   (Trans. J. H. Lesher)

An initial worry may be raised about Xenophanes' use of δέμας rather than Melissus' σῶμα for body. There was once a general consensus that in the Homeric epics δέμας connoted a living body while σῶμα solely signified a corpse.[24] This *communis opinio* has been vigorously challenged and should probably be largely discarded even if the two terms cannot be convincingly proved entirely synonymous in Epic.[25] Whatever distinction may be discernible in Homer, it seems clear enough that both δέμας and σῶμα are commonly used in Greek for a living human or animal body from at least the time of Hesiod.[26]

It is interesting to note that Xenophanes' denial of human bodies to the gods does not entail that he rejects their corporeality entirely. The criticism in both quoted fragments is aimed at the thought that the gods have bodies in any way similar to *humans* (οὔτι δέμας θνητοῖσιν ὁμοίιος). The possibility that the gods have bodily forms dissimilar to humans is implicitly affirmed. Indeed that god(s) has some kind of corporeal composition may be suggested by Xenophanes' ascription of the human faculties of seeing, thinking, and hearing to him in B24. Rather Xenophanes' primary interests seem to be to dispel anthropomorphic thinking about the gods and to draw attention to the uncritical epistemology that permitted the development of these fanciful theological

---

[24] 'σῶμα "Ομηρος οὐδέποτε ἐπὶ τοῦ ζῶντος εἴρηκεν', according to Aristarchus in the *Lexicon Homericum* of Apollonius Sophista. See also the LSJ entry on σῶμα.

[25] Renehan 1979.

[26] That δέμας is employed for this meaning in Homer is beyond doubt. For an early example of σῶμα used in a parallel sense, see Hesiod, *Works and Days* 539–40: 'τὴν περιέσσασθαι, ἵνα τοι τρίχες ἀτρεμέωσι μηδ' ὀρθαὶ φρίσσωσιν ἀειρόμεναι κατὰ σῶμα.'

conceptions. This first leg of this project is most strikingly accomplished in B16 and B15. In the former, Xenophanes remarks on the localised character of the ascription of human features to the gods by noticing that Ethiopians say their gods are snub-nosed and black, while the Thracians think their gods are blue-eyed redheads. In the latter fragment we may notice an even more pointed criticism of the subjective nature of anthropomorphic thinking about the gods. Here, using his characteristic counterfactual argumentation,[27] Xenophanes claims that if horses, cattle, or lions had hands, they would depict their gods just as they would themselves. What this suggests is that Xenophanes' target is not the corporeality of the gods *simpliciter* but, more narrowly, the understanding of them as organic in a way familiar to humans.

The thought that Melissus adopted a stance in opposition to an anthropomorphic understanding of what-is, following the model that Xenophanes established, is further supported by Melissus' B7.[28] Here he denies that what-is can suffer pain and anguish. Quite what this is supposed to signify I shall discuss later, but it is clear that these ailments threaten the unity and sempiternity of what-is. Therefore, we may say, with some security, that Melissus will not tolerate the attribution of anthropomorphic features to what-is. If this reading of Melissus is plausible and we accept that he proceeds at least partially along the same lines as Xenophanes, we have further confirmation that a narrow view of B9's σῶμα, discussed above, ought to be adopted. On this reading, Melissus is, like Xenophanes, denying that what-is possesses a familiar human (or perhaps animal) body, and he is not making the stronger claim that what-is does not have spatial extension of any kind.

So far my analysis has largely followed the lead of John Palmer. However, the second sentence of our fragment presents more intractable difficulties and occasions the divergence of our interpretations. The puzzle centres on Melissus' claim that what-is has no πάχος. We have established that it makes good sense for Melissus to deny that what-is has an organic or anatomical body,

---

[27] A similar pattern of argumentation can be discerned in B34 and B38.
[28] That Melissus had *a* body and not a wider notion of corporeality in mind is accepted by Sedley (1999: 129–30) and Palmer (2003: 4).

but it is puzzling that an infinite extension would have no 'thickness'. Palmer's suggestion is to excise the second sentence of the fragment, a solution which, while understandable under the weight of the interpretative difficulties, is both unfortunate and, I think, unnecessary. Palmer's response is nevertheless motivated by a real uncertainty about the original expression of our fragment. What is cited as B9 in DK is, in fact, a compilation of elements from two separate passages in Simplicius separated by some twenty pages in Diels' edition.

(a) ἀδιαίρετον γὰρ ὂν τὸ παρ᾽ αὐτοῖς ἓν ὂν οὔτε πεπερασμένον οὔτε ἄπειρον ὡς σῶμα ἔσται· καὶ γὰρ καὶ ὁ Παρμενίδης τὰ σώματα ἐν τοῖς δοξαστοῖς τίθησι, καὶ ὁ Μέλισσος ἓν ἐόν, **φησί**, δεῖ αὐτὸ σῶμα μὴ ἔχειν. εἰ δὲ ἔχοι πάχος, ἔχοι ἂν μόρια καὶ οὐκέτι ἓν εἴη. (Simplicius, *In Phys.* 87.5–7)

(b) ὅτι γὰρ ἀσώματον εἶναι βούλεται τὸ ὄν, ἐδήλωσεν **εἰπὼν** εἰ μὲν ὂν εἴη, δεῖ αὐτὸ ἓν εἶναι· ἐν δὲ ὂν δεῖ αὐτὸ σῶμα μὴ ἔχειν. (Simplicius, *In Phys.* 109.34–110.2)

Examining the two passages, we can see that B9, as it is printed by DK, is exactly paralleled in neither. Rather B9 is a synthesis of the underlined portion of (b) and the final sentence of (a). Another important discrepancy should also be noted: the ὂν in εἰ μὲν ὂν εἴη (b) has morphed into οὖν in B9. This is left unexplained by DK, but it makes good sense as ὂν for οὖν is an easy mistake to make; Melissus would have no doubt written the Ionic ἐόν,[29] and reading the participle makes the sentence unwieldy and repetitive.[30] In addition, we also have a parallel at B7.9 for support: εἰ μὲν οὖν χωρεῖ τι ἢ εἰσδέχεται.[31]

Yet, however we resolve ὂν, we are still left with two quotations of, broadly speaking at least, a similar argument but with crucial differences, in particular the mention of πάχος and μόρια in the one and not the other. It is this discrepancy that leads Palmer to argue for the excision of εἰ δὲ ἔχοι πάχος, ἔχοι ἂν μόρια καὶ οὐκέτι ἓν εἴη as a Simplician explication, probably inspired by a Zenonian

---

[29] Although, as I have argued earlier, I doubt Atticisation, on its own, is significant enough evidence to establish inauthenticity or corruption. Here, fortunately, we have more than one indication that ὂν ought to be read as οὖν.

[30] Some of these points are made by Palmer (2003: 6 n.13).

[31] οὖν also has superior manuscript authority as it is found in two of the fundamental manuscripts, E and F. ὂν appears only in D and the Aldine.

antinomy.[32] Certainly it is striking that Simplicius also uses the word 'πάχος' when quoting Zeno's antinomy that, were there many things, they would be so large as to be ἄπειρα τὸ μέγεθος and yet also so small as to μηθὲν ἔχειν μέγεθος: 'εἰ δὲ ἔστιν, ἀνάγκη ἕκαστον μέγεθός τι ἔχειν καὶ **πάχος** καὶ ἀπέχειν αὐτοῦ τὸ ἕτερον ἀπὸ τοῦ ἑτέρου. καὶ περὶ τοῦ προύχοντος ὁ αὐτὸς λόγος' (Simplicius, *In Phys.* 141.2–4).

However, *pace* Palmer, I see no reason, beyond this coincidence of vocabulary, to think that Simplicius is making use of Zenonian material in (a). Simplicius is unambiguously (φησί) quoting Melissus and there is no suggestion in the presentation of the fragment itself that verbatim quotation ends and exegesis begins. A final helpful point that should not be easily dismissed is that εἰ δὲ ἔχοι πάχος κτλ. is in the easily recognisable fashion of Melissan conditionals. Taken together, I submit, what this amounts to for us is an obligation to try and make sense of the whole of (a), however puzzling it may seem intially, as a genuine quotation from Melissus' treatise and not a Simplician conflation or confusion.

If the whole of (a) must be accepted, how are we to understand its relationship with (b)? The assumption, accepted since the beginning of modern scholarship on Melissus,[33] is that Simplicius' two quotations derive from the same piece of reasoning and that, thus, both should be treated as a single fragment. Such a view, of course, led to the pastiche DKB9 and is tacitly accepted by all subsequent commentators, including Palmer. However, the consensus stands on weak ground and should be questioned, if not overturned outright.

Our look at Melissus' argument for monism in the previous chapter suggests the way forward. Recall B5 and B6:

εἰ μὴ ἓν εἴη, περανεῖ πρὸς ἄλλο. **(B5)**

εἰ γὰρ εἴη, ἓν εἴη ἄν· εἰ γὰρ δύο εἴη, οὐκ ἂν δύναιτο ἄπειρα εἶναι, ἀλλ' ἔχοι ἂν πείρατα πρὸς ἄλληλα. **(B6, my text)**

---

[32] That Simplicius is conflating or, at least, using other Eleatic materials to interpret Melissus here is suggested by KRS: 401 n.1).

[33] To the best of my knowledge, this assumption has never been challenged.

Remember that commentators typically either treat B5 as a paraphrase of the more substantial B6 or simply ignore it as irrelevant. However, we saw that, far from being identical, each had a different role to play in Melissus' argument. It is Melissus' use of ring-composition (*demonstrandum*, argument, restatement of *demonstrandum*) in structuring his arguments that explains why we find quotations from Simplicius that appear similar, but not precisely the same. This means that overlap between different quotations need not entail different versions of the same source material from which we must work out an approximate reconstruction of a single original, but rather different elements of the same, longer argument. Therefore, (a) and (b) should, at least at this initial stage of reconstruction, be treated not as a single fragment but as two separate parts of a larger, more complex argument for the claim that what-is does not have a body. I distinguish the two quotations as B9 and B9*:

ἓν ἐόν, δεῖ αὐτὸ σῶμα μὴ ἔχειν. εἰ δὲ ἔχοι πάχος, ἔχοι ἂν μόρια καὶ οὐκέτι ἓν εἴη. (**B9**)

εἰ μὲν οὖν εἴη, δεῖ αὐτὸ ἓν εἶναι· ἓν δὲ ὂν δεῖ αὐτὸ σῶμα μὴ ἔχειν. (**B9***)

πάχος

Before we turn to a determination of the most plausible reconstruction of Melissus' argument from fragments B9 and B9*, the seemingly perpetual puzzle of the use of 'πάχος' must be considered. The thought that this word simply denotes 'thickness' for Melissus appears to render B9 particularly incompatible with B7, if we consider that Melisssus goes to some trouble in B7 to argue that what-is is πλέων (full). The heart of the worry is that it seems intuitive that something full must also have πάχος, understood as 'thickness'. Yet it is just this that Melissus denies. We might also be tempted to think, as many do in the case of σῶμα, that πάχος is to be understood quite abstractly as meaning nothing more than three-dimensionality. If this is the case, it is very difficult to see how B3 and particularly B7 can be comfortably accommodated.

The apparent inconsistency has led to some of the interpretations listed in option (4) in the introductory schema, most notably Gomperz's. He suggests that πάχος ought to be understood as a noun related to the verb πήγνυμι and thus connoting density rather than thickness.[34] This, however, is unlikely to be correct, as there is no persuasive evidence to suggest that πάχος does in fact come from this verb and we should note that Melissus uses the more familiar πυκνόν for 'dense' in B7.[35]

While the specific definition Gomperz suggests seems mistaken, the notion that πάχος does not stretch as widely as commentators have often assumed seems correct. However, we should not understand Melissus to be developing a special use of the word or employing it in a rare, secondary meaning. We shall see that Melissus, in fact, uses πάχος for its common denotation for something of 'determinable or measurable thickness'. Several examples may suffice to indicate that this meaning, more restricted than mere three-dimensionality, was perfectly standard in the fifth century. When describing a wall around the Peiraeus, Thucydides uses the word for a fortification's *observable* thickness: καὶ ᾠκοδόμησαν τῇ ἐκείνου γνώμῃ τὸ πάχος τοῦ τείχους ὅπερ νῦν ἔτι δῆλόν ἐστι περὶ τὸν Πειραιᾶ.[36] Thucydides' use of πάχος seems to suggest something like 'breadth' rather than the more expansive 'thickness'. A look to Pindar furthers our contention that a narrower meaning ought to be understood:

δράκοντος
δ' εἴχετο λαβροτατᾶν γενύων,
ὃς πάχει μάκει τε πεντηκόντερον ναῦν κράτει[37]

Pindar couples πάχει with μάκει (length) to describe the enormous jaws of a serpent. Notice how conveying the measurement of the serpent's jaw as both broader and longer than a ship of fifty oars is Pindar's object here. Thucydides and Pindar use πάχος not to suggest that a particular object is extended in space but rather to define the boundaries of something already assumed to have some determinate thickness. The distinction may appear slight, but it is essential if we are to make good sense of Melissus' fragment.

A final example from Herodotus confirms the emphasis on measurement and suggests a solution to the puzzle of why

---

[34] 1932: 158–9. For the related remarks of his father, see Gomperz 1906: 190. See also Guthrie 1965: 112.
[35] This is suggested by Palmer (2003: 5).   [36] 1.93.5.   [37] *Pythian Ode* 4.243–5

Melissus so clearly connects πάχος with σῶμα: ἑξακοσίους ἀμφορέας εὐπετέως χωρέει τὸ ἐν Σκύθῃσι χαλκήιον, πάχος δὲ τὸ Σκυθικὸν τοῦτο χαλκήιόν ἐστι δακτύλων ἕξ.[38] As in the Pindar example cited above, the passage concerns the description of an object of monumental scale, in this case a Scythian bronze vessel of enormous capacity. We can see that, once again, πάχος is used to describe a measurement of determinable thickness. This furthers the evidence of our first two passages and solidifies our contention that πάχος ought not to be understood as simply 'thickness'. What is truly striking here, however, is the connection that Herodotus establishes between this word and the capacity of fingers (δακτύλων) to act as instruments of measurement. This is certainly not an uncommon notion or one exclusive to ancient Greece; the length from the tip of one's thumb to its first joint is still frequently used as a rough measure corresponding to an inch and a quantity of spirit may be ordered at a bar by how many finger widths it ascends to in the glass. These are hardly accurate tools of measurement as fingers vary; however, they do provide a means of determining approximate extension.

We need not limit ourselves to fingers; a number of anatomical features have been used as measuring instruments. This may be observed by considering two of our standard units of measure, the foot and the hand. Both have now, of course, undergone a standardisation process that has given both an exact conversion to the fraction of a centimetre. However, a look to their anatomical names suggests how the units functioned prior to the International Standard of Units. If the usefulness of anatomical features is evident in the not so distant past, we might imagine how prevalent such tools were in Melissus' day before widely accepted standardisation was possible. The evidence that this is indeed the case is so plentiful that we need not dwell on the issue. However, one particularly instructive example may prove helpful.[39] We may again turn to Herodotus for assistance: ὁ δὲ βασιλήιος πῆχυς τοῦ

---

[38] 4.81.
[39] For another striking example of the anatomical basis of ancient Greek linear measurement see Plato, *Phaedo* 96d7ff. Here both heads and cubits are suggested to be common units of measurement.

μετρίου ἐστὶ πήχεος μέζων τρισὶ δακτύλοισι.⁴⁰ Here Herodotus is distinguishing between two different cubit lengths, the royal and the common kinds. The cubit is itself a unit of measure determined by an anatomical feature, the lower arm.⁴¹ Herodotus' description goes further though than merely providing evidence for another body part used as an instrument of measurement. It seems that the anatomical measurement of the cubit could be further subdivided into units of fingers (δάκτυλοι), possibly, though not mentioned here by Herodotus, with the transitional unit of the palm (παλαστή).⁴² What this passage of Herodotus suggests is that anatomical features not only were used as convenient means of approximating length, but were central to the system of ancient Greek measurement as a whole.

In the case of Melissus we have explicit confirmation that he was committed to such an anatomical understanding of measurement. We find in B7 that Melissus took the hair to be the smallest unit of measurement: εἰ τοίνυν τριχὶ μιῇ μυρίοις ἔτεσιν ἑτεροῖον γίνοιτο, ὀλεῖται πᾶν ἐν τῷ παντὶ χρόνῳ. On the basis of this evidence, we may say, with some safety, that anatomical features and measurement are very closely linked for Melissus.

How then does the anatomical foundation of measurement help us to understand our fragment of Melissus? If we keep in mind the intimate connection between the body and its role in determining linear extension, we can begin to make sense of why Melissus denies σῶμα to his understanding of what-is. πάχος need not be understood as a synonym or near synonym of σῶμα.⁴³ Rather something that has a σῶμα necessarily has the tools to determine a πάχος and, as these instruments are used for direct one-to-one comparison, they themselves have a πάχος. Therefore, it is not a construal of synonymy between σῶμα and πάχος that is desirable

---

⁴⁰ 1.178.
⁴¹ Given the approximate nature of anatomical units, it is not surprising that it is unclear in ancient sources whether a cubit is properly measured from the elbow to the wrist or, further on, to the middle finger. Frequently πῆχυς simply means the lower arm; see Plato, *Timaeus* 75a, for example. For some of the difficulties in understanding Greek units of linear measurement, see Bauslaugh 1979.
⁴² For the measurement of the cubit as six palms (παλασταί), which are themselves equal to four fingers (δάκτυλοι), see Pollux 2.158.
⁴³ The translation of πάχος as something like 'solidity' seems to be driven by this notion. See, for example, KRS: 400.

here but rather the understanding of an entailment relation. This fits in well with the rendering of the fragment I have advocated: *if* something has a body, *then* it has a πάχος understood as 'dimensions'.[44]

Does such an argument absolutely exclude the possibility that σῶμα had reached a more semantically rich stage of development for Melissus? Could the sense of σῶμα carry more than a mere anatomical implication? What the above considerations suggest is that it is one fundamental aspect of a σῶμα (that it has determinate dimensions and shape and is, thus, measurable) that is most relevant for Melissus' argument. Such an understanding of σῶμα does not eliminate the possibility that Melissus' use evidences some semantic development, but only that, if such abstraction had occurred, its use still carried with it a strong sense of determinate *shape* which the anatomical reading suggests. The thought that Melissus is especially keen to deny that what-is has a shape because of its impliciations of divisibility will be taken up in the following sections. In any case, I take it that the anatomical reading I have suggested is to be taken as primary, but it need not be taken to exclude *any* abstraction at all. What is crucial, as will become clear in the following section, is that it is the possibilty of division, implied by attributing a deteriminate shape to what-is, that must be taken away from Melissus' use of σῶμα.

Making Sense of the Argument

If the above analysis is along the right lines, Melissus' move from σῶμα to πάχος seems clear enough. Yet this move still does not lift the fog from our fragment. If the bodilessness of what-is is what is at stake in B9, why does Melissus focus on the impossibility of it having πάχος? It seems that if one wanted to counter the contention that what-is has a body, the most obvious move would be to

---

[44] This analysis does not demand that we need to transition from having a body to having a πάχος through the idea of bodily parts. Something needn't have bodily parts to have a πάχος. All I am committed to attributing to Melissus is the thought that a πάχος, understood as a 'determinate or measurable thickness' or 'dimensions', is intimately bound up with anatomical means of measurement and that, on such an understanding, an anatomical body is a paradigmatic example of something with a πάχος.

focus on the inherent mereological aspect of bodies. Bodies consist of arms, legs, fingers, and many other parts: in short, they are plural in constitution. Melissus could then deploy his argument against plurality, deduced from the predicate 'infinite', in B6. We might also imagine other routes to bodilessness as well; Melissus could deny what-is a body on the basis of homogeneity, of his prohibition of generation and destruction in B1, or, possibly, of the threat that pain and anguish pose to unity in B7. All three of these options seem plausible and perhaps more perspicuous than the logic of our fragment.

It is here that we enter murky territory. The above account posits that Melissus moves from the predicate 'uniqueness' established in B4, B5, and B6 to bodilessness through the thought that a body has a πάχος, and, if this is the case, it could not be one. This argument seems peculiarly round-about and unnecessarily complex. I agree that it is. However, a circuitous argument is not necessarily a confused argument. In addition, it is worth considering how far the evidence allows for definitive solutions to the puzzles of B9. All I hope for the reader to take away, at a minimum, is that there is good reason to think that the fragment(s) ought to be preserved and considered to contain a genuine Melissan argument. The place of πάχος within the structure of the argument may not be unassailably determinable. Yet this is no reason to chop our precious remains of Melissus crudely. In what follows I offer one argument for the rather tortuous and unparsimonious route Melissus takes from uniqueness to bodilessness. It is offered not as indisputable but rather as one possible construal, as well as an invitation for alternatives.

A look again at what I have termed B9 (i.e. without an asterisk) suggests a plausible reason why Melissus took what seems to be a peculiar route to bodilessness from uniqueness:

ἓν ἐόν, δεῖ αὐτὸ σῶμα μὴ ἔχειν. εἰ δὲ ἔχοι πάχος, ἔχοι ἂν μόρια καὶ οὐκέτι ἓν εἴη. (**B9**)

I have intimated that it is a close entailment relation, rather than synonymy, between σῶμα and πάχος, that is relevant for Melissus. Yet, even if my understanding of a πάχος as a 'determinable thickness' is correct, it is not immediately obvious why this should entail that something with a πάχος should have μόρια (parts). One factor often mentioned by commentators in this context is that Melissus may have not yet moved away from the obvious anatomical point of the fragment. After all, a human or animal body is a paradigmatic example of an object consisting of parts, e.g. head, hands, torso, etc. However, Melissus does *not* say that what has a body has parts, as we might expect, but rather chooses to deduce parthood from πάχος. For this reason we should be careful not to lean on σῶμα too heavily.

The reader may recall that I rejected much of the fourth class of interpretation I surveyed above. In particular I denied that it is fair to ascribe naïve or muddled notions of σῶμα and πάχος to Melissus. I do not wish to resurrect, for example, Gomperz's claim that πάχος ought to be interpreted as implying density and thus Melissus' point would be that not having a body entails that what-is is relatively unsolid. However, there may be a place for the thought that Melissus' mysterious move from uniqueness to bodilessness through an entailment of πάχος turns on something more abstract than I have previously suggested.

The fundamental question that we are considering, I take it, is why Melissus needs any notion of πάχος at all when it is clear that the essential parthood of organic bodies is sufficient to contradict the attribute of uniqueness he has already demonstrated. Πάχος, in short, seems unnecessary. Yet we might think that the same motivation I have attributed to B6 and the example of alteration by a single hair in B7 is at play here in B9. Both of those arguments acted as forceful supplementary arguments, marshalled as complementary proofs for theses already established. On such an account, Melissus would be taking it as obvious (or perhaps already demonstrated in a lost bit of reasoning) that if what-is had an organic body it could not be one because it would have parts. The introduction of πάχος, then, would be for the sake of making a more global point. It is of course the case that anything with a body would have a πάχος. Yet we might construe the apparently complex appeal to πάχος as eliminating not only corporeality, understood as having an anatomical or organic body, but also anything that has a determinable thickness and, necessarily, a shape. Such a view leaves the conception of σῶμα discussed above intact, while also pointing towards a solution to the mysterious appeal to something's πάχος. Why is having a πάχος incompatible with uniqueness? It is through Melissus' discussion of division that an answer emerges.

Indivisible

My suggestion is that in B9 Melissus is preparing the ground for his argument for the indivisibility of what-is. That argument undoubtedly depends on the proof of immobility found in B7; however, the argument is more complex and requires more premises to go through than has typically been appreciated by commentators. One such premise, I shall argue, is that what-is does not have a πάχος.

εἰ γὰρ διῄρηται, φησί, τὸ ἐόν, κινεῖται· κινούμενον δὲ οὐκ ἂν εἴη. **(In Phys. 109.32, B10)**

Melissus uses his characteristic conditional formula here to deny that what-is is divided on the basis of the impossibility of motion,[45] which is vigorously eliminated in B7. There Melissus argues that if motion were possible it would require void (understood as what-is-not) intermixed with what-is. If this were the case, there would be a spectrum of densities allowing what-is to compress and expand and thereby allow motion. However, void is nothing and cannot exist, what-is is full, and thus motion is denied.[46] But why should division result in motion? After all, England is divided up into counties, yet it would be absurd to imagine that Cambridgeshire had to be moved in any way to be divided from Bedfordshire. Stephen Makin has argued that B10 would provide a more substantial argument if Melissus were making a point about the *divisibility* of what-is.[47] I am not sure that this suggestion quite works. If Melissus were attempting to establish the modal conclusion here that what-is *cannot* be divided, we are still left with the unpalatable premise that division is necessarily the result of motion.

---

[45] I translate κινεῖται as 'it moves' on the evidence of Melissus' use of this word in B7, where motion is clearly what is meant. I see no reason why Melissus would be thinking of change-in-general here, *pace* Huby and Taylor 2011.

[46] I owe this understanding to Sedley (1982: 178–9).   [47] Makin 1993: 35–6.

Are we left then with a poor argument? Perhaps there is a way out. Makin extends Melissus' argument to a conclusion of indivisibility because of the alleged superiority of this line of thought over Zeno's arguments targeting division and plurality. According to Makin, Zeno needs both a premise of homogeneity and another one concerning the impossibility of infinite division in order to counter division. Melissus, according to Makin, needs neither and, therefore, presumably on the authority of *lex parsimoniae*, B10 is an advance on Zeno. This is a tempting line of thought. If Makin is right, Melissus introduces a novel argument against the division of what-is that proceeds without the claim of homogeneity that underpins the parallel arguments of both Zeno and Parmenides.

Can we accept Makin's construction of a 'neo-Melissan' argument? I do not think we can do so entirely. We are still left with the uncomfortable association between division and motion. In addition it seems mistaken to think that homogeneity is not assumed by Melissus in B10. After all, homogeneity certainly underpins much of the reasoning used to eliminate alteration in B7 and there is no persuasive reason why it should not be important to the argument in B10.[48] We know that Melissus did argue for homogeneity on the testimony of the paraphrase in the *MXG*[49] and we also have the summary found at the beginning of B7 (οὕτως οὖν ἀίδιόν ἐστι καὶ ἄπειρον καὶ ἓν καὶ **ὅμοιον** πᾶν). Therefore, as we know that B10 turns on the premise of 'immobility' established in B7, we can be sure that homogeneity was established by Melissus *prior* to indivisibility; this confirms that the premise 'immobile' was available to him in B10.

It perhaps attributes to Melissus a novel line of thought if we think that he argued that what-is is not undivided without recourse to homogeneity. However, it also leaves him with an insubstantial argument.[50] If we, following the lead of the evidence, assume that homogeneity plays a role in B10 as a suppressed premise, it might

---

[48] I note as well that Melissus' denial of motion later in B7 seems solely concerned with *internal* motion. Melissus can ignore movement into *external* space because he has already argued that what-is is infinite precluding this possibility. Each new argument Melissus provides is supported by previously established conclusions.

[49] *MXG* 974a12–14.

[50] We should note that Makin is not ultimately satisfied by his extended account of B10. He merely examines Melissus' argument to determine whether indifference reasoning

leave Melissus with a less original (vis-à-vis Zeno) piece of reasoning, but I think it also gives him a decent argument.

How does homogeneity fit into B10? We have seen that Melissus' assumption that division is necessarily the product of motion seems to be a weak contention. Yet if we add the premise that the world is completely homogeneous, we find a stronger argument. Imagine the universe is completely alike in every direction. There is no more here than there, in Parmenidean terms. Is this universe divided up into discrete parts? I think Makin is right here to appeal to Zeno's argument in B3: 'If things are a plurality, they will be infinite in number. For there will always be others between any of them, and again between these yet others. And so things are infinite in number.'[51] What concerns us here is Zeno's argument that distinct units must be separated and non-adjacent to be truly plural. This argument has a much greater punch in a homogeneous than a heterogeneous world. Separation is not required to mark out the stars from the stripes on the American flag. Yet in Melissus' universe it makes good sense. If what-is is divided, it must be so because one part has been separated from another. How does one separate one part from another? Motion. If there is no qualitative difference to mark out one spot from another, we would need to fall back on spatial difference as the criterion for separation. In a qualitatively homogeneous world, mere juxtaposition would not be sufficient to mark out a spatial difference. Thus a gap is required which, in turn, demands motion. This is impossible; therefore, what-is is not divided.

This account, which borrows much from Makin's presentation, only survives scrutiny if we assume an assertion of homogeneity. If this is correct, Melissus does not fall prey to the criticism that division necessarily requires motion. It does so only in a homogeneous world. Is it reasonable to think that Melissus constructed B10 to turn specifically on a consideration of homogeneity? Obviously, we do not have his words to that effect. Yet the evidence that both Zeno and Parmenides proceeded in this way

could be found in the fragment, and concludes that he must look elsewhere for explicit evidence.
[51] Translation by Lee 1936.

suggests that Melissus might have followed their formula. Parmenides' denial of division clearly hinges in some way on his claim of the homogeneity of what-is. Parmenides' remarks on division at B8.22–5 have posed a number of challenges for the interpreter. Is it the threat of temporal or spatial division that Parmenides is countering?[52] I think it is clear enough, from the language of the poem, that Parmenides does have spatial division in mind in these lines. However, whatever one's view on the notion of continuity Parmenides is advancing, we are concerned merely with the structure of his argument (i.e. what premises he is relying on) and it is unambiguous that he argues for the conclusion that what-is is undivided from a premise of homogeneity.[53] Line 22 bears this out: οὐδὲ διαιρετόν ἐστιν, ἐπεὶ πᾶν ἐστιν ὁμοῖον ('It is not divided, *since* it is all alike'). This is, of course, not conclusive evidence that Melissus followed in Parmenides' model. It does, however, suggest that this line of argumentation was available to Melissus.

If the account is along the right lines, Melissus appeals to homogeneity as well as immobility in B10. If we also consider what B9 contributes, I suggest that we will not only further strengthen the argument for indivisibility but also make good sense of the relation between πάχος and μόρια. I have offered the thought that Melissus need only have been committed to the notion that divisibility entails motion in a *homogeneous* world. However, we might wonder if the possibility of motion is the only necessary condition for division in such a world. Division requires not just a separation, and the means to effect it, but also a determination of where the division is to take place. It is on this last condition that B9 has something valuable to add to Melissus' argument. It also goes some way towards explaining why Melissus deduces parthood from having a πάχος and not directly from corporeality.

---

[52] For the temporal reading see Owen 1960: 97–100. For the spatial interpretation see Schofield 1970: 132–4. See Coxon (2009: 324) for the reading that Parmenides denies division in general as well as divisibility in lines 22–5.

[53] At the very least Parmenides maintains that there are no gaps of non-existence so that one area could be said to exist more than another. This is homogeneity of a kind. See Barnes 1982: 211–12.

Indivisible

Consider the following passages from Aristotle's *Physics* 3.5

ὥστε εἰ μὲν ὁμοειδές, ἀκίνητον ἔσται ἢ ἀεὶ οἰσθήσεται· καίτοι ἀδύνατον (τί γὰρ μᾶλλον κάτω ἢ ἄνω ἢ ὁπουοῦν;) (205a12–14)

So that, if it [an infinite body] were homogeneous, it will be immobile or it will always be moving. But this is impossible (for why will it move down rather than up anywhere whatsoever?).

ὅλως δὲ φανερὸν ὅτι ἀδύνατον ἄπειρον ἅμα λέγειν σῶμα καὶ τόπον τινὰ εἶναι τοῖς σώμασιν, εἰ πᾶν σῶμα αἰσθητὸν ἢ βάρος ἔχει ἢ κουφότητα, καὶ εἰ μὲν βαρύ, ἐπὶ τὸ μέσον ἔχει τὴν φορὰν φύσει, εἰ δὲ κοῦφον, ἄνω· ἀνάγκη γὰρ καὶ τὸ ἄπειρον, ἀδύνατον δὲ ἢ ἅπαν ὁποτερονοῦν ἢ τὸ ἥμισυ ἑκάτερον πεπονθέναι· πῶς γὰρ διελεῖς; ἢ πῶς τοῦ ἀπείρου ἔσται τὸ μὲν ἄνω τὸ δὲ κάτω, ἢ ἔσχατον καὶ μέσον; (205b24–31)

In general, it is obvious that it is impossible to say at the same time that there is an infinite body and that there is some place for bodies, if every perceptible body has either weight or lightness, and if it is weighty it has a natural tendency towards the centre, and if it is light, upwards. For this must apply to the infinite body too: but it is impossible that either everything be one or the other [weighty or light] or that each half has one of the two. For how could you divide it? **And how could there be an up and a down, or an extreme and centre, of what is infinite?**[54]

It is clear that in *Physics* 3.5 Aristotle advances a position very much in conflict with Melissus' view on the spatial infinity of the universe. Although he, unlike Anaxagoras, is not named specifically, nevertheless Aristotle raises a worry about division and divisibility with which Melissus, on my view, is in sympathy.

One of the many arguments raised by Aristotle in *Physics* 3.5 is that something infinite in extent, according to formal reasoning (λογικῶς ... σκοπουμένοις, 204b4),[55] is impossible because something with extent must have magnitude, and something with magnitude must be countable and therefore is not infinite.[56] It is just such a claim that Melissus wants to resist in B9 if we follow my reading of πάχος as 'determinate thickness' or 'dimension'. What is spatially infinite but not, for Melissus, an Aristotelian 'magnitude'. A look to the Aristotelian passages above gives us a plausible explanation why Melissus would want to resist the

---

[54] My translation, but owing much to Hussey 1983: 13.
[55] I take this to mean reasoning unconnected with any particular branch of science.
[56] This is a rough summary of the upshot of 204a34–b9.

thought that what-is could have a πάχος, which I take to be nearly synonymous with Aristotle's μέγεθος,[57] in so far as both imply countability and thus determination.

In the first passage quoted above, Aristotle poses a dilemma: if there is an infinite body, either it is immobile or it is always in motion. Both are impossible because there is no way there could be an up or a down or any other place. Presumably this is because, for Aristotle, his concept of natural place, to which he is firmly committed, cannot obtain in an infinite world and the existence of such a feature of the universe is a necessary condition of motion. We can see this further developed in the second passage. Aristotle denies here that there could be an up, down, extreme, or centre in what is infinite. In such a situation, how could what is light move away from the centre and what is heavy move towards it if such places cannot exist?

Aristotle also raises the problem of the division of an infinite body in the second passage quoted above: πῶς γὰρ διελεῖς; It might appear that this is done on the grounds of the absence of natural place: if there is no centre how could we divide something infinite? I don't think that this is quite right. The impossibility of division is explained not by the absence of natural place but presumably by Aristotle's commitment to the thought that what is infinite is inherently unknowable. Consider what τὸ ἥμισυ refers to. Surely it is τὸ ἄπειρον, found a few words earlier. Thus Aristotle is asking how we could divide the infinite so that one half has what is weighty and the other half what is light. The problem is that it is incoherent to expect to divide what never gives out (as Aristotle understands the infinite at 206b33ff) and is thus never determinable: e.g. if I cannot count how many pages I have written, I cannot determine half their number.

How does Melissus fit in here? Well, I want to suggest that the denial of σῶμα and, thus, a πάχος to what-is proceeds along similar lines. This is what I take to be the upshot of the connection between a πάχος and μόρια. If we take a πάχος to be the rough equivalent of Aristotle's notion of extension (and, as we have seen,

---

[57] Remember, of course, that Melissus is happy to use 'μέγεθος' in B3 without any assumption of finitism.

there are good semantic reasons to do so), it bears the intrinsic property of being countable (having determinate dimensions) and is therefore measurable. Something measurable has a determinate centre and is subject to division: division results in μόρια.

We may say as well that the anatomical nature of πάχος (measurable by fingers, cubits etc.) gives the further suggestion that something with a πάχος is subject to division at its organic joints. We should note too that the model of division in a homogeneous world I have attributed to Melissus requires actual spatial separation, i.e. non-juxtaposition. Yet in an organic body, we find just the opposite: the parts *must* be in contact. Thus we find the suggestion that in a heterogeneous subject something with a πάχος *does* have the qualitative differences necessary for division. In either case, what we ought to take away is that a πάχος entails divisibility and parthood.[58]

Even if the above is along the right lines, we are still left with the question why Melissus would be concerned with divisibility in B9 and B9* when he has an argument (B10) properly devoted to the subject. In that argument, as we have seen, it is motion and not magnitude that is relevant. I want to offer the thought, on the evidence of the appeal to homogeneity I have suggested above, that B10 does not offer the complete argument against the division and divisibility of what-is, but rather is the final nail in its coffin. We noticed how Melissus' argument, fully in conformity with his method throughout the treatise, relies on the prior establishment of homogeneity. In this way, one potential means of division, i.e. through heterogeneity, has already been ruled out. It is along similar lines that I propose that B9 is relevant: the denial of a πάχος to what-is establishes that it has no 'determinable thickness' and thus it lacks any distinctive point or plane, the determination of which is a necessary condition of division of a homogeneous subject.

Therefore, what I want to offer as an interpretation of the role of πάχος for Melissus is twofold, with both elements turning on issues of measurability. On the one hand, if we

[58] You might think, as well, that Melissus might have a Zenonian point in mind here. If it is divisible in one place, it is divisible in every place. By avoiding that first division, Melissus frees himself from anything paradoxical. I owe this point to Barbara Sattler.

say that something has a πάχος, we are saying that it has such and such a thickness and shape. Saying so entails that it has *metrically distinct parts* that constitute it as a whole and thus that what-is is a plurality and no longer one. Each of these parts, as we have seen, is for Melissus, determined by an explicitly anatomical system of measurement. On the other hand, I think we can attribute to Melissus a second, stronger claim. Let us consider an opponent who denies that something homogeneous has parts because of one's measurement of it. One might counter that there is *nothing intrinsic* to the thing that indicates where one measurement ends and another begins. Melissus could very well bite the bullet here and still have a perfectly good reply. If the very act of measurement as the origin of parthood is off the table, Melissus can adopt the Aristotelian position and respond that any measurement resulting in a determinate thickness gives a means of establishing parthood, i.e. at the very least, a middle point to divide at. Such a reading puts Melissus in a particularly strong position.

Why then add the argument in B10? After all, if we accept that a πάχος is necessary for division, no appeal to the impossibility of motion is strictly needed to counter division's possibility. However, B10 makes good sense as a final, conclusive repudiation of the notion of division. Such a multi-pronged approach is not alien to Melissus, as we saw previously in the last sentence of B2, and is evident in the introduction to B8, which I take to be the final fragment in the extant collection:

μέγιστον μὲν οὖν σημεῖον οὗτος ὁ λόγος, ὅτι ἓν μόνον ἔστιν· ἀτὰρ καὶ τάδε σημεῖα.

Therefore, this is the greatest proof that it is one by itself: but there are also the following proofs ...

We can see that it is clear from Melissus' words that he is comfortable providing multiple arguments for a single thesis. I take it that this is not in tension with the strict, deductive model I have attributed to his treatise. Rather it may simply be evidence that Melissus is concerned to persuade an audience with diverse prior commitments.[59]

---

[59] That Melissus is concerned to counter more than one opposing position I take to underpin Stephen Makin's 2005 study of B8.

Reconstruction

We may now, having considered the primary exegetical puzzles of B9, turn to a reconstruction of the text of the two fragments I have identified. The assumption that both instances of quotation derived from a single piece of reasoning is undoubtedly the product of the overlap between the two. My contention, of course, is that the differences are too significant to ignore. However, the striking congruence suggests that these pieces functioned as either beginnings or ends of arguments formed according to Melissus' favoured ring-composition model. Both fragments also explicitly indicate that Melissus is proceeding from his argument for monism to bodilessness. We may, then, safely say that B9 and B9* closely follow B6 in the reconstructed text.

It is more opaque how we are to proceed further. The striking similarity between the two sections emboldened below suggests that we accept the *communis opinio* that the argument is to be reconstructed by grafting onto this common element the beginning sentence of B9* and the final sentence of B9.

ἓν ἐόν, **δεῖ αὐτὸ σῶμα μὴ ἔχειν.** εἰ δὲ ἔχοι πάχος, ἔχοι ἂν μόρια καὶ οὐκέτι ἓν εἴη. **(B9)**

εἰ μὲν οὖν εἴη, δεῖ αὐτὸ ἓν εἶναι· **ἓν δὲ ὂν δεῖ αὐτὸ σῶμα μὴ ἔχειν. (B9*)**

One may recall that the argument for spatial infinity (B2) was similarly composed of words quoted differently in two, distinct locations in Simplicius' text. If this is correct, why then have I insisted above on treating B9 and B9* as separate fragments? I have done so because we find elements in the two fragments not only of the demonstration of the claim that what-is has no body *but also* of the previous argument for monism. This has not been suitably appreciated.

Let us consider again the first half of B9*, as we did in the previous section: εἰ μὲν οὖν εἴη, δεῖ αὐτὸ ἓν εἶναι. On the standard account, the sentence acts as the beginning of the argument for bodilessness. Two points tell against this. First, the particle οὖν, which we have determined to be very much the most plausible reading, is *conclusive* but not *inferential* in nature for Melissus.[60] What this suggests is that εἰ μὲν οὖν εἴη, δεῖ αὐτὸ ἓν εἶναι does not properly belong with the argument for bodilessness but rather acts as the conclusion to the argument for monism, on the model of the bridging function I have attributed to B3.

Let us look again at B6 to see how this works:

εἰ γὰρ εἴη, ἓν εἴη ἄν· εἰ γὰρ δύο εἴη, οὐκ ἂν δύναιτο ἄπειρα εἶναι, ἀλλ' ἔχοι ἂν πείρατα πρὸς ἄλληλα.

The reader will remember that it makes good sense to see B4 as immediately preceding B6 and this allows us to supply the predicates eternal and spatially infinite as jointly constituting the complements of εἴη. The upshot of this proposal is that it maintains Melissus' strategy of deducing each new predicate of what-is from the one previously established. If we did not have recourse to the complements in B4, we would be forced to contravene this standard model and accept the implausible thought that monism *is not* deduced from spatial infinity but from the murky premise that what-is *is*. Doing so would directly contravene the testimony of the two extant paraphrases.

We may now turn to the reconstruction of the argument for the claim that what-is lacks a body. After εἰ μὲν οὖν εἴη, δεῖ αὐτὸ ἓν εἶναι provides the bridge connecting the proof of monism with that of bodilessness, the element common to both B9 and B9* follows. It is clear that both instances of the quotation of this common piece are nearly identical but one small discrepancy must first be solved. In B9 we have ἓν ἐόν while in B9* we read ἓν δὲ ὄν. The obvious solution, given by DK, is that the correct reading is ἓν δ' ἐόν, simultaneously removing the asyndeton and the Atticisation of B9*. Finally, εἰ δὲ ἔχοι πάχος, ἔχοι ἂν μόρια καὶ οὐκέτι ἓν εἴη follows, serving as the heart of Melissus' argument. No doubt, a restatement of the conclusion of bodilessness, now lost, would have followed. Simply to reflect properly the original framework

---

[60] Loenen (1959: 163 n.72) is right that τοίνυν is the inferential particle for Melissus. However, I doubt that οὖν serves merely to reinforce a previous particle as he suggests. Other instances of οὖν in Melissus (7.1, 7.7, 8.1, and 8.6) indicate that it is used to restate conclusions *already* established. There is no instance in which οὖν acts as a straightforward inferential particle in the extant fragments of Melissus.

of Melissus' treatise, I add εἰ τοίνυν ἕν ἐστιν, σῶμα οὐκ ἔχει in angle brackets. Next, it makes good sense that B7 would follow. In particular, if we think that the argument for bodilessness immediately preceded B7, it gives us a good explanation for why Melissus thought it unnecessary to restate this predicate in the list at the beginning of that fragment. This provides a neat solution to the old question of why the purported fact that what-is lacks a body is not mentioned in B7.

Reconstruction Thus Far

Περὶ φύσεως ἢ περὶ τοῦ <ἐ> ὄντος

<Μέλισσος Σάμιος τάδε λέγει περὶ φύσεως ἢ περὶ τοῦ ἐόντος.> εἰ μὲν μηδὲν ἔστι, περὶ τούτου τί ἂν λέγοιτο ὡς <ἐ>όντος τινός; εἰ δέ τι ἐστίν, ἀεὶ ἦν ὅ τι ἦν καὶ ἀεὶ ἔσται. εἰ γὰρ ἐγένετο, ἀναγκαῖόν ἐστι πρὶν γενέσθαι εἶναι μηδέν. εἰ <δὲ> τύχοι νῦν μηδὲν ἐόν, οὐδαμὰ ἂν γένοιτο οὐδὲν ἐκ μηδενός. ὅτε τοίνυν οὐκ ἐγένετο, ἔστι τε καὶ ἀεὶ ἦν καὶ ἀεὶ ἔσται. καὶ ἀρχὴν οὐκ ἔχει οὐδὲ τελευτήν, ἀλλ' ἄπειρόν ἐστιν. εἰ μὲν γὰρ ἐγένετο, ἀρχὴν ἂν εἶχεν (ἤρξατο γὰρ ἂν ποτε γινόμενον) καὶ τελευτήν (ἐτελεύτησε γὰρ ἂν ποτε γινόμενον)· ὅτε δὲ μήτε ἤρξατο μήτε ἐτελεύτησεν, ἀεί τε ἦν καὶ ἀεὶ ἔσται, οὐκ ἔχει ἀρχὴν οὐδὲ τελευτήν· οὐ γὰρ ἀεὶ εἶναι ἀνυστόν, ὅ τι μὴ πᾶν ἔστι. ἀλλ' ὥσπερ ἔστιν ἀεί, οὕτω καὶ τὸ μέγεθος ἄπειρον ἀεὶ χρὴ εἶναι.

< ἄπειρον δ' ἐὸν ἓν ἐστιν> εἰ <γὰρ> μὴ ἓν εἴη, περανεῖ πρὸς ἄλλο, ἀρχὴν δὲ καὶ τέλος ἔχον οὐδὲν οὔτε ἀίδιον οὔτε ἄπειρόν ἐστιν· <εἰ τοίνυν μὴ ἓν εἴη, οὔτ' ἀίδιον οὔτ' ἄπειρόν ἂν εἴη.> εἰ γὰρ εἴη, ἓν εἴη ἂν· εἰ γὰρ δύο εἴη, οὐκ ἂν δύναιτο ἄπειρα εἶναι, ἀλλ' ἔχοι ἂν πείρατα πρὸς ἄλληλα. εἰ μὲν οὖν εἴη, δεῖ αὐτὸ ἓν εἶναι.

ἓν δ' ἐόν, δεῖ αὐτὸ σῶμα μὴ ἔχειν. εἰ δὲ ἔχοι πάχος, ἔχοι ἂν μόρια, καὶ οὐκέτι ἓν εἴη. <εἰ τοίνυν ἕν ἐστιν, σῶμα οὐκ ἔχει>.

Translation

On Nature or What There Is

Melissus the Samian says the following concerning nature or what there is. If it is nothing, what could be said about it as if it were something? But if it is something, it always was whatever it was and always will be. For if it came to be, it is necessary that prior to coming to be it was nothing. But if it happened that it were *now* nothing, at no time would anything come to be from (that) nothing. Since, therefore, it did not come to be, it both is and always was and always will be.

Since, then, it did not come to be, it both is and always was and always will be. And it has no beginning or end, but is infinite. For if it had come to be it would have a beginning (for it would have begun coming-to-be at some time) and end (for it would have ended coming-to-be at some time). But since it neither began nor ended, and it always was and always will be, it has no beginning or end. For whatever is not entire cannot be always. But just as it is always, so too must it always be infinite in magnitude.

<And being infinite, it is one. For> if it turns out not to be one, it will come to border another; but nothing that has a beginning and/ or an end is eternal or infinite; <Therefore, if it were not one, it would not be eternal and spatially infinite.> For if it were <spatially infinite>, if would be one. For if there were two, they would not be able to be infinite, but would have boundaries against each other. Therefore, if it were <spatially infinite>, it is necessary that it be one.

But being one, it is necessary that it not have a body. For if it had breadth, it would have parts and would no longer be one. <Therefore, if it is one, it does not have a body.>

B7: CHANGE, PAIN, AND MOTION

λέγει δ' οὖν Μέλισσος οὕτως τὰ πρότερον εἰρημένα συμπεραινόμενος καὶ οὕτως τὰ περὶ τῆς κινήσεως ἐπάγων

(1) οὕτως οὖν ἀίδιόν ἐστι καὶ ἄπειρον καὶ ἓν καὶ ὅμοιον πᾶν.

(2) καὶ οὔτ' ἂν ἀπόλοιτο οὔτε μεῖζον γίνοιτο οὔτε μετακοσμέοιτο οὔτε ἀλγεῖ οὔτε ἀνιᾶται· εἰ γάρ τι τούτων πάσχοι, οὐκ ἂν ἔτι ἓν εἴη. εἰ γὰρ ἑτεροιοῦται, ἀνάγκη τὸ ἐὸν μὴ ὅμοιον εἶναι, ἀλλὰ ἀπόλλυσθαι τὸ πρόσθεν ἐόν, τὸ δὲ οὐκ ἐὸν γίνεσθαι. εἰ τοίνυν τριχὶ μιῇ μυρίοις ἔτεσιν ἑτεροῖον γίνοιτο, ὀλεῖται πᾶν ἐν τῷ παντὶ χρόνῳ.

(3) ἀλλ' οὐδὲ μετακοσμηθῆναι ἀνυστόν· ὁ γὰρ κόσμος ὁ πρόσθεν ἐὼν οὐκ ἀπόλλυται οὔτε ὁ μὴ ἐὼν γίνεται. ὅτε δὲ μήτε προσγίνεται μηδὲν μήτε ἀπόλλυται μήτε ἑτεροιοῦται, πῶς ἂν μετακοσμηθὲν τῶν ἐόντων εἴη; εἰ μὲν γάρ τι ἐγίνετο ἑτεροῖον, ἤδη ἂν καὶ μετακοσμηθείη.

(4) οὐδὲ ἀλγεῖ· οὐ γὰρ ἂν πᾶν εἴη ἀλγέον· οὐ γὰρ ἂν δύναιτο ἀεὶ εἶναι χρῆμα ἀλγέον· οὐδὲ ἔχει ἴσην δύναμιν τῷ ὑγιεῖ· οὐδ' ἂν ὅμοιον εἴη, εἰ ἀλγέοι· ἀπογινομένου γάρ τευ ἂν ἀλγέοι ἢ προσγινομένου, κοὐκ ἂν ἔτι ὅμοιον εἴη.

(5) οὐδ' ἂν τὸ ὑγιὲς ἀλγῆσαι δύναιτο· ἀπὸ γὰρ ἂν ὄλοιτο τὸ ὑγιὲς καὶ τὸ ἐόν, τὸ δὲ οὐκ ἐὸν γένοιτο.

(6) καὶ περὶ τοῦ ἀνιᾶσθαι ωὑτὸς λόγος τῷ ἀλγέοντι.

(7) οὐδὲ κενεόν ἐστιν οὐδέν· τὸ γὰρ κενεὸν οὐδέν ἐστιν· οὐκ ἂν οὖν εἴη τό γε μηδέν.

(8) οὐδὲ κινεῖται· ὑποχωρῆσαι γὰρ οὐκ ἔχει οὐδαμῇ, ἀλλὰ πλέων ἐστίν. εἰ μὲν γὰρ κενεὸν ἦν, ὑπεχώρει ἂν εἰς τὸ κενεόν· κενεοῦ δὲ μὴ ἐόντος οὐκ ἔχει ὅκη ὑποχωρήσει.

(9) πυκνὸν δὲ καὶ ἀραιὸν οὐκ ἂν εἴη. τὸ γὰρ ἀραιὸν οὐκ ἀνυστὸν πλέων εἶναι ὁμοίως τῷ πυκνῷ, ἀλλ' ἤδη τὸ ἀραιόν γε κενεώτερον γίνεται τοῦ πυκνοῦ.

(10) κρίσιν δὲ ταύτην χρὴ ποιήσασθαι τοῦ πλέω καὶ τοῦ μὴ πλέω· εἰ μὲν οὖν χωρεῖ τι ἢ εἰσδέχεται, οὐ πλέων· εἰ δὲ μήτε χωρεῖ μήτε εἰσδέχεται, πλέων.

(11) ἀνάγκη τοίνυν πλέων εἶναι, εἰ κενὸν μὴ ἔστιν. εἰ τοίνυν πλέων ἐστίν, οὐ κινεῖται.

(Simplicius, *In Phys.* 111.18–112.15)

Introduction

B7 is probably Melissus' most well-known (and well-studied) fragment. It contains a host of arguments in favour of three main theses: what-is is unchangeable, impervious to pain, and immobile. These arguments appear to rely quite indiscriminately on the premises previously established. Melissus himself strongly gives this impression by listing in (1) that what-is is sempiternal, spatially infinite, one, and all alike. The argument for this final predicate, homogeneity, is not represented in the extant fragments; however, it is uncontroversial that Melissus did indeed accept homogeneity and we do have the testimony of the *MXG* to this effect:

ἓν δὲ ὂν ὅμοιον εἶναι πάντη[1] · εἰ γὰρ ἀνόμοιον, πλείω ὄντα, οὐκ ἂν ἔτι ἓν εἶναι ἀλλὰ πολλά. (974a12–14)

Being one it is alike in every way. For if it were unalike, being plural, it would no longer be one but many.[2]

The anonymous author, whose testimony is confirmed in its details by the Simplician paraphrase, suggests that Melissus deduced homogeneity from uniqueness. In the previous chapter, I suggested that bodilessness is similarly established from the predicate 'unique'. Where, then, did homogeneity originally fit within Melissus' treatise? On the account I have given of indivisibility in B10, there is very good reason to think that homogeneity was established *prior* to that fragment. B10 undoubtedly featured *after* B7 (because of its appeal to immobility, which is established in B7) and the argument for homogeneity obviously prior to B7 because of the evidence of (1). Thus we may say, with some safety, that homogeneity figured after B6 and B9, as both are argued on the strength of uniqueness and because B9 is continuous with B6 on my account.

The proposed reconstruction of the proof of bodilessness does *not* require that homogeneity was presumed. I suggested that the

---

[1] Graham (2010) suggests that πάντη should be taken locatively as 'everywhere'. It seems strange to limit Melissus' commitment to homogeneity in such a way. See Loenen 1959: 156 for the claim that homogeneity also implies a temporal aspect.

[2] The paraphrase found in Simplicius (at *In Phys.* 103.31–104.1) confirms the testimony of the *MXG*. See Solmsen 1969: 143 nn.18 and 19 for some (unwarranted) scepticism.

potential parthood of what-is is a function not only of a qualitative difference implied by something like heterogeneity, but also of a quantitative one, i.e. its measurability and thus separation into metrically distinct parts. Homogeneity *does* play a role in B10, on my account, because it goes a long way towards explaining why Melissus would think that division entails motion. On such an interpretation, motion is appealed to only as a last resort in a homogeneous world, and is not assumed to be an inseparable requirement, or element in the definition, of division.

However, the account in the *MXG* provides more than mere confirmation of the existence of an argument for homogeneity. Consider the conditional marshalled as the heart of the argument: εἰ γὰρ ἀνόμοιον, πλείω ὄντα. Heterogeneity is explicitly taken to entail plurality. This is striking. It appears, then, that Melissus takes the logical contradictory of plurality to be not only uniqueness but also homogeneity. We have seen how Melissus denies that what-is could be multiply instantiated simultaneously because it is all-encompassing: an all-encompassing entity cannot permit a second such entity because the two would border each other and no longer be each all-encompassing. Successive iterations of what-is are also ruled out because what-is cannot perish (assumed in B1 and B2, much as Parmenides does) and something new cannot come into being from nothing (B1).[3] Thus it is plain that uniqueness is to be contrasted with plurality.

Less clear is why we should think that a heterogeneous entity could not be unique. Yet if we keep in mind that Melissus is taking 'one' to mean both 'unique' and 'unified', the answer is at hand. This emerged in our discussion of B9. In that fragment it became clear that plurality, understood as the existence of multiple entities, is not the only threat to the predicate 'one' but is also violated by the parthood of what-is. This was the upshot of Melissus' somewhat mysterious denial of a πάχος to what-is. Thus being one, for Melissus, means that what-is is both unique and simple.

I take this to be a version of the 'generous' reading Jonathan Barnes has offered. If we accept that Melissus says that what-is is

---

[3] If, as I have suggested, temporal iterations are relevant in B4–6, we find further support for this hypothesis.

a unique entity, we may say that he is committed to the idea that qualitative heterogeneity would entail that what-is has at least two parts, i.e. one part with a specimen property (P) and one part without (P). If we take each of these parts as a distinct entity presumed to conform to Melissus' deductions, we can plainly see how heterogeneity would violate uniqueness.[4]

If this is a correct account of Melissus' (now lost) treatment of homogeneity, it reveals a rather extraordinary understanding of the so-called 'Eleatic One'. The view first attested in Plato,[5] though perhaps not original to him,[6] that Parmenides taught that all things are one or that the one *is*, and the difficulty of finding clear evidence of such a doctrine in the fragments are well-worn tropes of Eleatic studies. Whether what-is, for Parmenides, is unique, simply homogeneous, or neither is continually debated and probably cannot be resolved, on the evidence of the fragments, with any great degree of confidence.[7] It is often remarked, with some justification, that the monism of Melissus (or perhaps Zeno) is retrospectively attributed to Parmenides by the doxographical tradition or, more simply, that the fragments of Melissus reveal the final thoughts of his 'master', perhaps even reached in conversation between the two.[8]

Whatever the truth is for Parmenides, the explicit logical opposition between plurality and *both* uniqueness *and* homogeneity tells us that, for Melissus at least, these latter two predicates are nearly interchangeable. Both exclude plurality. We may conclude from this that Melissus takes his One (ἕν) to include both uniqueness and homogeneity, although he focuses on the language of homogeneity (ὁμοῖον) when necessary.

I have dwelled on an argument for homogeneity that admittedly does not survive as a fragment. I have done so because an understanding of the predicate ὁμοῖον is absolutely essential to an analysis of the arguments of B7, as we shall soon see. In (1) the list of four predicates of what-is suggests that each has equal status

---

[4] Barnes 1982: 208.   [5] See, for example, *Parmenides* 128d1ff.

[6] See Palmer 2009: 218–20.

[7] The literature on this is too voluminous to list in any detail. I point the reader simply to the helpful remarks of Jonathan Barnes (1982: 204–7) and John Palmer (2009: 1–50).

[8] See Reale 1970: 109ff, in particular, for the latter view.

in the arguments to come.[9] Yet this impression is belied by the absence of any significant role for spatial infinity in B7 and the claim, in (2), that the arguments to come directly follow from the predicate 'unique'. Let us consider this latter statement first:

καὶ οὔτ' ἂν **ἀπόλοιτο** οὔτε μεῖζον γίνοιτο οὔτε μετακοσμέοιτο οὔτε ἀλγεῖ οὔτε ἀνιᾶται· εἰ γάρ τι τούτων πάσχοι, οὐκ ἂν ἔτι **ἓν** εἴη.

ἀπόλοιτο provides our first hurdle. The reading has been vigorously challenged by Covotti who proposes to emend the text to ἀπολλύοι τι (nor would it lose *anything*) on the basis of an alleged opposition to μεῖζον γίνοιτο.[10] The thinking seems to be that Melissus is talking here not about simple destruction (as opposed to simple coming-to-be), but rather about piecemeal loss or decrease serving as a contrast to becoming greater. Thus the point is that what-is does not become diminished (presumably either qualitatively or quantitatively) nor does it become amplified or greater. The text does give some support to this interpretation at (3): ὅτε δὲ μήτε **προσγίνεται** μηδὲν μήτε **ἀπόλλυται** μήτε ἑτεροιοῦται ('and since nothing is being added, or being destroyed, or being altered', how could anything that is be rearranged?).

We may agree, then, that Melissus is, at the very least, including piecemeal loss, understood as diminishment of some kind, but this does not provide sufficient reason to adopt Covotti's emendation. What we seem to find is not a series of contrasts, as his thesis suggests, but rather simply a series of changes that are to be discussed and proved impossible. If ἀπολλύοι τι is intended to contrast with μεῖζον γίνοιτο, we would be led to expect that μετακοσμέοιτο contrasts with ἀλγεῖ, and this is obviously not Melissus' point.

In addition, we might consider the inference Melissus makes in (2). We shall have occasion to examine this argument shortly. However, it is clear, even at a superficial level, that any change, even the smallest of alterations, implies the possibility of, in the whole of time, the wholesale destruction of what-is. Taking the relationship between piecemeal and wholesale destruction that

---

[9] Solmsen (1969: 140) makes much of this.
[10] Covotti 1898: 219, app. crit. The emendation is accepted by KRS and Reale, and is looked upon somewhat favourably by Barnes (1982: 214 n.16).

Melissus wants to establish, it makes sense to leave the text intact so that it is wide enough in scope to accommodate both piecemeal and wholesale destruction. Thus the emendation is unnecessary and obscures Melissus' point.

However, there is also the question of the DK reading of the aorist ἀπόλοιτο. Elsewhere in B7 (see (2) and (3)), Melissus uses the present form of the verb. Thus Diels (though *not* DK) and Loenen decide to emend the text to ἀπολλύοιτο, making the verb coordinate with the present γίνοιτο and μετακοσμέοιτο.[11] I decline to adopt such an emendation for two reasons. (1) In Simplicius' paraphrase of the argument (103.31–104.1) he retains ἀπόλοιτο, confirming that the aorist was in his copy of the text. (2) The issue of aspect is not as relevant as it might appear to be as Melissus is merely introducing the changes he intends to discuss, and so it does not make sense to commit him to a view as to whether destruction is to be understood as a process or not.

Let us move on to the second sentence of the passage under consideration: εἰ γάρ τι τούτων πάσχοι, οὐκ ἂν ἔτι ἓν εἴη. The γάρ suggests that Melissus is providing the reason why what-is cannot ἀπόλοιτο οὔτε μεῖζον γίνοιτο οὔτε μετακοσμέοιτο κτλ. Thus it appears that uniqueness is to be the principal premise for the arguments to come. Friedrich Solmsen, in an important article, has vigorously challenged the accuracy of this assumption.[12] He goes to some lengths to provide a deflationary account of the importance of the 'Eleatic One' to B7 and, more broadly, to Melissus' treatise, generally speaking. Though Solmsen's account is problematical, particularly in its disregard of the deductive nature of Melissus' treatise, it does raise a conspicuous puzzle. Why does Melissus list four predicates in (1) but then pick out ἕν for particular attention in (2)? In addition, if ἕν is so central to the schema of the fragment, why does it seem to fade so quickly from prominence from (3) onward? After (2), as Solmsen notes, the focus seems to be on changes that are said to threaten ὁμοῖον not ἕν.[13] Even if my reading of the 'Eleatic One' and the near interchangeability of these two predicates for Melissus is correct, we

---

[11] Loenen 1959: 156 n.59. Unlike Loenen, I do not accept Covotti's addition of τι.
[12] Solmsen 1969.   [13] Solmsen 1969: 141.

are still left to answer why both ὁμοῖον and ἕν are listed individually in (1) before the latter is emphasised in (2), only to be upstaged by concerns specifically concerned with homogeneity as B7 continues.

The appearance of the equal status of the four predicates listed in (1) is easily explained. It is not a declaration of premises to be relied upon but a recapitulation of predicates already demonstrated, following Melissus' typical procedure. It is true that *some* of these predicates will prove to be essential in the arguments to come, but announcing which ones is not the aim of (1). Rather (1) is simply the standard Melissan summary, acting as a transition from one argument to the next. We may recall that Melissus frequently rehearses what he has proved previously, as we can see from B2 and B3.[14] Of course, the summary found in B7 is unique in its extent, but this is not a sufficient reason to think that it is playing a different role from the typical Melissan recapitulation.

More puzzling is the prominent role given to ἕν in (2). Are we really forced 'to accept so glaring a discrepancy between promise and performance' as Solmsen asks?[15] The heart of his interpretation, as I understand it, is that ἕν appears to occupy a privileged role in Melissus' argument in (2). If this is correct, the arguments that follow in B7 should be focused on threats to this predicate. Yet, for Solmsen, ἕν seems to disappear from prominence and is replaced by ὁμοῖον as the principal predicate violated by change.[16] Such a worry entails that there *is* a discrepancy between what Melissus promises and what he in fact goes on to argue. Let us take Melissus at his word in (2) when he says that the processes to be

---

[14] One might think that up to B7 Melissus only summarises singular predicates already established. Yet in B2 Melissus seems to think that sempiternity needs to be recapitulated by listing all three aspects of time. Also both sempiternity and spatial infinity are named in B3.

[15] Solmsen 1969: 141.

[16] It is worth noting that the apparent disappearance of ἕν from the argument is used by Solmsen in his effort to downplay the significance of the 'One' to the Eleatics and reinforce the point, perhaps in and of itself correct, that it is 'Being' that Parmenides focuses on in his poem. Whether this is true of Parmenides or not is largely irrelevant unless you think, as Solmsen seems to, that Melissus provides merely Parmenidean theses outfitted in new guises. My disagreement with this mistaken assumption should be plain.

discussed are a threat to ἕν, and explore whether Solmsen's alleged discrepancy cannot be overcome.

The most striking feature of the actions or properties Melissus discusses in B7 is their essentially negative character.[17] In most of the fragments we have thus far discussed, Melissus has aimed to demonstrate something positive about what-is, e.g. sempiternity, spatial infinity, uniqueness, and homogeneity. B7 marks a notable turn towards the exploration of what what-is is *not*; though, of course, if my proposal of the priority of B9 is accepted, such a shift would begin with that fragment. This negative character is important because it points the way towards a resolution to Solmsen's worry and an understanding of the argumentative schema of B7.

If we recall the paraphrase of the argument for homogeneity found in the *MXG*, Melissus assumed there that the logical contradictory of plurality was not only uniqueness but also homogeneity. This represents something of a fusion (though not necessarily a confusion) of the predicates ἕν and ὁμοῖον: anything that entails plurality violates both. Thus my reading of the 'Eleatic One' in Melissus goes some way towards diffusing Solmsen's worry.

The paraphrase found in Simplicius provides some help here:

ἀλλὰ μὴν εἰ ἕν, καὶ ἀκίνητον.[18] τὸ γὰρ ἓν ὅμοιον ἀεὶ ἑαυτῷ· τὸ δὲ ὅμοιον οὔτ' ἂν ἀπόλοιτο οὔτ' ἂν μεῖζον γίνοιτο οὔτε μετακοσμέοιτο οὔτε ἀλγεῖ οὔτε ἀνιᾶται. (*In Phys.* 103.30–104.1)

But if it is one, it is also unchanging. For what is one is always like itself, and what is <eternally> homogeneous could not be destroyed, become greater, or be rearranged, nor does it feel pain or grief.

We can see that, in the first sentence, Simplicius adheres to the letter of the text of B7: it is because what-is is one that it is unchanging. However, it is the last clause quoted that is striking. The reason why what is one is unchanging is explained by an appeal to homogeneity. Change violates homogeneity; what is one is homogeneous; therefore, what is one does not change.

---

[17] Graham (2010: 482) rightly makes this point.

[18] Simplicius seems to conflate the arguments against change and motion and presumably uses ἀκίνητον to cover both. I take them to be separate arguments, though they should still be regarded as parts of the same fragment. See Solmsen 1969: 144–5.

The question, then, is: why does he explicitly mention ἕν? If it is really homogeneity that is relevant for eliminating change, surely, on Melissus' deductive model, it would make more sense to claim that ὅμοῖον is the principal premise of the argument to come? What I would like to suggest is that plurality, as the shared contradictory of both uniqueness and homogeneity, provides an answer to these worries. The negative character of the arguments in B7 brings this to the fore. Let us consider the possibility that both uniqueness and homogeneity are relevant because *both* are the contradictories of what change entails, namely plurality. My proposal, then, is that the argument against change turns on its implication of heterogeneity and, thus, plurality. This is a novel reading, but its advantage is that it unifies Melissus' argument in a way previously thought impossible.

Before we go on, it is worth looking more closely at the structure of B7. Its unity has often been called into question.[19] Usually such a worry has been generated by Simplicius' implication at 111.18–19 that κίνησις is the umbrella topic under which all the changes discussed in B7 fall. This does not seem to harmonise with the arguments presented in the first half of the text, and it is thus often suggested that the second half of the fragment devoted to immobility ought to be treated as a separate argument, and perhaps a different fragment. I think this largely correct. Immobility is discretely established and bears the hallmark of distinct Melissan pieces of reasoning in its use of ring-composition. However, a single division does not go far enough: there are, in fact, three distinct arguments in B7. The first targets changeability and consists of two sub-arguments treating alteration and rearrangement respectively. The second aims to prove that what-is is impervious to pain and the third excludes motion through an elimination of void. All three show signs of ring-composition and are treated best as separate, and independently demonstrated, but not necessarily unrelated.

To return to changeability, the idea that I am proposing is that the predicate ἕν appears prominently in (2) because it is as vulnerable to the implication of plurality as is homogeneity, which seems

---

[19] See particularly Solmsen 1969: 144–5, Barnes 1982: 215 n.19, and Reale 1970: 386–8.

to take the lion's share of importance as the first section of B7 proceeds. Such a claim requires that both sub-arguments (*contra* alteration and *contra* rearrangement) pose threats to homogeneity because of the entailment of plurality. If my reconstruction of the argument for homogeneity correctly posits its logical contradictory as plurality, it should become obvious why uniqueness is also relevant: in short, plurality contradicts uniqueness and homogeneity equally.

Alteration

Melissus' first sub-argument in B7 targets alteration:

εἰ γὰρ ἑτεροιοῦται, ἀνάγκη τὸ ἐὸν μὴ ὁμοῖον εἶναι, ἀλλὰ ἀπόλλυσθαι τὸ πρόσθεν ἐόν, τὸ δὲ οὐκ ἐὸν γίνεσθαι. εἰ τοίνυν τριχὶ μιῇ μυρίοις ἔτεσιν ἑτεροῖον γίνοιτο, ὀλεῖται πᾶν ἐν τῷ παντὶ χρόνῳ.

We may provisionally translate:

(a) For if it is being qualitatively altered, it is necessary that what-is is not qualitatively alike, (b) but what was previously is being destroyed and what is not is coming-to-be. (c) Therefore, if it were to undergo qualitative alteration by a single hair in 10,000 years, in the whole of time it all would perish.

The passage begins with a resolutely Melissan counterfactual conditional stating that the previously proved predicate (ὁμοῖον) would be violated should there be alteration. Thus far, standard Melissan fare. Next in (b) we find the claim that alteration entails the destruction of what-is and the coming-to-be of what is not. What does Melissus have in mind here? Alteration is said to entail *both* destruction *and* coming-to-be. Why should an alteration to what-is mean any destruction at all? I can alter a painting by adding more paint but that does not entail that any of the original painting has been destroyed. Perhaps Melissus thought that any alteration to what-is must be understood as the complete destruction of its current iteration and the wholesale coming-to-be of a new iteration including the relevant alteration? Yet we could hardly attribute such a model of change to Melissus when he will happily discuss the possibility of a change by a single hair without any indication that for such a change to occur he would insist that what-is has been wholly and immediately destroyed. This is further suggested by the use of present-tensed verbs throughout the passage, which support the thought that Melissus had in mind alteration as a continuous *process* of coming-to-be and destruction.

Why Melissus thinks that alteration demands both destruction and coming-to-be becomes apparent if we consider the type of motion Melissus is to contemplate later in B7. David Sedley has pointed out that Melissus is there considering *internal* motion and not motion into the outside: Melissus had already demonstrated that what-is is spatially infinite in all directions and, thus, motion into anything external has already been ruled out.[20] On a similar line, we can understand why alteration necessitates destruction. What-is is infinite (both temporally and spatially), it is homogeneous, and we have also seen a clear indication in B2 that what-is is entire (πᾶν). With these predicates established, we are now permitted to think that an alteration is simply an addition to what is already, like a motion from the outside (for how could any new bit come about, or new space into which to add it?). Alteration then, like motion, is to be understood internally: if what-is is entirely homogeneous and the whole of what there is, an alteration must entail some destruction of what-is and the coming-to-be of what-is-not. Therefore, we can get an idea of how Melissus thought that homogeneity and uniqueness are threatened by altera-tion. On the former, the destruction of some piece of what-is violates the predicate ὁμοῖον because what-is would no longer be completely alike or like itself over space and time; on the latter, because the coming-to-be of any new piece plainly entails plurality.

The claim that, should what-is alter by a hair in ten thousand years, it would perish in the whole of time is obscure. Barnes remarks that the sentence to him is 'unintelligible'. Gomperz thinks that this is evidence of speculation founded upon empirical facts and congratulates Melissus for 'the elasticity of his mind' but chides him for introducing such *a posteriori* thinking into his

---

[20] Sedley 1982: 178–9. On many interpretations, it is mistakenly assumed that something 'retreats' to the outside of what-is, but of course Melissus has already ruled-out anything outside of what-is.

treatise.[21] Stephen Makin provides the most stimulating account thus far offered by introducing, as we have seen in previous chapters, indifference reasoning into the picture. His interpretation focuses on the temporal element of the sentence. The idea he presents is that, if any alteration is possible (even something as minute as alteration by a single hair), every alteration is then possible, and that, *given enough time*, the whole of what-is will be destroyed.[22] I think there is a great deal to say in favour of Makin's account, and my interpretation owes much to his exposition. A first point though, neglected or misinterpreted in most treatments of B7, is that τοίνυν needs to be appropriately construed. As we saw in our look at B1, there is a mistaken tendency to under-translate τοίνυν as a transitional particle in Melissus. Yet it is clear that Melissus invariably uses the particle with some inferential force.[23] This is plainly evident in B2, in B8, and *even elsewhere in* B7, and so it seems almost certainly to be the case here as well. If this is correct, we should be able to infer (c) on the strength of (a) and (b). The apparent difficulty of making such an inference has instigated the dominant non-inferential translations of τοίνυν. However, it is possible, and I believe true to Melissus' intentions, to make a valid inference, at least partially, from (a) and (b) to (c).

The only previous attempt known to me to read τοίνυν inferentially is Renzo Vitali's. He construes the particle as introducing a conclusion to the argument Melissus has been making throughout (2), i.e. that alteration is impossible. Vitali's claim is somewhat opaque, but the idea he suggests seems to be that emending ὀλεῖται πᾶν to ἂν ὄλοιτο πᾶν supports such a thesis because of an alleged correspondence between the use of the aorist and general conclusions in Melissus' fragments. He cites as supporting evidence the use of ἂν ὄλοιτο found in the conclusion to the argument against pain and suffering in (5). Against this emendation, we should note that, on the evidence of B5, mixed conditionals are perfectly normal for Melissus. In addition, it is clear that the sentence under consideration is not merely a conclusion, like (5), but also

---

[21] Gomperz 1906: 188–9.   [22] Makin 1993: 38–40.
[23] *Contra* Barnes 1982: 215 n.20. Loenen (1959: 163 n.72) gets this right.

a supplementary argument. If this is right, the comparison with (5) is largely irrelevant.[24]

The important question remains, despite the improbability of the details of Vitali's account, of whether τοίνυν can be understood to introduce a conclusion or draw an inference. It is easy to see why commentators have been hesitant to think so. Melissus appeals to the example of the most minute change conceivable, i.e. the alteration of something by a single hair. I say 'conceivable' because, as we have noticed in the previous section, Melissus is committed to a strongly anatomical understanding of measurement and a single hair is undoubtedly the smallest unit of measure in an anatomical model. Yet it is obscure how the provision of such an example could serve to conclude Melissus' discussion of alteration. It does not obviously restate the nature of the model of alteration Melissus adopts, nor does it serve any generalising function; in fact it seems to move from the universal to the specific. Reale, though understanding τοίνυν to introduce a logically independent claim, hits closer to the mark.[25] He argues that the upshot of (c) is the vivid description of the absurdity of *even the slightest change* to what-is. It certainly seems to be the case that Melissus chose the slightest of changes to make a point and no doubt it is at the service of demonstrating the absurdity of change.

Before we proceed further along these lines, let us look back to how Simplicius presents the text: εἰ τοίνυν τριχὶ μιῇ μυρίοις ἔτεσιν ἑτεροῖον γίνοιτο **τὸ πᾶν**, ὀλεῖται πᾶν ἐν τῷ παντὶ χρόνῳ. Extraordinarily, τὸ πᾶν, universally attested by the manuscripts of the *Physics* commentary (at least according to Diels), has been excised by DK. The reason for the omission seems to be twofold. Strikingly, Simplicius again quotes the sentence *without* τὸ πᾶν in his commentary on *De Caelo* and, as we saw in our look at Aristotle's interpretation of B2, Melissus takes his subject to be what-is and not τὸ πᾶν or τὸ ἄπαν (the universe) as Aristotle seems to understand it. Both points suggest that τὸ πᾶν is an

---

[24] Vitali 1973: 194–7. All manuscripts read ὀλεῖται. Mullach first offered ὄλοιτο. The *CAG* has ἄν for the πᾶν found in DK. According to the *apparatus* of the latter (271), this is a frequent mistake in the text of Simplicius' commentary on the *Physics* and, thus, should be unproblematically corrected.

[25] Reale 1970: 161–4.

unwarranted addition to Melissus' text. Yet both reasons stand on weak ground. A look at the quotation from the *De Caelo* commentary plainly suggests why τὸ πᾶν was omitted in that instance:

καλῶς γὰρ λέγει καὶ Μέλισσος, ὅτι "τὸ τριχὶ μιῇ μυρίοις ἔτεσιν ἑτεροῖον γινόμενον (**κατὰ τὴν οὐσίαν δηλον ὅτι**) ὀλεῖται ἄν²⁶ ἐν τῷ παντὶ χρόνῳ." (113.21–2)

At precisely the same place in the quotation where in the *Physics* commentary we find τὸ πᾶν, Simplicius supplies a gloss, making substance the object of Melissus' assertion of change. This is done, no doubt, in order to help make his needed exegetical point. Yet Simplicius obviously alters the sentence to conform to his present purpose in the *De Caelo* commentary. If this is right, there is good reason to disregard the quotation as it appears in the commentary on *De Caelo* on the grounds that it is too compromised by Simplicius' intervention to serve as adequate evidence for the addition of τὸ πᾶν in the rival quotation being unwarranted.

The second apparent motivation, far weaker in any case than the first, is generated by the very real concern that Melissus never elsewhere takes τὸ πᾶν as his subject but always rather τὸ ἐόν, or what-is. Independently, this should not be sufficient to warrant excision but, when it is taken in tandem with the misconstrued evidence of *In De Caelo*, one can easily see the strength of the concern felt by DK. The idea, then, is that Melissus would be discussing a hypothetical change not to τὸ πᾶν (the totality or the universe) but to his ordinary subject, what-is. Yet the addition here, in light of the context, makes sense. τὸ πᾶν serves the perfectly appropriate function of flagging the minute nature of the change Melissus is considering: it is not simply an alteration by a single hair to what-is but *an alteration by a single hair to the totality of what there is*. Melissus is raising not simply the counterfactual eventuality that what-is changes by a single hair but the more striking one that the whole of everything changes by the smallest possible fraction. It is essential for Melissus that the change discussed is presented as truly minute because this ensures

---

²⁶ The Greek is ungrammatical here and it is not clear from Heiberg's *apparatus* whether or not ἄν is universally attested with ὀλεῖται. One possibility may be that ἄν was an addition introduced as a result of the alternative reading of ὄλοιτο for ὀλεῖται. In any case, my point is unaffected.

the generality of his argument against any change, no matter how seemingly insignificant. Therefore, accepting the authenticity of τὸ πᾶν, as I believe the evidence suggests we must, changes the force of the sentence. I translate: 'Therefore, if the totality of what there is were to become altered by a single hair in ten thousand years, it . . .'

So where does that leave us? I have no doubt that Reale is largely correct about the *effect* of the sentence under consideration: the example of a micro-change by a single hair is intended to reinforce the argument targeting changeability. Indeed the incorporation of the transmitted τὸ πᾶν strengthens his point as we have seen. Yet it is not obvious to me that such an upshot cannot be logically inferred, at least partially, on the basis of (a) and (b).

So far on Melissus' argument in B7 against alteration we are entitled to make use of two conclusions, (1) and (2), and two reasons, (a) and (b), why these conclusions are true:

(1) Alteration excludes uniqueness.
(2) Alteration necessarily (ἀνάγκη) excludes homogeneity.
(a) Alteration entails the destruction what-is.
(b) Alteration necessitates the coming-to-be of what-is-not.

It is from these latter two that I submit we may make (at least partially) the inference to the claim offered in the τοίνυν sentence. We may put this in simple language by saying that any change, regardless of its scope, requires the destruction of what-is and the coming-to-be of what-is-not (understood *per impossibile* to be *ex nihilo*), both of which are impossible on the strength of B1.[27] Yet is this understanding of change sufficient evidence to imply Melissus' conclusion? Perhaps not. One may want a premise, or an argument, confirming that the existence of one possibility entails the existence of the possibility of every change, including the wholesale destruction of what-is. However, it is undoubtedly *necessary* for the argument to come that alteration includes elements of both perishing and coming-to-be. Melissus, on any understanding of the counterfactual event under discussion, makes a move from a minute alteration to the wholesale

---

[27] Of course, the destruction of what-is into nothing is not explicitly argued against by Melissus, just as it is not by Parmenides. It is, however, assumed in B2.

destruction of everything that there is. How he does so and whether he does so soundly are what we are trying to determine. However, it should be unobjectionable, and obvious from what we shall presently consider, to say that he can only do so if we have the understanding established that alteration is to be taken, at the very least and by definition, to entail destruction.[28]

Let us see how this works. Makin offers a number of competing understandings of how indifference reasoning is employed by Melissus in the counterfactual under consideration. At a fairly minimalist level, we might take Melissus to reason as follows: if one alteration occurs and there is no more reason for this alteration to occur than any other, then it follows that there is more reason to think that what-is will alter in every respect than not to think so. So, taking alteration as entailing destruction, there is reason to think that what-is will perish entirely. The deficiency (or, from some perspectives perhaps, advantage) of such a reading is that it views Melissus as committed not to any claims about the possibility of alterations but only to fairly basic epistemological notions implied by indifference reasoning. Yet Makin is right to note that this line of interpretation fails to grasp the emphasis Melissus plainly places on time.

To make sense of the temporal element, Makin introduces something like the Principle of Plenitude (PP) in order to help us follow Melissus' reasoning.[29] The idea proposed is that if any change can occur, given enough time, it must occur, at least in the case of possibilities that are eternally viable. This reading does not abandon indifference reasoning entirely: we still need some such principle to permit equating the possibility of alteration in one respect with <actual> alteration in every other respect.[30] Thus if any alteration (however minute) is possible and there is no reason

[28] I take it that alteration involves both destruction and coming-to-be. However, on the present argument Melissus really only needs the premise that alteration entails the destruction of what-is.

[29] Makin 1993: 38–40. I say 'something like' because Makin wants to make a number of distinctions about eternally viable possibilities that are not strictly relevant for our purposes, and because he never commits himself unambiguously to the claim that Melissus appeals to the Principle of Plenitude, but only that Melissus canvasses ideas about possibility and time provoked by an intuition we may grasp by using the framework of the Principle of Plenitude.

[30] Makin does not seem to recognise this point.

to think that the actualisation of this possibility is different from any other in a relevant way, then, on the strength of PP, in the whole of time alterations in every respect must be actualised. Indifference reasoning allows us to move from the possibility of alteration in one respect, however minute, to the possibility of alteration in every respect, while PP entails that every possibility must be actualised. Therefore, if one alteration is possible, all alterations are possible, and all alterations will and must take place, i.e. what-is will and must be destroyed if any alteration occurs.[31]

This is a very attractive line of interpretation and I submit that it is along these lines that Melissus' argument is best interpreted. However, there remains an unsolved puzzle. I have maintained that Melissus' introduction of this counterfactual event is intended as an inferential product of what is established previously and not simply as a vivid or explanatory example stated independently of his main line of reasoning. I have done so partly on the basis of the needed understanding of alteration as entailing both perishing and coming-to-be, something that is established in (a) and (b). Yet I have also maintained that both indifference reasoning and a commitment to PP in some form are needed to make the inferential structure of Melissus' text reasonably adequate and valid. Perhaps we can leave indifference reasoning to one side as simply a characteristic Melissan commitment, something we have seen in our discussion of B2; yet, if I am right, Melissus leaves (PP) unstated and we must supply it as a supressed premise or commitment. Is it reasonable that Melissus does not explicitly provide or state PP and yet expects his reader to make sense of his reasoning?

I am not convinced there is a truly dispositive argument in favour of answering in the affirmative here. PP may well seem to be a commitment that is far from obvious or intuitive, and in need of argument. Yet there is some evidence to suggest that having a belief or intuition that can be cashed out using PP was far from

---

[31] Such a view does not rescue Melissus completely from fallacious reasoning. We may agree that every single part of what-is may be non-existent in the future. However, it does not follow from this that every single part can be simultaneously non-existent: all things individually possible are not necessarily compossible.

unusual for ancient thinkers.[32] If this is correct, Melissus' omission of an explicit statement of commitment to PP perhaps seems less of a hurdle for the inferential reading I have offered.

I do not want to make the claim that PP, even only in regard to eternally viable possibilities, is an uncontroversial area of agreement for ancient philosophers, although I do maintain that it is more evident than one might think. The evidence is simply not available to make such a general claim. Rather I would like to point to a parallel argument in Plato that closely mirrors the Melissan argument we have been considering. It relies on both indifference reasoning and a belief (or an intuition at least) in PP. The upshot of the comparison should be, I hope, some support for the thesis that it is not implausible that Melissus would have made the inference I have claimed he does make in (c).

Consider a remarkable passage from *Republic* X:

Τοῦτο μὲν τοίνυν, ἦν δ' ἐγώ, οὕτως ἐχέτω· εἰ δ' ἔχει, ἐννοεῖς ὅτι ἀεὶ ἂν εἶεν αἱ αὐταί. οὔτε γὰρ ἄν που ἐλάττους γένοιντο μηδεμιᾶς ἀπολλυμένης, οὔτε αὖ πλείους· εἰ γὰρ ὁτιοῦν τῶν ἀθανάτων πλέον γίγνοιτο, οἶσθ' ὅτι ἐκ τοῦ θνητοῦ ἂν γίγνοιτο, καὶ πάντα ἂν εἴη τελευτῶντα ἀθάνατα. (611a4–8)

'Let us, then,' I said 'take this to be so. But if it is so, you will notice that these souls must always be the same ones. For if none is destroyed, they could surely not become fewer nor yet more numerous. For if any sort of immortal things becomes increased, you know that it would become so from what is mortal, and everything would ultimately become immortal.'

The argument here strikingly overlaps the Melissan passage we have been considering.[33] We can discern traces of both indifference reasoning and a commitment to PP. On the former, Plato

---

[32] Discussions of the Principle of Plenitude or, more broadly, of the necessary actualisation of possibilities, in Aristotle and others (particularly Diodorus Cronus) can be found in Prior 1967, Sorabji 1980: 128–40, and Waterlow 1982. It seems safe to say that, for Aristotle at least, it is fairly clear that he agrees that all eternally viable possibilities must be actualised in the whole of time: see *De Interpretatione* 9 on the difference between transient subjects like a cloak and eternal subjects like the stars whose capacities last for the whole time and *De Caelo* 1.12 on the similar, but not identical, argument that what is eternally standing is not capable of sitting. For a reading of a stronger commitment to PP in Aristotle, see Jaakko Hintikka (1973), who argues that PP applies even to transient, non-eternal things. I remain agnostic on this point, but I suggest that such a reading, if correct, would further my claim that PP is a far more prevalent commitment than one might assume it to be at first blush.

[33] This has been noted, but only partially explored, by Eric Brown (1997: 236–8).

seems committed to the Melissan notion that if there is any possibility of the increase of an immortal class of things (understood as necessarily the product of mortal things), it is possible that every mortal thing could become immortal. The idea is that if one mortal thing can become immortal, there is no reason to think that that thing is different in a relevant way from any other mortal thing. If this is the case, Plato can use indifference reasoning to conclude that it is possible that every mortal thing should become immortal. Finally, on the strength of PP, if it is possible that every mortal thing *can* become immortal, then it is necessary that every mortal thing *will* become immortal. Though we get no explicit mention of time here as we do in Melissus, it is plain from the language of the passage (τελευτῶντα) that we may take it for granted that he is arguing on the basis of eternity.[34] Therefore, if this reconstruction is correct, we find the same basic mode of argument here that we do in Melissus.

The upshot of the comparison is that Melissus is not alone in employing an argument using indifference reasoning as well as a commitment to PP. This suggests, I hope, that the inference I claim Melissus makes in (c) is not as outlandish as commentators have taken it to be. Obviously, one may still deny the soundness of the argument; yet it should be reasonably clear that Melissus is not alone is seeing a tension between eternally viable, but unactualised, possibilities and an infinite temporal expanse.

Rearrangement

ἀλλ' οὐδὲ μετακοσμηθῆναι ἀνυστόν· ὁ γὰρ κόσμος ὁ πρόσθεν ἐὼν οὐκ ἀπόλλυται οὔτε ὁ μὴ ἐὼν γίνεται. ὅτε δὲ μήτε προσγίνεται μηδὲν μήτε ἀπόλλυται μήτε ἑτεροιοῦται, πῶς ἂν μετακοσμηθὲν τῶν ἐόντων εἴη; εἰ μὲν γάρ τι ἐγίνετο ἑτεροῖον, ἤδη ἂν καὶ μετακοσμηθείη.

We may provisionally translate:

---

[34] This is different from the ostensibly similar argumentation at *Phaedo* 72c–d. There we might find a trace of PP: if sleep is possible but not waking, eventually everyone will be asleep, or if death is possible but not waking from the dead, eventually everyone will be dead. Yet we do not find any hint of the move from any instance of one possibility to actualisation of every instance of this possibility that seems to underpin both Melissus' argument and the one found in the *Republic*.

But neither is it possible for it to be rearranged. For the order which was previous is not perishing, nor is one that is not coming to be. And since nothing is either being added, or being destroyed, or being altered, how could anything that is be rearranged? For if it became different in any respect, it would then be rearranged.

The text is reasonably sound with the exception of the rhetorical question (πῶς ἂν μετακοσμηθὲν τῶν ἐόντων εἴη;). The manuscript reads πῶς ἂν μετακοσμηθέντων ἐόντων τι ᾖ which Diels, in the *CAG*, alters by separating off the article τῶν before ἐόντων (τῶν ἐόντων). Mullach corrected ᾖ to εἴη (accepted by DK, though without τι). This was subsequently challenged by Heidel, who thought μετακοσμηθὲν εἴη intolerably periphrastic.[35] He dismisses ᾖ as a marginal correction and argues that τι has been misplaced and reads instead πῶς ἂν μετακοσμηθείη τι τῶν ἐόντων.[36]

Clearly there is some uncertainly over the correct reading. What is striking in the various attempts to make sense of the text is the absence of any discussion of how one could reasonably adjudicate between the various options. Yet the criterion we should appeal to is nevertheless clear. The rhetorical question is obviously acting as a transition between two separate elements. On the one hand, we have Melissus' initial statement that rearrangement is not possible (ἀνυστόν), recalling the language of the argument for spatial infinity in B2. Rearrangement is impossible because it would entail destruction of one order (κόσμος)[37] and the creation of a new one. At the other end of the argument we learn that since nothing is being added (προσγίνεται), destroyed/lost (ἀπόλλυται), or altered (ἑτεροιοῦται) there is no rearrangement. Thus there is a move from a consideration of the nature of rearrangement itself to a claim of its connection with those species of change we have considered above, i.e. alterations. My suggestion, then, is that if we can make sense of the transition evident in the rhetorical question, we should be on firm ground to make best sense of the text.

---

[35] Mullach 1883: 263.   [36] Heidel 1913: 724–5. Reale (1970) and KRS follow suit.

[37] The use of κόσμος has encouraged some cosmological readings. See Reale 1970: 164–6 for further details. Kahn (1960: 229) takes κόσμος, for Melissus, as 'the immutable structure of the one Being, eternally identical with itself'. This is far too strong. It is true that this description will fit the κόσμος Melissus ascribes to what-is. However, Melissus in no way thinks that this is the only 'positive sense' of the term. It is clear from the fact that he uses the word in a counterfactual scenario that he understands it absolutely neutrally as simply an arrangement of what there is, real or not.

So in the first part of the argument we learn that rearrangement necessitates the destruction of one order and the coming-to-be of a new one. The discussion seems designed to respond, at least in part, to a question one might naturally ask of Melissus in response to his remarks on alteration. Perhaps one might agree that alteration, understood as entailing both destruction and coming-to-be, is impossible. Yet surely mere rearrangement entails no such thing? Nothing is destroyed by rearrangement, but rather something is only shifted around like the contents of a jar of marbles after it has been shaken. Melissus responds to such a worry by redeploying the same machinery he does for alteration but with the explicit understanding that rearrangement is to be understood as a change of the order (κόσμος) of what-is.

This points towards something even more significant that is evident here. If we look back to our examination of the argument targeting alteration, it was clear that Melissus was concerned with *qualitative* change, i.e. that what-is becomes qualitatively other (ἑτεροιοῦται) than what it was previously and is no longer ὁμοῖον. This is not, of course, to deny that qualitative changes do not have a quantitative feature. I take it that, should a new quality come into being, rearrangement would be implied to simultaneously (ἤδη) occur. This is plain from the last sentence of (3). Rather, the idea is that while the framework used to target rearrangement may be the same as that deployed for alteration (i.e. the impossibility of generation and destruction), as I have indicated above, there is a fundamental difference. Rearrangement is said to require the wholesale destruction of one order and the coming-to-be of a new one. This suggests that Melissus has in mind the thought that rearrangement entails successive iterations of *kosmoi*. Yet such successive *kosmoi* cannot be cashed out satisfactorily as equivalent to either qualitative or a quantitative change and this seems to get to the heart of Melissus' argument.[38] Even when no part or quality comes into being or perishes (i.e. there has been qualitative or quantitative change), rearrangement entails that there still is the generation and destruction of arrangements.

---

[38] Loenen (1959: 155–60) makes something of what kinds of change Melissus is interested in in B7, though our conclusions differ.

So, on this account, Melissus has not transitioned from a consideration of qualitative change to one of quantitative change. Clearly though we have species of change (alteration and rearrangement) that have qualitative and quantitative characteristics. Yet the example of rearrangement, understood as entailing successive arrangements, demonstrates that this is an example of a change that is reducible to neither its qualitative nor its quantitative aspects.

Perhaps the idea I am suggesting would be clarified by making a distinction between 'synchronic' and 'diachronic' versions of homogeneity and uniqueness. 'Synchronic' homogeneity is simply the notion that what-is is all alike: no part is qualitatively different from any other. 'Diachronic' homogeneity, on the other hand, necessitates that what-is is alike itself over both space *and time*. It is this second understanding that rearrangement threatens. Even though no new quality comes to be, what-is is clearly not the same as it was previously after it has been rearranged. 'Synchronic' and 'diachronic' ideas of uniqueness work in parallel. The 'synchronic' version only demands that what-is be unique and singular at a given time; while 'diachronic' uniqueness means that what-is is its only instantiation through space and time. Once again, it is the latter the rearrangement is said to threaten.

We can see then how Melissus proceeds in the fragment. Alteration violates the synchronic versions of both homogeneity and uniqueness. If we leave aside the thought that what-is may change all over simultaneously, part of what-is becomes different from another part, implying both heterogeneity and the existence of distinct parts, both of which entail a kind of plurality. Rearrangement, on the other hand, tackles the diachronic versions described above. What-is need not gain or lose any quality, yet may still violate the 'strong' version of homogeneity because rearrangement demands that what-is no longer be identical to what it once was.[39] Uniqueness follows suit. Rearrangement means that one arrangement is destroyed and another comes to be. Even though the arrangements are not simultaneously

---

[39] I take it that qualitative change certainly entails rearrangement while the reverse is not necessarily true. This is clear from the last sentence of (3): εἰ μὲν γάρ τι ἐγίνετο ἑτεροῖον, ἤδη ἂν καὶ μετακοσμηθείη.

instantiated, nevertheless the diachronic version of uniqueness is violated.

One might reasonably ask here why it is that rearrangement should threaten the uniqueness of what-is and not, more modestly, the uniqueness of its current state. We may agree that rearrangement entails the destruction of one arrangement of what-is and the coming-to-be of another. Yet this does not entail that what-is is itself destroyed and regenerated in a different form. One answer to this sort of worry would be to think that it is merely diachronic homogeneity that is relevant here and not the uniqueness of what-is itself. Rearrangement on such a reading would then be no threat to the diachronic model of uniqueness canvassed above.

Obviously, even a violation to the claim that what-is is diachronically homogeneous would be a threat to the Eleatic 'One'. Yet I don't think we should put uniqueness off to the side here. Taking different arrangements of what-is as the product of successive iterations where what-is itself endures, but its various *kosmoi* are generated and destroyed, necessitates that these *kosmoi* are in some sense separable from, and non-identical with, what-is. This, on the face of it, suggests an implication of plurality that Melissus would be keen to avoid.

Let us now return to the text of the rhetorical question. The first puzzle is the presence of the plural ἐόντων. Does this commit Melissus to a plurality of things that are? Surely not, as he is in the process of considering a counterfactual, i.e. that what-is is rearranged. The procedure is in two steps. First, as we have seen, we are made to see that rearrangement is the destruction of one *kosmos* and the coming-to-be of a new one. The next move is an exploration of how one would even come to a rearrangement in the first place: Melissus is inquiring *per impossibile*, much as he does later in B7, by entertaining the counterfactual existence of void (εἰ μὲν γὰρ κενεὸν ἦν). Such a method is also employed in B2, B6, and B8, suggesting that it is a highly typical Melissan mode of argument. If this is the case, Melissus is in no way committing himself to any position about monism or plurality.[40]

---

[40] Loenen (1959: 160 n.65) recognises this point. However, his suggested text is also too problematic to accept. He retains the manuscript reading, with Mullach's correction of ἢ to εἴη, and translates: 'how then could it (something that is) be, if the things that are were

Heidel argues that the correction of ἦ to εἴη is unnecessarily periphrastic and inadequate Greek. Yet his solution of eliminating ἦ altogether as a marginal correction is over-hasty. Melissus is, in fact, quite fond of using εἴη in similar counterfactual enquiries. Consider the last sentence of B8: οὕτως οὖν, εἰ πολλὰ **εἴη**, τοιαῦτα χρὴ εἶναι, οἷόν περ τὸ ἕν, and the last of B9: εἰ δὲ ἔχοι πάχος, ἔχοι ἂν μόρια, καὶ οὐκέτι ἓν **εἴη**.[41] Undoubtedly, in both of these examples εἴη is taking an adjective and not a participle as its complement. Yet it is clear that Melissus is using the aorist passive participle form of the verb μετακοσμέω much as he does any other predicate under consideration, whether it is πολλά, ἕν, or ὁμοῖον. With this in mind, my suggested text is as follows: πῶς ἂν μετακοσμηθέν τι τῶν ἐόντων εἴη;. I translate: 'how could anything rearranged be among what-is?' Such a text preserves more of the manuscript reading than the alternative proposals: the only change is the straightforward correction of ἦ to εἴη.[42] So, then, the answer to the question should be obvious from what immediately precedes: there could be nothing rearranged because what has been rearranged has perished and therefore is not one of the ἐόντα.

The last sentence of (3), εἰ μὲν γάρ τι ἐγίνετο ἑτεροῖον, ἤδη ἂν καὶ μετακοσμηθείη, brings alteration together with rearrangement. Here we find the claim that any alteration implies a simultaneous rearrangement. This is clear enough. If any property were to come-to-be or perish, what-is would no longer be alike itself in the diachronic sense outlined above. Melissus is not explicitly committed to the reverse entailment – that the rearrangement of what-is entails its alteration – but it seems likely that this must also hold true for him. If what-is is rearranged, at the very least, the new iteration would contain spatial relations different from the previous order. Once again, this would violate the notion of

to be rearranged?' I am not convinced this is a possible translation of the Greek. In any case, such a thought does an injustice to Melissus' point. It is not that if something were rearranged it would no longer *be*, but that were it to alter, it would be rearranged. This is made plain by the text that follows: 'for if it became different in any respect, it would then be rearranged'.

[41] Other examples can be found throughout B7.

[42] Of course, we must also accept τῶν as an article belonging with ἐόντων rather than as an element in the participial construction 'μετακοσμηθέντων'. I take it that this is an uncontroversial decision.

diachronic homogeneity that demands that what-is be eternally like itself at all times.

If such a solution to the textual worries is along the right lines and the above reading of the passage sound, we come to see the primary benefit of the interpretation we have been sketching. Melissus argues that rearrangement, like qualitative change, is impossible because it too entails coming-to-be and destruction. Yet we can see that progressively more demanding understandings of both homogeneity and uniqueness are assumed in successive pieces of the argument. This supports my solution to Solmsen's anxiety about the apparent initial prominence and subsequent fading of the predicate ἕν. It is not the case that the issue of plurality is abandoned; this is in any case clear from the near conflation of unity and homogeneity as the dual contradictories of plurality made evident in the *MXG*. Rather unity and plurality are tightly knitted together and equally relevant in both arguments we have considered (*contra* alteration, *contra* rearrangement). Next we shall consider how the argument against pain and suffering caps off this section of the treatise devoted to eliminating those changes that threaten the predicate ἕν.

Pain and Grief

Sections (4), (5), and (6) of B7 are typically presented as something of an oddity.[43] Thus far in the fragment, we have found arguments with easily explicable aims, even if their means have needed some investigation. However, pain and grief are resolutely zoological, if not distinctively human, notions that seem irrelevant to a consideration of what-is. It is unclear, for instance, what pain and grief would amount to when their subject is the whole of what there is. In addition, Melissus nowhere else presents what-is as animate or intelligent, something we might expect to be preconditions for even a consideration of its suffering pain or grief.

The motivation for this curious line of argument is made less opaque if we recall Melissus' insistence on denying a body to what-is. It became clear from our examination of B9 that it makes

---

[43] Cf. Barnes 1982: 216–17 and KRS: 397.

sense to think that he was following the lead of Xenophanes by denying that what-is should be understood to be anthropomorphic in any way. There is also a hint in ancient reports of Melissus' treatise that he may have additionally followed Xenophanes in conceiving of the universe as divine.[44] We shall take up this connection fully in due course.

The motivation for Melissus' denial of pain and grief may be opaque, at least superficially, but the structure of the argument itself is relatively clear.[45] The same framework (the assumption of homogeneity, uniqueness, and the impossibility of both coming-to-be and destruction) deployed against alteration and rearrangement is brought to bear against pain and suffering. In addition, we shall see once again how both homogeneity and uniqueness are at stake for Melissus.

We learn from (6) that both pain and grief are taken to be dismissed, using the same piece of reasoning (ὡυτὸς λόγος). This reasoning is itself in three parts: let us take each in turn.

οὐδὲ ἀλγεῖ· (a) οὐ γὰρ ἂν πᾶν εἴη ἀλγέον· οὐ γὰρ ἂν δύναιτο ἀεὶ εἶναι χρῆμα ἀλγέον· (b) οὐδὲ ἔχει ἴσην δύναμιν τῷ ὑγιεῖ· (c) οὐδ' ἂν ὁμοῖον εἴη, εἰ ἀλγέοι· ἀπογινομένου γάρ τευ ἂν ἀλγέοι ἢ προσγινομένου, κοὐκ ἂν ἔτι ὁμοῖον εἴη.

Nor is it in pain. (a) For if it were in pain it would not be entire, for a thing in pain could not be eternal, (b) nor does it have equal power with what is in health. (c) Nor would it be homogeneous if it were in pain; for it would be in pain either because something was taken from it or added to it, and it would no longer be homogeneous.

The first step of Melissus' argument turns on the thought that pain depletes the completeness (πᾶν) of what-is. Why he might think this we shall examine shortly. Our first step though is to determine how incompleteness implies that what-is cannot be eternal. The answer is apparent if we remember the example of a change

---

[44] In *Metaphysics* A (986b21–5), Aristotle ascribes to Xenophanes the view that 'the One', understood in connection with the whole of heaven, is god: Ξενοφάνης δὲ πρῶτος τούτων ἐνίσας (ὁ γὰρ Παρμενίδης τούτου λέγεται γενέσθαι μαθητής) οὐθὲν διεσαφήνισεν, οὐδὲ τῆς φύσεως τούτων οὐδετέρας ἔοικε θιγεῖν, **ἀλλ' εἰς τὸν ὅλον οὐρανὸν ἀποβλέψας τὸ ἓν εἶναί φησι τὸν θεόν**. We find a similar thought (that the universe is divine) attributed to Melissus in our collection of *testimonia*: μίαν τοίνυν ἀκίνητον <καὶ> ἄπειρον ἀρχὴν **πάντων τῶν ὄντων ἐδόξαζεν Μέλισσος τὸ θεῖον**. (DK30A13, Aëtius, Olympiodorus).

[45] Reale 1970: 171.

by a hair considered above. There, on the strength of both indifference reasoning and the Principle of Plenitude, a single alteration entailed the destruction of the whole of what-is in the whole of
time. A similar interpretative approach makes good sense of the
present argument:

Melissus takes it that, by definition, pain depletes (or at the very
least alters, as the disjunction in (c) makes clear) its subject in
some respect. On the strength of indifference reasoning, it would
follow that there is reason to think that pain could deplete what-is
equally in any other respect. If we add in the Principle of
Plenitude, Melissus is entitled to the claim that if it is possible
that what-is can be depleted in any respect, in the whole of time it
will be depleted in every respect. What-is cannot, then, be in pain
and also be eternal.[46]

Melissus' next sentence (b) is not an argument but merely
a claim apparently unsupported by any reasoning: what-is in
pain does not have equal power (ἴσην δύναμιν) to that which is in
health (or is healthy). What does this add? It is certainly an
intuitively plausible notion but one that seems unnecessary for
the argument to go through. Perhaps the idea is something like
this.[47] Not only does pain entail that what-is is incomplete, it also
means that its capacities (understood as constituting its power) are
diminished. If this is right, we can run through the same argument
we rehearsed above. If pain diminishes its subject's capacities in
one respect, there is reason to think that it could do so in any
respect, and so, in the whole of time, the capacities of what-is
would be completely destroyed. The upshot of such a claim is
further clarified if we remember that in the Hippocratic corpus –
especially relevant given the subject matter here – something's
φύσις is strongly associated with its δυνάμεις.[48] A diminution of
capacities then correlates with a threat to something's very nature.
If this is representative of Melissus' understanding, it is plausible

---

[46] This account is similar to, but different in some aspects from, the interpretation offered
by Barnes (1982: 217). He suggests that pain weakens its sufferer and so in time will
destroy her. Using indifference reasoning and PP gives us a clearer reason why the
sufferer will eventually be destroyed.

[47] The following account borrows much from Reale (1970: 172).

[48] See Schiefsky 2005: 226–8 for a discussion and a list of relevant examples.

that he takes the complete loss of the capacities of what-is as identical, in practice, with its destruction. This is merely one suggestion, but if it is along the right lines, we can begin to see the mileage Melissus gets out of targeting anthropomorphic conceptions of what-is.[49] The entirety of what-is understood as the perfection of both itself and its power has been affirmed.

Our next section, (c), recalls the arguments against alteration and rearrangement considered above. Parallel to the former we find that it is homogeneity that is explicitly at stake and, like the latter, we are to understand that addition and destruction are necessary elements of the counterfactual change being considered. I take it that this goes some way towards confirming the close connection between alteration and rearrangement I have suggested, because, just as in those two arguments, homogeneity and uniqueness are equally relevant in the case of pain.

However, we have yet to determine why Melissus thinks that pain requires that something in its subject be added to (προσγινομένου) or taken away (ἀπογινομένου).[50] That a physiological theory is in the background seems clear enough, and it is likely that the most relevant place to find such a theory will be in the Hippocratic corpus. Our best bet is to turn to the well-known treatise *On the Nature of the Human Being*, where Melissus is explicitly mentioned in the first chapter.[51] Almost immediately after the mention of Melissus' name, we find an intriguing account of the nature of pain:

ἐγὼ δέ φημι, εἰ ἓν ἦν ὁ ἄνθρωπος, οὐδέποτ' ἂν ἤλγεεν· οὐδὲ γὰρ ἂν ἦν ὑφ' ὅτου ἀλγήσειεν ἓν ἐών· εἰ δ' οὖν καὶ ἀλγήσειεν, ἀνάγκη καὶ τὸ ἰώμενον ἓν εἶναι· νυνὶ δὲ πολλά.[52]

And I claim, if a man were one, in no way could he be in pain. For, being one, there is nothing from whose agency he could suffer pain. So that, even if he were

---

[49] A further suggestion, developed later in this chapter, is that if the One is assumed to be a god, it must, like a god, be all-powerful.

[50] I take it that there is no real difference to be found in the opposition between προσγίνεται and ἀπόλλυται in (3) and (προσγινομένου) and (ἀπογινομένου) here.

[51] For our purposes whether Hippocrates himself, his son-in-law Polybus (to whom Aristotle, in *Historia Animalium* III.3, ascribes the description of veins found in chapter 11, cf. *Anomymus Londiniensis* XIX), or someone else is the author is beyond our scope. For convenience's sake I refer to the author as Hippocrates, but without committing myself to the authenticity of his authorship.

[52] I use the text of Littré 1849: vol. 6, 34–6.

to suffer pain, it is necessary also that the cure be one. But, in fact, they (the cures) are many.

There are crucial differences between the account of pain presented here and what we find in Melissus' B7. Importantly, Melissus does *not* appeal to any causal force or external agent, as we find in the quoted passage here. Yet there is a fundamental agreement that what is one cannot suffer pain. This suggests that the unity of the subject of disease (and equally of its cure) was a live issue in medical enquiry, helping to situate Melissus' ostensibly mysterious claims.

In Melissus, we find the understanding that pain requires its subject to lose or gain something. In Hippocrates, we find the idea that there is nothing by whose agency (ὑφ' ὅτου) that which is one could suffer pain. The reasoning seems to be that disease (which I take to be the cause of pain for Hippocrates) requires a causal component. Causation requires two elements: an agent and a patient. The argument seems to be, then, that if the body were constitutively simple, there would be no distinctive component that could act as the cause of pain. Pain requires, as Hippocrates immediately goes on to emphasise, that the body contains many constituents (πολλὰ γάρ ἐστιν ἐν τῷ σώματι ἐνεόντα), just as the cures for suffering are many.

How does this help us make sense of Melissus' understanding of pain? Well, in Hippocrates we find confirmation that the existence of pain requires some causal element distinct from the subject of pain and that hence the subject can be neither homogeneous nor unique. We can see how Melissus might be deploying a similar sort of argument. He takes it that pain requires addition to or subtraction from what-is. What this amounts to is the claim that pain requires an alteration to what-is and, as we have seen above, this constitutes a violation to both homogeneity and uniqueness. What the Hippocratic parallel helps to clarify is why we should think that pain and unity cannot coincide. For Hippocrates, it is a distinct causal component that necessitates the heterogeneity of the human body. Melissus does not adopt a causal approach but, nevertheless, we find the related notion that pain requires two distinct components, either the subject and an addition or the subject and something subtracted from it. Therefore, for both authors, pain requires heterogeneity and plurality.

In (5), Melissus continues:

οὐδ' ἂν τὸ ὑγιὲς ἀλγῆσαι δύναιτο· ἀπὸ γὰρ ἂν ὄλοιτο τὸ ὑγιὲς καὶ τὸ ἐόν, τὸ δὲ οὐκ ἐὸν γένοιτο.

Nor could the healthy come to be in pain, for the healthy (i.e. what-is) would be destroyed, and what-is-not would come to be.

The broad strokes of the argument are clearly following the formulae we have considered above. In the previous argument, it emerged that it was alteration that pain necessitated. Here we seem to find a parallel to the account of rearrangement in so far as both arguments turn on a consideration of illicit coming-to-be and perishing. The idea, then, is that if the healthy subject were to become pained, something would have to be destroyed and something would be generated. We might imagine that this works on multiple levels. If pain necessitates alteration, some part or property of what-is would need to be destroyed and a new part or property would need to come-to-be. This also works for rearrangement: the healthy arrangement is destroyed and a pained arrangement comes-to-be.

We do find, however, something unusual, at least superficially, in the second sentence: ἀπὸ γὰρ ἂν ὄλοιτο **τὸ ὑγιὲς καὶ τὸ ἐόν**, τὸ δὲ οὐκ ἐὸν γένοιτο. Melissus seems to name two distinct subjects of destruction here: both the healthy and what-is. This would suggest that he is adopting the healthy as a new subject, thus making this piece of reasoning somewhat tangential to the main business of the deductive account of what-is.[53] A better interpretation, which avoids attributing to Melissus multiple subjects and thus the dangerous implication of pluralism, takes the καί between **τὸ ὑγιὲς** and **τὸ ἐόν** epexegetically: the healthy *is* what-is and is *not* a distinct subject.[54] The identification makes perfect sense; it is only if the two are the same that the argument can be said to follow.

---

[53] The thought that the healthy and what-is are two different subjects is often encouraged by translations: McKirahan (1994) has 'For what is healthy *and what-is*'. KRS bracket τὸ ὑγιὲς καί.

[54] Reale (1970: 171) captures this in translation: 'infatti perirebbe ciò che è sano, *cioè l'essere*'.

If, for example, the healthy were not understood to be the *whole of what there is*, one would be right to challenge the claim that its pained state particularly requires *its* destruction and coming-to-be.[55]

(6) καὶ περὶ τοῦ ἀνιᾶσθαι ὡυτὸς λόγος τῷ ἀλγέοντι

In typical Melissan style, we are left to construct a parallel argument for suffering. I translate, 'and the same argument applies to grief as to pain'. It is not explained why grief should follow in parallel, but it seems clear enough that, just as pain requires two distinct components, grief would as well. If this is right, we can easily construct an argument that demonstrates how suffering, like pain, violates both homogeneity and uniqueness.

Despite the appeal to the same argumentative framework, it is worth asking how ἀνιᾶσθαι (grief) is meant to differ from pain on Melissus' account. Clearly, the two are not understood as synonymous or (6) would be unnecessary. Rather I take it that the argument we are left to run through here is intended to eliminate *mental* pain or anguish in addition to the *physical* suffering considered in (5). This is not to say that the semantic range of ἀλγέω only refers to physical pain while ἀνιάομαι solely connotes mental distress. Such a claim would be impossible to demonstrate incontrovertibly. Yet it is clear enough from the *general use* of these two verbs that this distinction *largely* holds true and my point is simply that from their use in conjunction it seems plain that Melissus intends to eliminate both from his picture of what-is.[56]

We may now take up the promise made above to pick up on the connection with Xenophanes. In our look at Melissus' demonstration of bodilessness in B9, I suggested that Xenophanes' criticism of anthropomorphic conceptions of the divine played a crucial background role in the argument. My point there was that Melissus was following Xenophanes in denying not *any* body as

---

[55] It is worth noting that the *MXG* (974a20) also understands Melissus to claim that what-is is healthy: ὑγιές τε καὶ ἄνοσον εἶναι.

[56] For example, Herodotus uses ἀλγέω at 4.68 for bodily illness, and ἀνιάω at 4.130 for mental distress.

such to what-is, but only a more narrow anthropomorphic notion. Xenophanes again figures in our present look at pain and suffering. Consider B25:

ἀλλ' ἀπάνευθε πόνοιο νόου φρενὶ πάντα κραδαίνει

but without toil he shakes everything by the thought of his mind.

Xenophanes' divinity here is explicitly said to be free from distress/toil (πόνος), very much in line with Melissus' elimination of pain and suffering from what-is. The overlap is striking and it is certainly worth asking whether the connection here is deliberate, but the more important question is whether Melissus is himself endorsing Xenophanes' implicit claim of the perfection of divine life and intelligence. In short, does Melissus imply, through the denial of pain and suffering in B7, that what-is is alive, intelligent, and divine? The very great advantage of answering this question in the affirmative is that the motivation for Melissus' remarks on pain and suffering is made obvious. This does not suggest that the preservation of unity and the parallel with *On the Nature of the Human Being* are irrelevant, but rather that Melissus had especial reason to deny pain and anguish to what-is if it is taken as a divine being.

A. A. Long makes the argument that Melissus does indeed follow Parmenides in attributing divine mind to what-is. He notes that the absence of physical and mental pain is the primary characteristic of the divine in ancient Greek thought and, as such, Melissus' explicit denial of both to what-is is therefore an incontrovertible indication of the divine status of what-is.[57] David Sedley makes a similar claim, on the basis of the elimination of pain and grief, saying that the 'One is being assimilated to a deity.'[58]

It is crucial that it is in conjunction with Parmenides that divinisation of what-is in Melissus is considered. On its own, the comparison between Xenophanes and Melissus yields a mixed picture: certainly Xenophanes criticises human misconceptions of the divine but, importantly, he does *not* discard many of the

---

[57] Long 1996: 141.   [58] Sedley 1999: 128.

traditional attributes of the divine. He retains a body (though it is unlike a human's) (B23), has cognitive capacities superior to humans (B23, B24), and is an active force in the world (B25). Indeed Xenophanes' god seems not different in *kind* from what we learn from the traditional Homeric/Hesiodic picture, but rather different in respect of his level of similarity to humans. Yet, if we see Xenophanes as inaugurating a philosophical tradition of theological criticism, we might be able to conclude how Melissus could embrace some of his conclusions, while taking others further, sometimes in very different directions. This is particularly true if the inauguration of the tradition I have ascribed to Xenophanes is filtered through Parmenides.

Parmenides, on the account Long and Sedley give, makes the crucial step of assimilating what-is with the divine. This is certainly distinct from what we can glean from the fragments of Xenophanes,[59] but it is not evidence of a totally distinct project either. To see how this works, let us take up the motion of the gods. Certainly, the ability to travel at tremendous speed is a hallmark of divinity in Homer. Xenophanes' turns this traditional conception on its head: 'always he remains in the same place, moving not at all' (B26). Xenophanes, then, makes god motionless while allowing him to retain active powers in the world outside himself through his capacity of thought. Parmenides, on this picture, by a very different means, extends the motionlessness Xenophanes attributes to god to the whole of what there is, eliminating the need for an external world outside of the divine.

With the help of Xenophanes and Parmenides, then, it seems Melissus could attribute divinity, very much counter to tradition, to what-is, understood as immobile, unchanging, and with nothing external to rule over or control. These seem rather extraordinary qualities to attribute to the divine; yet if we take it that Parmenides had made the identification between divine thought and being in his B3, and the fact that it is exceptionally common in early Greek

---

[59] We do find, of course, such an assimilation ascribed to Xenophanes by Aristotle at *Metaphysics* 986b24–5. Yet it very difficult to see how such a view would tally with the claim that, while god is motionless, he moves all things with thought. It seems likely that Aristotle's reading is a distortion, produced by a misunderstanding of the nature of Xenophanes' influence on Parmenides and Melissus.

philosophy to think that one's proposed *arche* is divine,[60] this non-traditional conception of divinity is not so very surprising.

This view is, it should be said, at odds with a leading interpretation in the secondary literature. Loenen, for example, denies that there is any indication that Melissus conceived of what-is as a conscious being and doubts that his method could permit such an understanding. KRS leave open the possibility that Melissus follows Xenophanes in thinking of being as divine but strongly dismiss the possibility that what-is is to be taken as sentient.[61]

I think Long and Sedley are largely correct in their assessment and indeed it is unclear whether the issues of divinity and sentience can be as easily distinguished as KRS suggest: perhaps there is non-divine intelligence but a divine, non-sentient being? Yet I doubt that the theory that Melissus' commitment to divine being is simply a rather casual, obvious, and somewhat unconscious inheritance from Parmenides gets the issue right. The evidence suggests a different conclusion: the divinity of what-is is not an afterthought or a hollow cultural commitment but rather, I will suggest, the product of an elegant solution to a pressing worry.

The pressing worry I take to emerge from Xenophanes' criticism of anthropomorphic conceptions of divinity. I have already suggested that Melissus echoes such criticism in his denial of a body to what-is in B9. The heart of Xenophanes' criticism is that traditional views of the divine are hopelessly relativised and inappropriate/unfitting (ἐπιπρέπει B26) for such an august and unimpeachable subject matter. The worry generated, then, is how one is to speak about the divine *at all* from a human perspective: if we cannot move from the evidence of our experience towards an understanding of the divine, we seem to be left with no access to theological truth.

Undoubtedly, such a concern plays a large part in the scepticism evident in Xenophanes about acquiring knowledge of and speaking about reality, particularly of the divine (cf. B34–6). Though it is little commented upon, we have evidence that Melissus

---

[60] Sedley (1999: 120) makes this point. See, for example, Aristotle, *Physics* 203b10–15. Examples include Anaximander, Anaximenes, and Heraclitus.

[61] KRS: 397.

harboured a similar worry. Near the end of Diogenes Laertius' entry on Melissus (IX.24), we find an intriguing claim: 'ἀλλὰ καὶ περὶ θεῶν ἔλεγε μὴ δεῖν ἀποφαίνεσθαι· μὴ γὰρ εἶναι γνῶσιν αὐτῶν' ('Also he said one should not speak about the gods, for there is no knowledge of them'). It is striking that these words come after a rather perfunctory account of Melissus' arguments largely conforming to what we learn from the surviving fragments, though of course highly influenced by intermediary accounts.[62] This raises the possibility that Melissus offered a now lost argument for the position, though the absence of any indication of such an argument in either one of the paraphrases suggests caution. It is also worth noting that Diogenes lists the familiar doctrines as what Melissus 'thought' (ἐδόκει), while the claim about the gods is described as what he 'used to say' (ἔλεγε). Thus the possibility is left open that Diogenes is reporting an anecdote and not indicating something Melissus included in his book. This does not necessarily diminish the value of the report but it does permit us to remain sceptical that an argument from the written book has been lost.

Whatever we make of how Diogenes' claim might have fitted within Melissus' treatise, it suggests an important link with Xenophanes' criticism. The evidence might lead us to think that Melissus entirely dismissed discussion of the divine from his purview and devoted his treatise to the more accessible realm of naturalistic speculation. However, Melissus' strict monism suggests something richer and more robust. He is committed to the thought that what-is is *all encompassing*; this is the rational product of his deductions and requires no particular view on the accessibility of knowledge of the divine. Such a position requires Melissus either to equate what-is with the divine, or to declare himself to be an atheist. The latter option would be unlikely for a figure of Melissus' period[63] and, in any case, the evidence of Diogenes clearly implies that it is *knowledge* of the gods, not their *existence*, which Melissus disclaims.

Therefore, taking Diogenes' report and Melissus' monism in tandem results in something remarkable. Monism of Melissus'

---

[62] For example, the assumption made here that Melissus' subject is the universe (τὸ πᾶν) rather than what-is seems to go back to at least Aristotle.

[63] The same, of course, goes for Xenophanes. See Lesher 1992: 115.

stripe provides a solution to Xenophanes' worry about speaking about the gods. The epistemic gap between man and the divine is indirectly bridged by the deductively transparent conclusion that what-is is one and all encompassing. Melissus can agree that we have no direct knowledge of or acquaintance with the divine, yet also insist that rational deduction from undisputed premises requires, of necessity, that what-is be identified with the divine. An attraction of seeing Xenophanes and Melissus in such a light is the possibility of adding some weight to the idea, apparent in both Plato and Aristotle, that Xenophanes was the founder of the 'Eleatic School'.[64] While it is unlikely that the so called 'Eleatics' were members of a formal philosophical school, it seems plausible that Melissus thought himself to be the heir of an intellectual tradition that included Parmenides as well as Xenophanes.[65] If this is accepted, Melissus may, then, be thought to have elaborated Xenophanes' view just as he does Parmenides'.

On such an account, Melissus is committed to a rational theology much as Xenophanes is, and the rationale for strict monism is further elucidated. Importantly, such an account also properly situates Melissus within his intellectual milieu. The distorting effect of the doxographic accounts of early philosophy in Aristotle and Theophrastus is often and rightly bemoaned; this is particularly acute in their relative neglect of what the Presocratics thought about the divine.[66] The effect of this treatment is the commonplace assumption that the natural philosophy of thinkers like Melissus shares a commitment to the continuing diminution of God's place that has been evident in scientific enquiry since the early modern period. Yet it is just the opposite that is true: natural philosophy is thought to be serious and valuable because it undertakes to make the divine accessible to reason. Sarah Broadie puts this very well: 'We cannot dismiss the identity [between divine reality and the subject matter of natural science] as an alien feature of these philosophers' thought – dead weight from the past or a hollow form ... A better theory is that the identity between gods

---

[64] Cf. Plato, *Sophist* 242c8–d7 and Aristotle, *Metaphysics* 986b21–3.

[65] Schofield (2003: 44–5) has made a case for the existence of some interaction between Xenophanes and Parmenides.

[66] Long (1996: 127–9) makes an excellent argument for this.

and natural principles was never allowed to fade because it helped make sense of the philosophers' deep commitment to the enterprise of scientific enquiry.'[67]

Void and Motion

Melissus' argument against motion on the basis of the impossibility of void has a good claim to be his most influential. Parmenides had, of course, maintained much the same position at B8.26, and many commentators have assumed that void plays an essential role in his argument. This consensus has been vigorously challenged.[68] For our purposes, it should be enough to say that if something like void figures in the background of Parmenides' thinking, or even if an assumption of void makes best sense of his position, it is not obvious from the letter of text that this is the case.[69] What is clear, in any event, is that it is, at least partially, on the basis of the illegitimate notions of division (claimed at line 22), coming-to-be (γένεσις), and perishing (ὄλεθρος) that Parmenides eliminates change in general, and motion in particular, from his picture of Being or what-is.[70] What is striking is that Melissus does *not* follow suit despite the preponderance of the same argumentative machinery (the appeal to the impossibility of coming-to-be and perishing) in the first half of B7. Indeed it is because Melissus noticeably differs from Parmenides in his approach to motion that there has been speculation[71] that it is the former who

[67] Broadie 1999: 206–7.

[68] An appeal from the inference of the impossibility of empty space, or the absence of what-is, to the impossibility of motion is attributed to Parmenides by Guthrie (1965: at 33 and 36 n.1) and Burnet (1930: 181). This reading, partly based on a misreading of Plato's *Theaetetus* 181e3, has been vigorously challenged by a number of interpreters. See, in particular, Kirk and Stokes 1960, Tarán 1965: 110–13 and 196, and, especially, Malcolm 1991: 75–7 for some of the relevant points. (NB Malcolm himself does *not* ultimately endorse the non-void reading.) This does not ultimately mean that Parmenides had no concept of the void, only that the fragments do not present it as having a role in his argument against motion.

[69] There is, of course, no explicit mention of 'void' in Parmenides' text.

[70] There is some debate whether ἀκίνητον in B8.26 refers to motion in particular or change in general or something in between. The details of the debate (see Tarán 1965: 109–10, in particular, for an account) need not concern us too much. However, it is clear that Parmenides, at the very least, does intend to include a denial of locomotion within the scope of his argument for ἀκίνητον. This is made plain at B8.41 (τόπον ἀλλάσσειν).

[71] See Barnes 1982: 217–19 in particular.

first made the vital conceptual connection between void and motion, which proved so prominent in the systems of the atomists and later physicists. I shall have some comments on this connection shortly. However, let us first get a grasp on the argument Melissus makes.

(a) οὐδὲ κενεόν ἐστιν οὐδέν· (b) τὸ γὰρ κενεὸν οὐδέν ἐστιν· (c) οὐκ ἂν οὖν εἴη τό γε μηδέν.

(a) It is not in any way empty. (b) For the empty is nothing. (c) Well what is nothing could not very well exist.

The upshot of this first piece of the argument is clear enough: what-is contains no void (τὸ κενεόν). In (a) and (b) we find a lovely example of rhetorical *epanados* or *commutatio* in which there is a chiastic and reciprocal exchange of the syntactic functions of κενεόν and οὐδέν. The result is a neat and rhetorically pleasing argument. This, if nothing else, is a strong reproof to Aristotle's claim of the 'crudeness' of Melissus.[72]

However, the details of the text are less than straightforward. The first worry is the subject of (a), which yields a number of possible construals. One may take οὐδέν as the subject. This suggests a translation in the vein of Burnet's 'nor is anything empty'.[73] Another possibility is to follow Graham by translating the sentence expletively as 'nor is there any void'.[74] A third possibility adopted by both Loenen and Sedley is to take what-is as the subject of this first sentence of the argument. They argue that the final sentence of B7 unambiguously suggests that it is Melissus' typical 'what-is' that is the relevant subject in the argument.[75] Loenen is also right to note that what-is is certainly Melissus' subject by the time he writes οὐδὲ κινεῖται a few

---

[72] See Lausberg 1998: Section 801. The use here is not strictly an *antimetabole*, a term reserved for an *epanados* which is also an antithesis. We might think of a famous example from Herodotus, where Xerxes is quoted after seeing the daring (and deceptive) exploits of Queen Artemisia of Halicarnassus at Salamis: οἱ μὲν ἄνδρες γεγόνασί μοι γυναῖκες, αἱ δὲ γυναῖκες ἄνδρες. A useful English example that, like the one in Melissus, is not strictly antithetical is 'I mean what I say, and I say what I mean.'

[73] Burnet 1930: 323.

[74] Graham 2010: 473. One might think here that the lack of the article before κενεόν, as in (b), slightly discounts his translation.

[75] Loenen 1959: 163 and Sedley 1982: 178 n.7. Note also that Melissus is clearly taking what-is as the subject in the subsequent argument against motion: οὐδὲ κινεῖται (nor does **what-is** move).

sentences hence, suggesting that the subject is consistent throughout the argument. Such a reading takes οὐδέν adverbially, as the
translation provided above suggests.[76]

I follow Loenen and Sedley in adopting this translation, but
I would suggest that the greatest argument in its favour is neither
the final sentence of the fragment nor the subject of οὐδὲ κινεῖται,
though both points certainly suggest such a translation. Rather it is
the fact that such a construal yields what I will argue to be
Melissus' central thesis, as it will be developed in the coming
argument. It is not simply the twin claims that there is no void and
that void is nothing that he wishes to aver, but also that none of
what-is is empty, i.e. constituted by void. That Melissus is concerned with internal void mixed in with what-is will emerge in the
below interpretation.

The second sentence, (b), is more straightforwardly construed as
'for what is empty is nothing'. Here we find the essential identification of void with the nothing. For the moment, I hold off on further
discussion of what this identification amounts to. It is (c) that has
been subject to the greatest uncertainty. The appearance of the
particle οὖν has encouraged the thought that Melissus had it in
mind to make an inference on the strength of the previous two
claims, i.e. (a) and (b).[77] Yet a sound inference is not readily
apparent. We might, if such an inferential reading of οὖν were
correct, expect Melissus to move from the dual claims that what-
is is not empty and that the empty is nothing to the conclusion that
what-is is not nothing. Yet such a claim has no obvious place in the
context of the argument in B7, since we have already agreed, on the
basis of Q, that what-is is something. It is rather the identification of
the *void* with nothing that is at stake in the argument.

In any case, the search for an inference in (c) is unnecessary
because οὐκ οὖν followed by γε is not to be construed inferentially
but rather as the negation of γοῦν meaning 'at any rate not'.[78]
The above remarks follow the lead of Sedley and, to a lesser

---

[76] That Melissus would be satisfied which such a construction of the Greek is confirmed by
comparison with B8: καὶ ταῦτα πάντα ἑτεροιοῦσθαι, καὶ ὅ τι ἦν τε καὶ ὃ νῦν **οὐδὲν** ὅμοῖον
εἶναι.

[77] Barnes (1982: 218) takes it thus and calls it 'logical nonsense'.

[78] Loenen 1959: 163 and Sedley 1982: 178 n.7. See Denniston 1959: 422–5.

extent, Loenen.[79] We might ask though what we are meant to take away from (c). The grammar and the sense of the sentence suggest that the claim made is not be supported (at least not entirely) by (a) and (b); (c) itself is, or at least appears to be, a highly plausible but unsubstantiated claim. Why does Melissus deploy the optative mood here? As we have seen, optatives typically function within hypothetical counterfactual reasoning in Melissus' fragments and not, as here in B7, in supposed statements of fact. An answer emerges if we remember how **Q** prepares the way for B1 by getting Melissus' reader to agree to the unobjectionable hypothesis that what-is *is* on the basis that only if so can we say something about it. It is from this fundamental agreement that the nest of arguments we have considered emerge. The optative mood then invites us to apply the same reasoning we accepted in **Q** to justify (c). Thus Melissus takes it as read that void, understood as nothing, cannot be. On this line of interpretation, the absence of an inferential move from (a) and (b) to (c) is absolutely natural and evidences no logical confusion.

What we find then in (c) is not an inference made on the basis of the previous two clauses, but rather the introduction of a piece of evidence to justify the claim made in (a) that what-is is in no way empty. If we agree on the strength of (b) that void is nothing, we can arrive at (a) by accepting that the nothing cannot exist. Therefore, the particle γοῦν functions unsurprisingly in its commonest use as introducing a 'part proof' for, but not as the inferential product of, the preceding statement.[80]

The void then is nothing and has no place within what-is. I say 'within' because the adverbial reading of (a) implies that Melissus has in mind the thought that what-is is empty or intermixed with the empty. That this 'internal' reading of the void is correct is supported not only by (a) but also by the appeal to 'dense' and rare' in the coming argument against motion. In any case, it must

---

[79] Loenen develops a reading of (c) that takes what-is as its subject. This requires taking τό γε as referring to what-is. I leave further details aside except to say that this takes the grammar past its breaking point for little interpretative gain.

[80] Denniston 1959: 451: 'Much the commonest use of γοῦν is to introduce a statement which is, *pro tanto*, evidence for a preceding statement. This has been well termed "part proof".'

be right because Melissus, by B7, has already established that what-is is spatially infinite in all directions. External void, then, is not on the agenda.[81] This will become clearer as we go through in detail the argument targeting motion.

If this correctly charts the shape of Melissus' argument against the place of void within what-is, we ought to wonder precisely what he means by the claim that the void is nothing. We might consider, in this context, the interesting suggestion David Sedley has made that the conceptual difficulties of grasping the notion of the void were worked out over a period of time. As such, he maintains that there is evidence for an early understanding of the void as something like a space/place occupier and a later, more developed view where void is viewed purely *as* 'empty space' and not as emptiness *in* a space or a place.[82] On Sedley's view of the argument in B7, Melissus' understanding of the void, though it possibly appears to be equated with the mature concept of empty space, is at least as well matched to the emptiness *in such-and-such space/place*.

Why is such a distinction relevant for our account of Melissus? Well if he did indeed understand void as internally intermixed with what-is, it does not seem likely that he understood the void as *absolutely nothing*, i.e. that of which we cannot predicate anything. Presumably internal void, understood as a space/place occupier, could be said to be in such and such location and occupy such and such measureable space.[83] The point then, if we again keep **Q** in mind, is not that we cannot say anything at all about the void, but that we cannot say anything at all about the void as *if it were what-is*. As we have agreed that what-is exhausts what there is, in both time and space, we are obliged to agree that the void cannot be.

Motion: Text and Translation

(a) οὐδὲ κινεῖται· ὑποχωρῆσαι γὰρ οὐκ ἔχει οὐδαμῇ, ἀλλὰ πλέων ἐστίν. εἰ μὲν γὰρ κενεὸν ἦν, ὑπεχώρει ἂν εἰς τὸ κενεόν· κενεοῦ δὲ μὴ ἐόντος οὐκ ἔχει ὅκη ὑποχωρήσει.

---

[81] Again, this reflects the readings of Loenen and Sedley.   [82] Sedley 1982.
[83] Loenen 1959.

(b) πυκνὸν δὲ καὶ ἀραιὸν οὐκ ἂν εἴη. τὸ γὰρ ἀραιὸν οὐκ ἀνυστὸν πλέων εἶναι ὁμοίως τῷ πυκνῷ, ἀλλ' ἤδη τὸ ἀραιόν γε κενεώτερον γίνεται τοῦ πυκνοῦ.

(c) κρίσιν δὲ ταύτην χρὴ ποιήσασθαι τοῦ πλέω καὶ τοῦ μὴ πλέω· εἰ μὲν οὖν χωρεῖ τι ἢ εἰσδέχεται, οὐ πλέων· εἰ δὲ μήτε χωρεῖ μήτε εἰσδέχεται, πλέων.

(d) ἀνάγκη τοίνυν πλέων εἶναι, εἰ κενεὸν μὴ ἔστιν. εἰ τοίνυν πλέων ἐστίν, οὐ κινεῖται.

(a) Nor does it move. For it cannot give way at any point, but is full. For if there were the empty, it [i.e. what-is] would give way into the empty; but as there is no such thing as the empty, it can nowhere give way.

(b) Dense and rare could not be. For it is impossible for what is rare to be equally full as what is dense, but already the rare thereby becomes emptier than the dense.

(c) And this must be made the mark of what is full and what is not full: if something yields or accommodates, it is not full. But if it neither yields nor accommodates, it is full.

(d) So then, it is necessary that it is full, if it is not empty. Therefore, if it is full, it does not move.

Melissus begins in (a) by announcing that the aim of the subsequent reasoning is to deny motion. While it is not explicitly stated, it is unambiguous that he makes an inference from the non-existence of void to the impossibility of motion. This becomes evident in the argument itself (cf. (d) in particular) and is certainly how Simplicius understood Melissus' reasoning (*In Phys.* 104. 3–5). In (a) we find the heart of the argument: it is fullness that is the impediment to motion. If there were such a thing as emptiness it would intermix with what-is and make it less than completely full. This would allow for something like springiness or resilience. What-is, if intermixed with void, could compress and allow for movement.

Such an understanding of motion, which for Melissus I take to be limited to *internal* motion (for what could be outside what-is?), does have a good deal of intuitive plausibility, as Barnes notes.[84] Yet does such an argument successfully eliminate the possibility of motion? Well, in the first place, we have to grant to Melissus the

[84] Barnes 1982: 219.

premise that it is impossible for two bodies to occupy the same place simultaneously. Perhaps this is just an innocuous and uncontentious thought that no one would think to challenge. Yet even if the impossibility of co-location is accepted, why, for example, should we think that motion is impossible within a plenum? If I drop a penny in a bottle, fill the bottle to its brim with water, and ensure that there is no internal empty pocket of air, the coin may still move within the water.

On the latter point, Melissus does have a reply. In (c) we are told that the necessary mark or criterion of what is full is its inability to yield or receive. On such a definition the water in the bottle would count not simply as full but as something intermixed with void: this is a fairly natural understanding of the state of liquids. If a stack of bricks of a solid, e.g. gold, is one's model of fullness, it is easy to see why the apparent receptivity of water to the coin would make the liquid seem less than completely full and thus intermixed with the empty. Melissus does, of course, also have recourse to his denial of alteration and rearrangement earlier in B7.

Melissus' notion of the full (πλέων) is worth examining. Perhaps one natural view of what he has in mind, in hypothetically considering motion and the void, is something like a fifteen puzzle. In such a puzzle there are fifteen sliding squares, arranged in a four by four configuration, with one space empty. The puzzle is solved by manipulating the squares, one by one, into the recurrent empty space until the numbered squares are in the correct order. The thought, then, is that what-is would have a discrete pocket of void that would shift within what-is after its previous location became occupied in the course of the action of locomotion. Yet, appealing as it may seem, we can safely discount the possibility that this is analogous to the Melissan model.

Such a view, though an entirely plausible view of internal void, and indeed of something less than completely full, cannot, I maintain, be what Melissus has in mind. One concern is that it is unclear if the fifteen puzzle model can adequately capture the non-particulate theory of matter that is evident here. Importantly, we do not find any hint that the target location of motion would require a minimum amount of empty space (say, for instance, something the size of an atom) for something to move into it.

Additionally, the fifteen puzzle analogy fails because such a model has already been ruled out by the argument for homogeneity and would make the reasoning here superfluous. We have already agreed that what-is is entirely qualitatively uniform; if this is taken as read, a discrete pocket of void could not even hypothetically be a possibility in B7.[85] Rather the point I take Melissus to be making is that motion and void are impossible *even if* the void is entirely blended in with what-is so as to ensure qualitative uniformity throughout. So, then, we ought to think not of the internal, discrete pockets of air in the sponge as a useful analogy but rather of something like a meringue where the air has been uniformly blended throughout the egg and sugar mixture. Thus Melissus' concept of fullness implies that what-is is completely solid without intermixed void, and also impenetrable.[86]

I stress the above interpretation of Melissus' understanding of a, *per impossibile*, uniform, homogeneous mixture composed of what-is and the empty because it is essential to making sense of the progression of the argument. There is a mistaken assumption, evident in much of the secondary literature, that (a) is intended as an argument against the fifteen puzzle view of what-is and the empty.[87] On such accounts the introduction of the dense and the rare in (b) is said to be a mere supplemental, largely unnecessary addition rather than an important explication of the model of motion and void Melissus has in mind.[88] Such an interpretation is no doubt the reason, as Sedley rightly maintains, for the strained rendering of ὑποχωρεῖν and χωρεῖν as simple verbs of locomotion rather than as the standard 'to give way'.[89] In Burnet, for instance, we find the second sentence of (b) translated as 'for it has nowhere to betake itself'.

Since the verb ὑποχωρεῖν first appears in (a) and its various forms continue to be found throughout the argument, it makes

---

[85] Of course the atomists will bite the bullet here as they are not committed to homogeneity. They will agree that void is what-is-not but allow it in addition to what-is.

[86] See Barnes (1982: 224–6) for an excellent discussion of Melissus' notion of solidity and impenetrability.

[87] See Barnes 1982: 219 and Burnet 1930: 323 for two instances among many.

[88] Barnes (1982: 219) claims: 'The sentences about "dense" and "rare" ... muddy the waters of the argument.'

[89] Sedley 1982: 178.

better sense to think that a single model of motion is to be understood in B7 and that this model is one of compression or springiness. This helps to make best sense of the argument in (a) for why what-is cannot give way into the empty.

What sort of hypothetical notion of motion does Melissus canvass? The understanding evident in the secondary literature is that we ought to think of local motion as the relevant concept, i.e. there is some part of what-is less than completely full, permitting, by giving way, another part (presumably adjacent) to move into it.[90] Thus the coming discussion of the dense and the rare is intended to suggest that what-is does not have different degrees of density in different spatial regions. My discussion above of the inadequacy of the fifteen puzzle is partially intended to tell against this attribution of *per impossibile* local motion. Melissus has no reason to discuss any concept of motion that entails parts or gaps, just as he has no reason to discuss the possibility of external void: what-is is homogeneous and exhausts what there is. This brings us back to the meringue: a blend of void and what-is could compress and rarefy, *as a whole*, while still maintaining qualitative homogeneity at any given instant. Such a model of motion is surely more relevant to Melissus' argument at this point in the treatise.[91] In addition, such a reading makes better sense of why he moves from the standard word for motion (κινεῖται) in (a) to the more

---

[90] See Loenen 1959: 165 and Barnes 1982: 226. Barnes provides a fascinating and very illuminating discussion of Melissus' notion of fullness as impenetrability and examines its validity in the face of a Leibnizian objection. The worry is that it seems imaginable and perhaps even logically possible that a body can move into a location, though completely full and in no way empty, were it penetrable in some way. Fullness on such an account would not be sufficient without an argument for impenetrability that Melissus arguably lacks. My point is simply that, whether or not Melissus' notion of fullness holds up to scrutiny, Melissus has no need to consider parts or degrees here, as such things have clearly been eliminated from the conversation earlier prior to B7.

[91] In this way, it is one version of 'weak' homogeneity that Melissus targets (what-is is at any given time homogeneous but not homogeneous through time, i.e. different iterations of what-is, on comparison, would not be identical). Surely, though, Melissus in the first half of B7 has already eliminated such a possibility? This is true if we are taking the first half of B7 as necessary for the argument against motion and void to go through. I maintain rather that the two halves of B7 work *in parallel* to develop the 'strong' version of homogeneity I have canvassed. If this is so, nothing established in the first half of B7 is needed to make sense of the second half; this makes best sense of our evidence because it is unclear if the argument targeting motion did indeed follow as it does in Simplicius. For example, in the *MXG*, motion is discussed prior to alteration, pain, and anguish.

specific notion of giving way (ὑποχωρεῖν). It seems clear that 'giving way' is the only species of motion left that could pose a difficulty for Melissus' picture, and presumably this is because such motion need not entail heterogeneity or rearrangement in the synchronic senses described above.[92]

In (b) we find a discussion of the rare and the dense. The rejection of these concepts I take to be in support of the compression model of motion developed in (a). Were void inter-mixed with what-is, this would allow for different degrees of density at different stages of compression.[93] Yet, in the second sentence of the section, we find that Melissus seems to equate degrees of density with degrees of fullness: 'for it is impossible for what is rare to be equally full as what is dense'. If density is to correspond with fullness, it seems that something completely dense would also be completely full, i.e. Melissus is not, in fact, eliminating the concept of dense at all. We would, then, be obliged to translate πυκνὸν δὲ καὶ ἀραιὸν οὐκ ἂν εἴη as something like 'nor is it both dense *and* rare', signalling that what-is cannot at one time or place be dense and at another become rare.[94]

Must we accept this conclusion? Perhaps it may be objected that the comparative (κενεώτερον) suggests caution, as it arguably implies that both the rare and the dense contain void in some respect. However, this is far from definitive, as the dense is not in turn said to be fuller than the rare and it is quite clear that it is rarity alone that Melissus is determined to eliminate. I submit that the text is ambiguous on this point and leaves us with no compelling reason to prefer one reading over another.

---

[92] My interpretation of the argument against rearrangement probably would *not* allow for compression or springiness. However, such a model of motion comes closest to preserving what Melissus has already established. It is worth remembering that he does *not* strictly need an argument against motion: the fragments, including the first half of B7, are sufficient to eliminate any possibility of motion. This suggests that the latter half of B7 is intended to provide a secondary or parallel argument serving as reinforcement. It follows then that Melissus may, for the sake of argument, not be taking for granted the particularly strong understanding of rearrangement I have attributed to him in the first half of B7.

[93] This, of course, does not imply that we need to resort to any discussion of degrees of density at different *parts* of what-is at any given instant.

[94] Loenen (1959: 168) takes this view.

Yet a look at an intriguing report from Aristotle might suggest a solution to this worry about the status of the concept of the dense, while also throwing some light on the compression model of motion I have attributed to Melissus.

εἰσὶν δέ τινες οἳ διὰ τοῦ μανοῦ καὶ πυκνοῦ οἴονται φανερὸν εἶναι ὅτι ἔστι κενόν. εἰ μὲν γὰρ μὴ ἔστι μανὸν καὶ πυκνόν, οὐδὲ συνιέναι καὶ πιλεῖσθαι οἷόν τε· εἰ δὲ τοῦτο μὴ εἴη, ἢ ὅλως κίνησις οὐκ ἔσται, ἢ κυμανεῖ τὸ ὅλον, ὥσπερ ἔφη Ξοῦθος. (Physics 216b22–6)

There are some who think it is evident from rarity and the density that there is void. For if rarity and density do not exist, nothing can compress or contract. But if this were not to take place, either there will be no motion at all, or the universe will swell up, just as Xuthus said.

This tantalising report is marshalled by both Barnes and KRS as a curious but rather obscure parallel to Melissus' argument.[95] About Xuthus we can say little more than that Simplicius (*In Phys.* 663.24) calls him a Pythagorean and that he may be the Xuthus called the father of Ion of Chios (DK36A3), placing him in the first half of the fifth century. From Aristotle's wording it is not entirely clear how much of the reported argument we can attribute to Xuthus: is it just that the universe swells up, or the fuller point that were there no rarity or density either there would be no motion at all or the universe will swell? I am inclined to attribute, speculatively it must be said, the core of the argument to Xuthus on the evidence that, by mentioning him by name, Aristotle is surely including him among those (τινες) he is reporting, implicating Xuthus fully in the report.

If this is along the right lines, two points emerge. First, Aristotle is describing an argument that eliminates degrees of density not the concept of the dense itself. It is *relative* rarity and density, i.e. degrees less dense than absolute density, which are at stake. Indeed the idea that absent density and rarity nothing could compress or contract implicitly affirms the idea of something absolutely dense. That Melissus might have had such an argument in view is further supported by the disjunction between motionlessness and swelling that is said to result from the elimination of relative rarity and

[95] Barnes 1982: 226 n.30 and KRS: 398 n.1.

density; this suggests a close overlap with B7. Both Xuthus and Melissus can agree that there is such a thing as absolute density and that there are no degrees of density. Where they differ, as we shall see, is that Xuthus maintains that the elimination of degrees of density still allows for swelling.

Barnes and KRS see a possible criticism of Parmenides' full and finite universe in Aristotle's report. Perhaps Xuthus suggested that Parmenides failed to counter the possibility of internal swelling thus allowing expansion without breaking the limits of what-is. This makes some sense but we can say little more. On firmer ground though might be the thought that Melissus is countering the understanding of motion that Aristotle describes here. Xuthus, or someone among his number, is said to permit a species of motion (swelling) despite the non-existence of degrees of density and rarity. Combatting such a position makes a good deal of sense of the progression of Melissus' argument and the seeming parenthetical remarks on density and rarity. Therefore, appealing to the compression and expansion model of motion I have attributed to the argument is perfectly in keeping with a response to the kind of position Aristotle reports.

Locomotion from one region to another is not what is most important here but rather the idea that fullness does not eliminate the swelling up of what-is.[96] One suggestion is that Melissus countered such an argument by proposing that what-is is spatially infinite.[97] Certainly this takes the bite out of Xuthus' argument, but it hardly tackles the core of the proposed model of motion. A more direct line might be to think that Melissus' emphasis on fullness and the description of its criterion (κρίσις) are a response to the Xuthan position that the absence of degrees of density is not a sufficient condition to eliminate the possibility of swelling. This would help to explain why the verb εἰσδέχεται is introduced in (c). Unless we were to think that Melissus intends χωρεῖ and εἰσδέχεται to be synonyms, something the twice repeated disjunction

---

[96] I take it that by 'bulging' or 'swelling' the thought is not that one bit expands and this is compensated for by the contraction by another bit (Aristotle's remarks in the context of his report perhaps suggest such a reading). The words of the report itself make it plain that without density and rarity there can be *no* contraction but there *can* be swelling.

[97] Barnes 1982: 226 n.30.

between the two strongly tells against, it should be clear that he wants to eliminate two *distinct* species of motion that would mark something out as less than full. Both verbs then jointly serve to demonstrate that fullness (i.e. the absence of any attribution of degrees of dense and rare) *is* sufficient to counter both contraction and expansion; the latter, of course, taken as equivalent to Xuthus' swelling. Such an argument is perfectly at home in B7, even without the assumption of a dialectical context. Yet if we see Xuthus or his ilk in the background, Melissus' strategy becomes even more readily explicable.

(d) concludes Melissus' argument. In absolutely standard form, he completes the ring of his demonstration by repeating the theses that what-is is full and that motion is impossible. We find a characteristic modalisation of the conclusion with the introduction of ἀνάγκη (necessity) and the reiteration of the inferential structure of the argument: there is no such thing as empty, *therefore* what-is is full, *therefore* it does not move. However, we also find something new in B7: the argument is, strictly speaking, unnecessary. The first half of B7 is independently sufficient to prove motion impossible. The 'strong' notions of homogeneity and unity clearly eliminate the possibility of motion. Why, then, does Melissus provide such a detailed argument? What seems likely is that the dialectical context that frames B8 is emerging here.

My reading of the argument has insisted that homogeneity and unity *are* assumed but only in their synchronic senses, as the two halves of B7 operate in parallel rather than in succession. This suggests that Melissus is adopting a new strategy of hypothetical concession. The idea seems to be something like this. He can back off, at least temporarily, from the strong theses I have attributed to him in the first half and still show that motion is impossible on the basis of fullness. This puts him in a better position because he is reliant on fewer contestable premises. Such a strategy is well-suited to a particularly hot-button position, directly in contravention of the evidence of sense experience, like the impossibility of motion. We shall see next how the assumption of such a method makes best sense of B8.

B8: SENSE EXPERIENCE AND PLURALITY

(1) μέγιστον μὲν οὖν σημεῖον οὗτος ὁ λόγος ὅτι ἓν μόνον ἔστιν· ἀτὰρ καὶ τάδε σημεῖα.

(2) εἰ γὰρ ἦν πολλά, τοιαῦτα χρὴ αὐτὰ εἶναι οἷόν περ ἐγώ φημι τὸ ἓν εἶναι. εἰ γὰρ ἔστι γῆ καὶ ὕδωρ καὶ ἀὴρ καὶ πῦρ καὶ σίδηρος καὶ χρυσός, καὶ τὸ μὲν ζῶν τὸ δὲ τεθνηκός, καὶ μέλαν καὶ λευκὸν καὶ τὰ ἄλλα, ὅσα φασὶν οἱ ἄνθρωποι εἶναι ἀληθῆ, εἰ δὴ ταῦτα ἔστι, καὶ ἡμεῖς ὀρθῶς ὁρῶμεν καὶ ἀκούομεν, εἶναι χρὴ ἕκαστον[1] τοιοῦτον οἷόν περ τὸ πρῶτον ἔδοξεν ἡμῖν, καὶ μὴ μεταπίπτειν μηδὲ γίνεσθαι ἑτεροῖον, ἀλλὰ ἀεὶ εἶναι ἕκαστον οἷόν πέρ ἐστιν.

(3) νῦν δέ φαμεν ὀρθῶς ὁρᾶν καὶ ἀκούειν καὶ συνιέναι· δοκεῖ δὲ ἡμῖν τό τε θερμὸν ψυχρὸν γίνεσθαι καὶ τὸ ψυχρὸν θερμὸν καὶ τὸ σκληρὸν μαλθακὸν καὶ τὸ μαλθακὸν σκληρὸν καὶ τὸ ζῶν ἀποθνήσκειν καὶ ἐκ μὴ ζῶντος γίνεσθαι, καὶ ταῦτα πάντα ἑτεροιοῦσθαι, καὶ ὅ τι ἦν τε καὶ ὃ νῦν οὐδὲν ὁμοῖον εἶναι, ἀλλ' ὅ τε σίδηρος σκληρὸς ἐὼν τῷ δακτύλῳ κατατρίβεσθαι ὁμουρέων, καὶ χρυσὸς καὶ λίθος καὶ ἄλλο ὅ τι ἰσχυρὸν δοκεῖ εἶναι πᾶν, ἐξ ὕδατός τε γῆ καὶ λίθος γίνεσθαι· <ὥστε συμβαίνει μήτε ὁρᾶν μήτε τὰ ὄντα γινώσκειν.>

(4) οὐ τοίνυν ταῦτα ἀλλήλοις ὁμολογεῖ. φαμένοις γὰρ εἶναι πολλὰ καὶ ἀίδια καὶ εἴδη τε καὶ ἰσχὺν ἔχοντα, πάντα ἑτεροιοῦσθαι ἡμῖν δοκεῖ καὶ μεταπίπτειν ἐκ τοῦ ἑκάστοτε ὁρωμένου. δῆλον τοίνυν, ὅτι οὐκ ὀρθῶς ἑωρῶμεν οὐδὲ ἐκεῖνα πολλὰ ὀρθῶς δοκεῖ εἶναι·

(5) οὐ γὰρ ἂν μετέπιπτεν, εἰ ἀληθῆ ἦν· ἀλλ' ἦν οἷόν περ ἐδόκει ἕκαστον τοιοῦτον. τοῦ γὰρ ἐόντος ἀληθινοῦ κρεῖσσον οὐδέν.

(6) ἢν δὲ μεταπέσῃ, τὸ μὲν ἐὸν ἀπώλετο, τὸ δὲ οὐκ ἐὸν γέγονεν. οὕτως οὖν, εἰ πολλὰ εἴη, τοιαῦτα χρὴ εἶναι οἷόν περ τὸ ἕν.

Introduction and Section (1)

Melissus' B8, like his B6, is quoted by Simplicius in his commentary on Aristotle's *De Caelo*, rather than in the *Physics*

---

[1] Aristocles F7 (Chiesara) reads εἶναι ἐχρῆν καὶ τὸ ὄν for εἶναι χρὴ ἕκαστον. With Reale (1970: 400), I see no reason to prefer this over Simplicius' text.

commentary, where 80 percent of Melissus' fragments (as a percentage of distinct fragments and not total word count) are found.[2] This may suggest that a central problem we face – the place of B8 within the overall structure of the treatise – is particularly challenging, as the fragment is quoted independently of the majority of what survives. From (1) it is clear, for example, that B8 is somehow distinct from our other fragments, and perhaps a part of a separate section of the original text. Fortunately, our surviving paraphrases are of some help. The *MXG* (974a24–974b9) seems to suggest that an argument, corresponding in principle to what we find in B8, followed immediately from B7, and acted as a complementary proof. In addition, Simplicius' introduction to the fragment explicitly confirms his belief in its placement after B7.[3]

The *MXG* account suggests that following what is found in B7 came an argument against construing what-is as a composition of multiple entities, either in the form of a mixture or as made up of distinct layers of discrete elements. What is striking is that the argument described by Anonymous is not immediately apparent in B8; yet there are strong overlaps in the language and details of both, suggesting that they correspond to each other. The *MXG* (974a29–974b1) dismisses the putative layered account of what-is using the language of rubbing away (ἐπιπροσθήσεως δ' οὔσης ἐν τῇ τρίψει γίγνεσθαι ἂν ἕκαστον φανερόν), much as iron, thought to be tough, is rubbed away with a finger in (3) (σίδηρος σκληρὸς ἐὼν τῷ δακτύλῳ κατατρίβεσθαι ὁμουρέων). A further example (mysterious but arresting) is found in the resemblance of the statement found in the *MXG* that it is only in certain ways (e.g. what-is as a mixture, or composed of layers) that what-is could be plural and yet appear as one to the final sentence of B8:

---

[2] Intriguingly, we find part of this text quoted by Aristocles of Messene in a discussion of those that dismiss sense experience, alongside the criticism that Melissus must trust in the evidence of the senses in order to criticise sense perception as he does. See Chiesara 2001: 40–5 and 155–60. We shall below turn to this point. It is clear enough, however, that Simplicius' text is to be preferred, as Reale (1970: 400) accepts. The differences, in any case, are largely stylistic.

[3] εἰπὼν γὰρ περὶ τοῦ ὄντος, ὅτι ἕν ἐστι καὶ ἀγένητον καὶ ἀκίνητον καὶ μηδενὶ κενῷ διειλημμένον, ἀλλ' ὅλον ἑαυτοῦ πλῆρες, ἐπάγει· 'B8'.

διὰ τούτων δὲ τῶν τρόπων κἂν εἶναι πολλὰ κἂν ἡμῖν οἷ' ἔστι φαίνεσθαι μόνως.

In these ways could they both be many and appear to us singular, as they are. (974b2–3)

οὕτως οὖν, εἰ πολλὰ εἴη, τοιαῦτα χρὴ εἶναι οἷόν περ τὸ ἕν.

Therefore, if there were many, they ought to be of just the same sort as the One is.

Whatever we make of the precise nature of these similarities, we must contend with the tension between the claim found at the beginning of B8 that 'the greatest proof' that what-is is one has already been given and that the following fragment consists of others of lower status, and the impression evident in the *MXG* that the argument corresponding to B8 is no different in kind or motivation from what was paraphrased previously.

It is common in the literature to think that B8 is representative of a different section of Melissus' treatise outside of (or at least distinct from, if not independent of) the deductive structure we find in the other fragments. Karl Reinhardt has suggested that B8 is a not rejection of plurality but an attempt to offer a systematic account of the sensible world in parallel with the second half of Parmenides' poem.[4] Stephen Makin sees a dialectical strategy at work targeting an anti-Eleatic position not evident in the other fragments.[5] Another reading, evident in KRS, Barnes, and Palmer, is that B8, though aimed at plurality, is an attack upon the evidence gained about reality through sense perception: the fragment is aimed at the common assumptions humans make about reality and not at any particular Presocratic natural philosophy.[6]

There are merits to these interpretations and my indebtedness to them will be obvious. However, in the following account of the argumentative strategy of B8, I will try to emphasise a number of points that have not been given

[4] Reinhardt 1916: 71–4.
[5] Makin 2005: 263–88. Palmer (2009: 213 n.37) offers a strong criticism of Makin's assumption that Melissus and Parmenides were Eleatic 'allies'. I think Palmer is probably correct to reject the close association between the Eleatics that Makin seems to think obvious. However, it should become clear that, although we disagree on many details, I think that Makin is correct to hold that some dialectical strategy is in place in B8.
[6] KRS: 400, Barnes 1982: 298–302, and Palmer 2009: 210–16. That the unreliability of sense perception is the main point of B8 is also suggested by Simplicius.

sufficient attention. First, I submit that B8, as the *MXG* suggests, is *not* separate from the deductive strategy we have seen in the other fragments. Rather it is entirely consistent with what is demonstrated up to B7 and follows naturally on from that fragment. Secondly, I will emphasise that the criticism of the validity of sense perception is invoked for the sake of demonstrating that what-is is not a plurality. This constitutes the heart of the proposed interpretation: B8 is not ultimately about the sensible world but rather about the attempt and inevitable failure to make the evidence of the senses cohere with what Melissus has previously demonstrated about the uniqueness of what-is. Thirdly, I will propose (*contra* Palmer, KRS, and Reale) that, while assuming that rival Presocratic systems are relevant is not necessary to make sense of B8, the argument developed in the fragment is perfectly consistent with its targeting rival Presocratics as well as everyday ontologies.

Melissus' strategy in B8 bears a close resemblance to what we have identified as his use of complementary or supplemental arguments in earlier fragments. In the argument for uniqueness, for example, we noted that B4 and B5 are jointly sufficient to demonstrate that attribute independently. B6, then, considered the minimal example of plurality (namely that what-is is two), and was marshalled as a vivid but, strictly speaking, deductively unnecessary reinforcement. Much the same approach was found in the consideration of a change by a single hair (the smallest alteration conceivable) in B7.

Consider the start of (2):

εἰ γὰρ ἦν πολλά, τοιαῦτα χρὴ αὐτὰ εἶναι οἷόν περ ἐγώ φημι τὸ ἓν εἶναι.

For if there were many things, they ought to be such as what I say the One is.

At first blush, it seems that Melissus is hypothetically posing the possibility that what-is, as it has been described heretofore in the treatise, is multiply instantiated. Yet the manner in which he proceeds belies this reading. In order to demonstrate that what-is is as described and also unique, all Melissus would be obliged to point out is that what-is is spatially infinite (all-encompassing) and that this eliminates the possibility of plurality. B4, B5, and B6 have already covered this ground. The argument in B8 suggests that he is considering for argumentative reasons only a restricted subset of the attributes of what-is, namely sempiternity and immutability.[7] In (5), we shall see that Melissus returns to this point and adds an argument for why what-is (whether one or many) must exhibit these attributes.

Why, at this point in the work, would Melissus ignore or temporarily put to one side much of what he has purported to demonstrate? The logic of B8 turns on dismissing the reality of the objects of our experience.[8] This is done by appealing to the mutability and instability of these objects as they appear to us. In the wake of B7, this makes good sense. In that fragment, species of change (alteration, rearrangement, and locomotion) were eliminated from Melissus' picture of what-is and this was done for the explicit end of further establishing uniqueness.[9] B8 works in parallel: change is considered, as the apparent datum of sense experience, in order to eliminate it and, by discounting the evidence of the senses, prove uniqueness. Yet, in addition to the exploration of the illicit entailments of change (e.g. *ex nihilo* coming-to-be), we find a look at the tension between holding that everyday objects of experience are real and the mutability of these objects according to their presentation to the senses. In short, B8 is an attempt, by a different means, to reinforce the arguments of B7. If this is correct and change plays a crucial role in B8, it makes sense that only those attributes that are vitiated specifically by the existence of change, i.e. sempiternity and immutability, should be on the table.

Section (2): Text and Translation

Section (2) continues by posing the possibility that the objects of our experience are real:

---

[7] Palmer (2009: 212) rightly makes this point.

[8] I reiterate that, at this point, I do not mean to restrict these items to so-called 'everyday' ontologies of common experience or to the metaphysical results of Presocratic theoreticians.

[9] καὶ οὔτ' ἂν ἀπόλοιτο οὔτε μεῖζον γίνοιτο οὔτε μετακοσμέοιτο οὔτε ἀλγεῖ οὔτε ἀνιᾶται· εἰ γάρ τι τούτων πάσχοι, οὐκ ἂν ἔτι ἓν εἴη.

For if there is earth, water, air, fire, iron and gold, and one thing living[10] and another dead, and black and white, and all the things people say are real – if indeed there are these things, and we see and hear correctly, each of these must be just as it first seemed to us, and they cannot change or become different in quality,[11] but each must always be just as it is.

The list of hypothetical entities listed by Melissus here includes the canonical four elements, natural kinds, and contraries. Such a list encourages speculation about who Melissus thinks holds these objects of experience to be real. Does the inclusion of the four elements suggest Empedocles, or that of the opposites Anaxagoras, or perhaps other Presocratic philosophers? Such a view has received sustained criticism from Reale and Palmer, who both take the mention of what people say to be real (ὅσα φασὶν οἱ ἄνθρωποι εἶναι ἀληθῆ) as strong evidence that it is only the common opinions of ordinary people that are under consideration.[12] I hold off from detailed consideration here except to point out that the text encourages us not to decide actively between the theories of rival Presocratics and everyday, ordinary opinions, but rather to *include* all those people (philosophically inclined or not) who rely on the testimony of sense experience.[13] The list of entities coupled with the dragnet clause (ὅσα φασὶν οἱ ἄνθρωποι εἶναι ἀληθῆ) suggests such a broad view.

---

[10] The text here (τὸ μὲν ζῷον) demands some consideration. Both here and in (3), Heiberg (in the *CAG*) prints τὸ ζῷον. Presumably, this is understood as the Ionic neuter present participle of ζῶ, which DK translates as 'lebend'. I think this understanding and translation are along the right lines, but I take the alternative manuscript reading of ζῶν, attested in both cases in D (codex Coisilianus 166), to be more probable as the Ionic participle, cf. Heraclitus B26 and B88.

[11] The translation here is intended to emphasise that it is *qualitative* differentiation that I take Melissus to mean. Melissus' point, as I understand it, is that each thing must remain exactly the same and not simply that it must stay the same *kind* of thing, e.g. it is not only that a seed cannot become a flower but also that the seed cannot change qualities like size, shape, or colour.

[12] Reale 1970: 243–4 and Palmer 2009: 212–13. See Loenen 1959: 169–70: 'Now I see no reason to think, as is commonly done, that he is attacking Anaxagoras and/or Empedocles in particular. On the contrary, it is quite clear that he is refuting a *communis opinio*.'

[13] Barnes (1982: 299) wisely makes this point, but backtracks in n.4 by claiming that no *particular* philosophical school is intended. I certainly agree that we need not assume such a school or person for the argument to go through. This, however, is not the same as saying that Melissus *certainly* did not have a professional opponent in mind along with ordinary, everyday opinions. This seems as likely to me as not.

Before we consider the strategy apparent in the passage, it is worth considering what Melissus means when he speaks of whether or not the entities people hold truly exist or are real (εἶναι ἀληθῆ). We find an existential εἶναι here along with the predicative εἶναι ἀληθῆ which Melissus seems to treat as interchangeable. Is Melissus evaluating whether the list of putative plural things can truly be said to be as what-is is said to be, and perhaps in the process leave open a third option between what-is and what-is-not? John Palmer considers something like the latter option by claiming, 'the passage is not concerned with the mere existence of earth, water, air, and the rest, but with the question of whether any of these things can be properly said to "be", that is, whether any of these things *really* are ... This is not immediately equivalent, however, to denying that entities subject to change do not exist.'[14] Our look at the deductive structure of the treatise suggests that such a distinction is illicitly formed in Melissus' case. All of the attributes of what-is have been ultimately reached from the fundamental hypothesis 'something is'. In short, Melissus' point is that if anything is, it is as he has presented his subject, what-is. There is no possibility that something could exist and not be identical, in terms of existence, predication, or modality, to what-is. We must say, then, that, *contra* Palmer, Melissus' decision to consider only a subset of the attributes of what-is in B8 does not suggest any intention to distinguish between ontologically or modally distinct states of being.

Rather Melissus is simply testing whether or not our sense experience is reliable and compatible with the results of arguments thus far in the treatise. It is the unreliability of the results of sense experience that emerges as the central point in the passage under consideration and the argument to come. The strategy is as

---

[14] Palmer 2009: 211–13. Palmer does, though, ultimately think that Melissus' argument amounts, at least in part, to a denial of the very existence of these entities. But this is understood merely as an 'entailment' of the argumentation. Alexander Mourelatos (1965: 362–3) makes a similar argument: 'When Melissus says "if there were earth and water" he does not, of course, mean the paradoxical and self-contradictory thesis that this to which I point (the earth, the sea) does not exist. The verb "to be" here has a special sense.' Barnes (1982: 299 n.4) is right to respond that Melissus' thesis is not self-contradictory and, although perhaps it is paradoxical, this certainly would not trouble an Eleatic.

follows: people say there are many things like earth, water, air, and so on, and if this is so and our eyes and ears are good witnesses, these things must always be as they were at our first encounter with them. Why is this latter requirement necessary? Perhaps Melissus is simply taking it for granted that if we say that there is water, the simple fact that that water changes into ice in the cold of winter eliminates it from contention for the status of what really and not deceptively is. Yet this does not seem to cohere with how the argument proceeds. Rather it seems to be the case that the veracity of the testimony of the senses requires that they provide a *stable* and reliable insight into the natures of their objects.

It is just this point about the *instability* of the results of sense experience that Melissus needs to emphasise. This is because simply stating that the hypothetical entities do indeed appear to change is not sufficient to generate the desired result of the argument: it is not simply change but also uniqueness that is at stake ultimately. Melissus needs to eliminate the very thing (i.e. sense experience) that is responsible for the postulation of plural entities in the first place. This is accomplished by demonstrating that sense experience produces contradictory results. Much like in B7, B8 exploits an argument concerned, at least in part, with change, put at the service of demonstrating that what-is is unique.

Perhaps nowhere else in Melissus' fragments do we find so close a parallel with Parmenides. We may recall his B6:

πρώτης γάρ σ' ἀφ' ὁδοῦ ταύτης διζήσιος <εἴργω>,
αὐτὰρ ἔπειτ' ἀπὸ τῆς, ἣν δὴ βροτοὶ εἰδότες οὐδὲν
πλάττονται, δίκρανοι· ἀμηχανίη γὰρ ἐν αὐτῶν
στήθεσιν ἰθύνει πλακτὸν νόον· οἱ δὲ φοροῦνται
κωφοὶ ὁμῶς τυφλοί τε, τεθηπότες, ἄκριτα φῦλα,
οἷς τὸ πέλειν τε καὶ οὐκ εἶναι ταὐτὸν νενόμισται
κοὐ ταὐτόν, πάντων δὲ παλίντροπός ἐστι κέλευθος.   (Text as in DK)

We find a number of intriguing overlaps between this fragment and what we learn in Melissus' B8.[15] In both we have an attack made

---

[15] It is interesting that the connection between the two fragments rarely receives much scholarly attention. See Mourelatos (1965: 362–3) for an honourable exception. It is worth noting that Palmer (2009: 215–16) uses B8 as further evidence that Melissus' position is a 'deformation' of Parmenides ontology. My suggestion is that Melissus is largely sympathetic to a Parmenidean position in B8 and that the fragment therefore reveals one of the closest ties between the two.

against generic, broadly construed opponents (in Melissus' case ἄνθρωποι; in Parmenides βροτοί) and in both the instability of their enemies' claims is emphasised. It is also striking that we find in both fragments references to seeing and hearing that suggest people fail to appreciate the deception and unreliability that are inherent to sense experience. Of course, the strategies apparent in the two fragments are not exactly aligned: Parmenides is simply declaring that mortals are confused and hold contradictory positions, while Melissus attempts to demonstrate more specifically that one cannot hold both that what-is is sempiternal and immutable and that sense experience is reliable. Yet the overall aims in both are remarkably alike and suggest, if nothing else, that Reinhardt's reading of Melissus' B8 as corresponding to Parmenides' *doxa* is not corroborated by his fragments, as B6, on any account firmly in the Way of Truth, is its closest parallel.

Section (3): Text and Translation

In (3), Melissus proceeds to demonstrate how the initial results of sense experience (namely that there is a plurality) are self-contradictory, insofar as sense experience also reveals that the putative plural entities are subject to change.

But, as a matter of fact, we say that we see and hear and grasp correctly, yet it seems to us that what is hot becomes cold and what is cold hot; what is hard becomes soft and what is soft hard; that the living dies and comes-to-be from what is not living; and that all these things alter and that what they were and what they are now are in no way homogeneous. It seems that iron, though hard, is rubbed away when it comes into contact[16] with a finger, and so too gold and stone and everything else that seems to be strong, so that it follows that we neither see nor recognise what is, and that earth and stone come-to-be from water.

Melissus' strategy in this *reductio* is often called 'ingenious' and rightfully so.[17] But how does it work? On any account, Melissus' aim is to generate a contradiction inherent to the pluralists' position. This contradiction is typically cashed out on the level of change. Barnes, whom I take to have formulated the standard

---

[16] I translate ὁμουρέων conjectured by Bergk. The manuscripts universally read ὁμοῦ ῥεων *separatim*.

[17] See, for example, Barnes 1982: 300 and KRS: 400.

view with the greatest precision, and thus to be an ideal representative, takes the contradiction to consist in the conjunction of two propositions:

(a) No one of the putative plural entities ever changes (established in (2)).
(b) On the strength of (3), sometimes the putative entities change.[18]

KRS opt for a similar reading of B8 by arguing that one cannot both accept the results of B7 (i.e. the impossibility of change, broadly construed) and hold that the senses are veridical.[19]

Such an interpretation, by assuming that the hypothetical pluralist accepts the elimination of change, suggests that B8 is little more than a continuation of B7. Certainly, as I have suggested, B8 does follow naturally from B7; yet this approach fails to take into account sufficiently the explicit transition Melissus makes at the beginning of the fragment. The desire to establish uniqueness is common to both fragments, but Melissus is absolutely clear that the argument in B8 is different in kind from what has come before.

With this in mind, I submit that a better reading of the text is gained if we find the contradiction Melissus intends to exploit not in change but in the reliability of sense experience itself. The benefits of such an approach hopefully will soon become clear. For the moment, I would like to sketch out a potential difficulty of the standard reading found in Barnes and KRS and show how focusing on sense experience may help dissolve the worry. For Barnes the contradiction of the two propositions stated above is intended by Melissus to demonstrate the falsity of *both* elements of his hypothesis, i.e. that there are several entities and that our senses are veridical. Yet, as Barnes acknowledges, Melissus achieves no such strong conclusion but only the negation of their conjunction. So all the argument compels the opposing party to do is to drop one half of the hypothesis while allowing it to retain the other. Melissus does, of course, have the means to target whichever half of the hypothesis is retained, but the fact that he does not do so in B8 suggests that the standard reading forces us to

[18] Barnes 1982: 299–301.
[19] KRS: 400. Makin (2005: 270), though hostile to the orthodox position, seems to accept that the relevant contradiction concerns change.

conclude uncharitably that the argument he thinks he is entitled to is at least *prima facie* unsound.[20]

So the assumption that the salient contradiction is to be found in holding two conflicting views about change leads to an undesirable consequence. My proposal is that the contradiction is better interpreted as generated from the account of how sense experience must be (in order to be reliable) in (2) and how it really is, as presented in (3). This brings us back to the argument in (2) where it is claimed that, if there is a plurality and we see and hear correctly, each entity must be just as it always is and not susceptible to change. This is a slightly mysterious piece of reasoning. Why is it necessary that the senses be veridical for it to follow that each of the plural entities be unchanging? Sketched in this way, the reasoning is indeed difficult to grasp; however, if we look closely at the text a way through emerges. The conclusion of the reasoning is said to be not just that the plural entities do not alter, but *also* that they remain just as they first appeared. These two stipulations are, of course, compatible, but the latter provides a crucial clue to what Melissus means when he speaks about seeing and hearing correctly.

We might think, as most interpreters do, that the point about seeing and hearing correctly is simply a straightforward continuation of B7. There is no change, so if we see and hear change, we hear and see incorrectly. I suggest an alternative that does not appeal quite so strongly to B7 and thus has the benefit of finding something of an independent argument: if one sees a leaf as green at t^1 and red at t^2, the relevant point is not that the leaf has changed but that perception fails to grasp the leaf properly. The idea is that, if sense perception is indeed both reliable and veridical, it must provide for the understanding of the essential or eternal nature of

---

[20] Barnes (1982: 301–2) is absolutely correct that Melissus has at his disposal the means to eliminate whichever half of the hypothesis is retained by means independent of the text of B8. If an opponent is committed to the reliability of the senses, he must *ipso facto* accept that things are plural and Melissus' arguments up to B8 can be deployed. If one accepts plurality and not that the senses are veridical, a similar difficulty is generated in so far as plurality suggests that the evidence of the senses is indeed reliable. I take it that part of the worry expressed by Makin (2005) as to how the argument about perception, whether veridical or not, relates to each element of the hypothesis turns on a similar line of thought.

its object. It is this point that is suggested by Melissus when he seems to equate the verb εἶναι with εἶναι ἀληθῆ in (2). Such a use is of course familiar from Plato and perhaps already present in Parmenides.[21] It is not that Melissus separated the consideration of mere being from that of being fundamental and ontologically basic, or that he trades on the ambiguity of the verb 'to be' to this effect, as Palmer seems to suggest.[22] Rather the point is that these two things are coextensive: what-is is also and necessarily that which is genuinely true and real. This is the upshot of beginning the treatise from the basic hypothesis 'something is'. Thus if sense experience cannot provide access to its object in the informatively rich way Melissus demands, it also cannot tell us anything reliable about its mere being. If iron, for example, seems hard at one time and soft at another, my perceptions of its qualities must surely be eliminated as insufficient to the task of understanding what iron really is like. Thus the examples provided in (3) serve to demonstrate not merely that sense perception suggests that change is real, but that the results of the senses fail to provide access to information about the world in the way that we think they do.

In this way, Melissus is setting up sense experience as a rival to the rationalist method of argumentation he has adopted thus far in the prior fragments. This makes good sense of the strategy apparent in the text. The first sentence of (2), εἰ γὰρ ἦν πολλά, τοιαῦτα χρὴ αὐτὰ εἶναι, οἷόν περ ἐγώ φημι τὸ ἓν εἶναι, sets up the conclusion Melissus aims to demonstrate. In the remainder of (2) what this amounts to is explored. He reasons that, if we are to accept the finding of sense perception that there is a plurality of entities, the senses need to be reliable and accurate guides to how the world is.

---

[21] For Parmenides, see B8.39, ὅσσα βροτοὶ κατέθεντο πεποιθότες εἶναι ἀληθῆ. For Plato, the argument in *Republic* 5, which attempts to convince the 'lovers of sights and sounds' that they do not possess knowledge of what-is, turns on the identification of what-is with what-is real.

[22] Palmer (2009: 212–15) does think, as I do, that there is an intended equivalence between 'being' and 'being real'. He does suggest though that there is relevant ambiguity for Melissus in εἶναι ἀληθῆ between mere existence and a stronger sense of being without qualification or without deficiency in any respect. The point Melissus would then be making is that the ordinary way of speaking about the world (saying, for instance, that earth *is*) needs to be corrected. While this is attractive, I can't help worrying that such a reading presupposes that Melissus would be comfortable distinguishing the verb 'to be' in such a manner, and that he would entertain, even only to discount the point, the thought that one could assert that something 'merely is'.

In (3) the total failure of the senses to live up to this basic stipulation is demonstrated, with the result that (4)–(6) firmly discount the twin hypotheses of the existence of change and of plurality.

On such a reading, the results of B7 are not strictly needed to generate the relevant destructive contradiction in the opposing party's position (though, as we have seen, B7 is not entirely irrelevant), and the worry described above about the failure of the argument to meet Melissus' expectations is significantly weakened. Eliminating sense experience as a reliable guide to reality should be independently sufficient to cast doubt on both change and plurality. This is an essential point we shall have occasion to return to: if it is right that the contradiction in the pluralists' position can be generated without assuming their acceptance of the Eleatic prohibition of change, the dialectical strategy of the argument is made much clearer and some of the worries raised by Makin are dissolved.[23]

The text of (3) makes it clear that it is the contradictory results of sense perception, and not primarily change, which are in sight. This is suggested from the very beginning of the section: Melissus is concerned with how we can coherently think that we grasp or understand (συνιέναι) the world using sense perception. The examples marshalled, largely following the list of putative entities in (2), adhere closely to the model of the leaf suggested above. At one time (t^1), we believe x is f, and at another (t^2), we think x is g. Our sense experiences are plainly said to be in conflict and it is from this conflict that we come to believe that change is real.

However, the leaf example fails to capture a crucial detail that has not been given due consideration in the literature. Melissus does *not* consider examples where the results of sense experience are merely altered at different times, but examples where the results are in *direct* opposition: warm to cold, hard to soft, and living to dead. Melissus seems to confirm that it is contrariety that

---

[23] For example, Makin (2005: 269) claims: 'The Striking Fact is that if Melissus is defending *one* Eleatic claim, that just one thing exists, then he is doing so by appealing to some *other* Eleatic claims.' On the interpretation I have suggested, the fact that objects of perception violate an Eleatic claim is not strictly relevant. It is that their change eliminates sense experience from our philosophical tool kit that is the point.

it is relevant and not simply difference: καὶ ὅ τι ἦν τε καὶ ὃ νῦν οὐδέν ὁμοῖον εἶναι. Why make such an exceptionally strong claim? After all, an opponent could respond that he thinks that plurality and change are real but not that things altered are *in no way* the same as they once were: the red leaf may still share properties like size and texture with the green leaf.

Perhaps Melissus has in mind the model of alteration discussed and eliminated in B7, whereby any alteration amounts to rearrangement and, thus, to the coming-to-be of an entirely new iteration of its subject. Yet such an appeal does not seem necessary to make sense of Melissus' method. The examples of sense experience that are directly contrary to each other seem rather to function within the structure of the *reductio*. The point is that sense experience goes further than merely suggesting that entities change; in fact, Melissus argues, it commits us to thinking that, in their putative plurality, things are entirely unlike their former selves at different times along the relevant spectrum. Making such a point is essential to his programme of entirely eliminating the senses as useful windows into reality. This is all in line with what we found in Parmenides' B6: the senses are not just useless, they are actively harmful to philosophical activity.

The very last sentence of the section is in doubt. The manuscripts universally read: ὥστε συμβαίνει μήτε ὁρᾶν μήτε τὰ ὄντα γινώσκειν, ἐξ ὕδατός τε γῆ καὶ λίθος γίνεσθαι. The ὥστε clause makes little sense in its manuscript location and Karsten wisely suggested transposing it to follow γίνεσθαι. Yet even if Karsten is right in his transposition, we must face the charge levelled by Jonathan Barnes that the clause is a later marginal gloss and ought to be deleted from the text.[24] He offers three reasons why the clause is linguistically suspect: let us take each in turn.

The most serious worry about the authenticity of the clause under consideration is the sense in which συμβαίνει is used with ὥστε. Clearly the verb is used here to indicate logical or argumentative consequence, an absolutely standard sense in the fourth century, particularly in Plato and Aristotle, but unparalleled in

---

[24] Barnes 1982: 299 n.4. KRS (399 n.1) follow Barnes. Makin (2005) brackets off the clause.

Melissus' period. This objection cannot be easily eliminated, but two considerations tell against taking it as wholly destructive. The first, echoing our look at B9, is that attempting to determine the precise date of semantic shifts, especially given the state of evidence, is a very uncertain practice. The second, and far more compelling consideration, is that there is strong evidence that a sentence corresponding in principle to the ὥστε clause was echoed by the nearly contemporaneous[25] author of the Hippocratic treatise *De Arte* in an apparent rebuke to Melissus' argument[26]:

δοκέει δή μοι τὸ μὲν σύμπαν τέχνη εἶναι οὐδεμία οὐκ ἐοῦσα· καὶ γὰρ ἄλογον τῶν ἐόντων τι ἡγεῖσθαι μὴ ἐόν· ἐπεὶ τῶν γε μὴ ἐόντων τίνα ἄν τίς οὐσίην θεησάμενος ἀπαγγείλειεν ὡς ἔστιν; εἰ γὰρ δὴ ἔστι γ᾽ ἰδεῖν τὰ μὴ ἐόντα, ὥσπερ τὰ ἐόντα, οὐκ οἶδ᾽ ὅπως ἄν τις αὐτὰ νομίσειε μὴ ἐόντα, ἅ γε εἴη καὶ ὀφθαλμοῖσιν ἰδεῖν καὶ γνώμῃ νοῆσαι ὡς ἐστιν· ἀλλ᾽ ὅπως μὴ οὐκ ᾖ τοῦτο τοιοῦτον· **ἀλλὰ τὰ μὲν ἐόντα αἰεὶ ὁρᾶταί τε καὶ γινώσκεται, τὰ δὲ μὴ ἐόντα οὔτε ὁρᾶται οὔτε γινώσκεται.**

It is true that the last sentence of this extract does not replicate the ὥστε construction found in Melissus. However, the overlap between the two sentences is too striking to be dismissed as a mere coincidence. Both authors use verbs of seeing and under-standing to make directly opposed points about the relationship between what-is and human sense capabilities. For Melissus, we can neither see nor recognise what-is using our senses *at any point in time.* Hippocrates seems to respond by claiming that we can *always* see what-is and understand it. What we seem to find then, in the Hippocratic passage, is a dialectical reworking of the Melissan material. The similarity of language and subject matter, while perhaps not a guarantee that Hippocrates knew Melissus' sentence, is certainly a strong clue that he did.

While this echo does not confirm that Melissus' ὥστε construc-tion is linguistically plausible, it certainly does strongly tell

---

[25] For a survey of the arguments which have been raised for dating *De Arte* to the second half of the fifth century, see Mann 2012: 37–8. Cumulatively, the linguistic evidence is convincing.

[26] That the language and style of argument of this section of *De Arte* are 'Eleatic' in nature is a common theme. See, for example, Hankinson 1998: 77. Mann (2012: 25) takes a weaker view of Melissus' connection to this passage than others, but admits, none-theless, that 'the sentiment expressed in *De Arte* seems directly opposed to that voiced by Melissus'.

against deleting the sentence as merely a later gloss. Barnes' second and third objections are more easily tackled. τὰ ὄντα for the Ionic τὰ ἐόντα is no doubt incorrect for Melissus but, as we saw in our look at **Q**, the absence of the epsilon is far less suggestive of a spurious addition to the text than many scholars seem to believe. After all, even a brief look at the apparatus of Parmenides' text, for example, reveals several places where the manuscripts are divided between readings of ἐόν and ὄν,[27] yet this in no way suggests that we should adopt a sceptical attitude towards the authenticity of the text.

Barnes' final point is that γινώσκειν misinterprets the earlier instance of συνιέναι. However, this is only a worry if we think that γινώσκειν was intended to mirror συνιέναι in a particularly strong way. A better reading takes γινώσκειν to follow on from the argument Melissus has just made that sense experience is unreliable because it indicates that something at one time is x and at another the opposite of x. Taking γινώσκειν as a verb of cognitive success ('recognise') very nicely captures this point by emphasising that sense experience fails to grasp its object in the way that the pluralists must be committed to if they accept that sense experience is good evidence for plurality.

So, on balance, the evidence suggests that we retain the disputed sentence as a genuine reflection of something Melissus did include in his argument. There is, of course, the possibility that the text has been couched in later language, but the single doubt about the authenticity of συμβαίνει, especially when weighed against the evidence of *De Arte*, does not demand deletion. I do, however, angle bracket the sentence, as Karsten is undoubtedly right that the manuscript location of the clause cannot be correct. I follow his lead and transpose it to follow γίνεσθαι.

Section (4): Text and Translation

So then these things do not agree with each other. For we say that there are many things that are eternal and have their own forms and strength, and yet it seems to us that they all alter in quality and change from how

---

[27] DK2.7, DK8.12, DK8.46, and DK8.47. In the latter two, the manuscripts are completely agreed in omitting the epsilon.

they are each time they are seen. Therefore, clearly we have not seen correctly, nor do those things correctly seem to be many.

This section makes the contradiction in the pluralists' position explicit. Melissus proceeds from the ὥστε clause in (3) to his conclusion that those who rely on sense experience are committed to thinking that it is both reliable enough to justify the inference that there is a plurality, yet so unstable that it presents contradictory results each time it is employed.[28] This conclusion to the argument also lends further support to the interpretation of the contradiction I have sketched above, as we see, once again, a strong emphasis on the failure of sense experience to produce consistent results. In fact, Melissus seems to be committed to the stronger claim that *each* instance of sense perception (ἑκάστοτε ὁρωμένου) produces different results. It is not, then, simply that sense experience is unreliable, it is indeed *reliably* unreliable.

Melissus makes it plain in this section that 'we' (i.e. those that are committed to the use of sense experience as a reliable guide to reality) hold that the plural entities which exist are eternal, and have both forms and strength.[29] As I have suggested above, we think this not because we are already necessarily committed to other Eleatic claims about change but because Melissus insists in (2) that this must be the case if we do indeed see and hear correctly. The choice of vocabulary here (εἴδη, ἰσχύν) is arresting; the introduction to the argument did not specifically mention form or strength but rather sempiternity and unalterability. This suggests, then, that Melissus is cashing out these latter two qualities in the language of 'form' and 'strength'. Yet there is more. The language here is explicitly theological and, as we shall soon see, marks an attempt at critical theology.

---

[28] One further reason for retaining the ὥστε clause is that Melissus' inferential τοίνυν follows much more smoothly if such a conclusion is indeed reached in (3).

[29] It should be clear by now that I take it that Melissus' assumption that his pluralist opponent accepts that what-is (whether a unity or a plurality) is eternal turns on the equivalence of εἶναι with εἶναι ἀληθῆ discussed above. Indeed this equivalence is put into the mouths of οἱ ἄνθρωποι. He is taking it as read that his opponent agrees that to say 'something is' is to say that it truly is so, with the understanding that this includes eternality and indestructibility. This is what Melissus means when he says, 'for if there were many things, they ought to be such as what I say the One is'. The assumption will be further reinforced in (5).

It is also worth noting how well this conclusion to the argument coheres with the end of the argument against void and motion. In both we find a nested structure employing a double use of τοίνυν. In B7 the intermediate conclusion states that fullness precludes void, before this claim is in turn used to conclude that what-is does not move. A parallel structure is apparent in this section of B8. Melissus begins by concluding that what sense experience *must* be like and what it in fact *is* like are contradictory because of the presence of alteration. This conclusion then is used to derive not just the point that we do not see correctly *but also* that there cannot, as we had supposed, be many things. It is here that the interpretation of the argument sketched above bears fruit. The objection Barnes raises about whether the argument is indeed sufficient to eliminate both hypotheses (i.e. that there are many things and that the senses are veridical) and not simply their conjunction proves to be irrelevant. The structure of the argument makes it clear that Melissus takes the elimination of sense experience as a reliable guide to reality as sufficient to remove a potential obstacle to the previous elimination of plurality in B7. This can only be because sense experience, if reliable, would subvert the previous denial of plurality.

Section (5): Text and Translation

For they would not change, if they were real, but each thing would *be* just as it seemed to be. For nothing is stronger than what is real.

This section confirms the fundamental metaphysical assumption Melissus has made throughout B8 and adds an argument in its support. Sense experience has been shown to be contradictory and unreliable. It seems that, if we can agree that it was through the testimony of the senses alone that change is suggested as something that is, it can now be safely eliminated as unsupported. We shall soon find in (6) that the correlated elimination of plurality, explored already in B7, is reinforced. Yet in (5) we find that the argument does not immediately suggest that the mere existence of change or plurality or the veridicality of the senses is targeted. Rather there is an effort to reinforce the understanding of the real (i.e. εἶναι ἀληθῆ and related verbal forms) as eternal and indestructible and further the claim that were there many things they would be just as Melissus has said the One is.

In Makin's dialectical reconstruction of Melissus' argument in B8, the claim offered in (5) is dubbed the 'Nothing Stronger' (NS) principle.[30] On his account, the principle functions within a clever strategy intended to entrap an anti-Eleatic opponent who accepts both that the senses are veridical and that the Eleatic arguments for denying this are false. Melissus, though, in such a dialectical context can use NS to generate an Eleatic denial of change and thus of the veridicality of the senses, yet the opponent (Makin's 'Bluff Realist') cannot reject NS without also discarding his commitment to the claim that the senses provide privileged and veridical access to what is true and real. Thus the acceptance of the claim that sense experience is reliable amounts to a commitment to NS and the 'Bluff Realist' is in a bind.[31]

This interpretation relies on the assumption that Melissus' argument that what-is is one, accomplished through the elimination of sense experience, is defended by appealing to a previously established Eleatic claim that change does not exist. This is Makin's so-called 'Striking Fact'. As we have seen, this assumption is not necessary to make sense of Melissus' argument and, in fact, misconstrues why sense experience is eliminated as unreliable. I think that Makin *is right* to find a crucial piece of the overall argument of B8 in (5). However, it is not a dialectical strategy that is apparent but a suggestive indication of an argument for the Eleatic prohibition of change that crucially does not turn on the purported impossibility of *ex nihilo* generation. The fact of such an argument's place in B8 further tells against Makin's 'Striking Fact'.

In B7 change (understood as alteration, reconstruction, and motion) was considered and shown to be non-existent because it necessitated, for each of its species, the destruction of what-is and the coming-to-be of what-is-not and, thus, the implication of plurality: alteration, for example, entailed rearrangement which

---

[30] Makin 2005: 282–6.
[31] Of course, the converse (a commitment to NS entails the acceptance of the reliability of sense experience) does not hold for Makin's reading of Melissus.

required the coming-to-be of a new iteration of what-is for Melissus. Here in (5) we find a different kind of argument, supplemental in nature and nested within the already supplemental B8, that appeals to neither coming-to-be nor the threat of plurality. This is further evidence that Melissus does *not* proceed from or attribute to an opponent an assumption that change is impossible on the grounds of a previously established point, whether earlier in the treatise or in the 'Eleatic' tradition.

The argument itself recalls and, perhaps, helps to clarify the appeal to the absence of pain and anguish in B7. This makes sense against the increasingly physical and anthropomorphic language (εἴδη, ἰσχύν) found in (4). Once again Melissus is appealing to the imperviousness to external forces of what-is, using language that strongly recalls Greek descriptions of divinity.[32] Just as the absence of physical and mental pain is closely associated with the divine,[33] so are the three qualities discussed here: ἀίδια (everlasting), εἶδος (form, understood as a visible appearance)[34], and ἰσχύς (strength). One could hardly list three more characteristic qualities associated with the traditional Homeric/Hesiodic depiction of divinity: each traditional god (e.g. Athena or Apollo) is everlasting with a unique, visible appearance and peculiar strength.

It seems, then, that Melissus is taking the opportunity to engage in theological criticism as he simultaneously attempts to eliminate any notion of plurality from his picture of the world. This is remarkable but hardly surprising in the light of the elimination of pain and anguish in B7. If Melissus is indeed attempting to criticise the concept of a pantheon of gods, distinguished by their anthropomorphic features, we find a strong and absolutely appropriate commitment to monotheism, understood as the coextension of god with the universe. Once again postulating a connection between Melissus and Xenophanes is irresistible.

---

[32] Cf., for example, κρεῖσσον οὐδέν applied to fate at Euripides, *Alcestis* 965.

[33] Long (1996: 141) makes this point.

[34] Herrmann (2007: 127 n.231) suggests that Melissus has in mind 'visible appearance' here. This is confirmed by the verb of seeing (ὁρωμένου) at the conclusion of the sentence. This is completely in line with the dominant Presocratic use of the term, philosophical or otherwise.

What, then, does the argument here amount to and why should Melissus think that the One has more claim to reality than a plurality of things and the means that bring about their accumulation and separation? Why, for example, should Empedocles' elements plus Love and Strife not have an equal claim to reality? One might respond with the *communis opinio* that Melissus had in mind only a naïve, or popular view about destruction and reformation, and not the theories of those like Empedocles and Anaxagoras who attempted to combine Parmenides' prohibition of coming-to-be and destruction with a plural ontology of things. Perhaps, but I think Melissus' appeal here to strength and imperviousness suggests a different answer, one that is worth fleshing out.

Empedocles and Anaxagoras may eliminate 'genuine' change understood as the destruction and coming-to-be of what they take to be ontologically basic (the roots and Love and Strife in the former and the homoeomerous stuffs/the opposed qualities in the latter). However, neither postulates a completely stable, unchanging system as Melissus does. If, then, one were to choose which of the two (plural or unitary) has a greater claim to reality, understood as the strongest and most powerful thing that is, it would follow that the One would be preferred, as its stability and imperviousness to change must be associated with superior power. Such a reading is closely in line with the appeal to the theological characteristics discussed above. Though speculative, once again we can see that absolutely eliminating rival theoretical philosophy from Melissus' dialectic frame is not necessary to make sense of the argument.

Section (6): Text and Translation

But being changed, what-is is destroyed, and what-is-not has come to be. Therefore, if there were many, they ought to be of just the same sort as the One is.

In this final section, we find the standard Melissan method of ring composition. He circles the argument around from the innovative NS claim in (5) back to his standard remark that change, as it involves the coming-to-be of what-is-not fatally compromises a belief in the plurality of things. B8 ends with a close paraphrase of the principal claim that Melissus makes in the second sentence of the fragment and this is somewhat curious. Of course, it is entirely in line with the method of the other fragments to find such a repetition of the point that has been demonstrated and was first canvassed at the start of the fragment. Yet Melissus, of course, does *not* accept, even as a remote possibility, that there could be a plurality of things. Indeed, if my account is along the right lines, one of the fundamental motivations for B8 is to reinforce the denial of plurality so assiduously made in B7.

The status of B8 as primarily supplemental seems to help answer this worry. The aim of the fragment is not to repeat what has already been made clear in B7 but rather to reinforce that fragment's conclusions and address those readers who accept only part of what has been argued. For this purpose, what is immediately desirable is the acceptance of the counterfactual claim made in B8 that each member of a plurality would be just as the One is. If this is granted to Melissus, the putative fact of a plurality is easily dismissed using whichever of the two sorts of argument he had at his disposal. He could appeal to the uniqueness argument in B4–B6 or use the unreliability of sense experience to eliminate the testimony that gives rise to the belief in a plurality of things in the first place. B8, in short, by way of eliminating sense experience from the philosophical tool kit, expands Melissus' means of countering the closely related notions of change and plurality.

APPENDIX 1

Melissus' Περὶ φύσεως ἢ περὶ τοῦ <ἐ>όντος:
The Reconstructed Text

SIGLA

Simplicii in Aristotelis Physicorum Commentaria
D   Laurentianus LXXXV 2
E   Marcianus 229
F   Marcianus 227
a   Aldina

Simplicii in Aristotelis De Caelo Commentaria
A   Mutinensis III E 8
D   Coislinianus 166
E   Marcianus 491
E²   Marcianus 491 correxit Bessario adhibita interpretatione latina Guilelmi
     de Morbeka
F   Marcianus 228

Authorities Cited

BA   Barnes, J. (1982) *The Presocratic Philosophers*. London: Routledge.
BR   Brandis, C. A. (1813) *Commentationum Eleaticarum pars I: Xenophanis
      Parmenidis et Melissi Doctrina Exposita*. Altonae.
CH   Chiesara, M. L. (2001) *Aristocles of Messene*. Oxford: Oxford University
      Press.
CO   Covotti, A. (1898) 'Melissi Samii Reliquiae.' *Studi Italiani di
      Filologia Classica* 6. 213–27.
HE   Heidel, W. A. (1913) 'On Certain Fragments of the Pre-Socratics'.
      Proceedings of the American Academy of Arts and Sciences 48. 681–734.
KRS   Kirk, G. S., Raven, J. E., and Schofield, M. (1983) *The Presocratic
      Philosophers*. Cambridge: Cambridge University Press.
LO   Loenen, J. H. M. M. (1959) *Parmenides, Melissus, Gorgias*. Assen:
      Royal Van Gorcum.
MU   Mullach, F. W. A. (1883) *Fragmenta Philosophorum Graecorum*.
      Paris: Ambrosio Firmin Didot.
PA   Palmer, J. (2009) *Parmenides and Presocratic Philosophy*. Oxford:
      Oxford University Press.
RE   Reale, G. (1970) *Melisso: Testimonianze e frammenti*. Florence: La
      Nuova Italia.

216

VI   Vitali, R. (1973) *Melisso di Samo: Sul mondo o sull'essere*. Urbino: Argalìa Editore.

The following text and *apparatus criticus* are intended as a guide to the results of my reconstruction. I include only those manuscripts and authorities that serve to illustrate how the text offered relates to those examined in the main body of the book. Therefore, what follows is intended to be *selective* and to help clarify points I have made in the course of the reconstruction and commentary. For ease of comparison, I print Mullach's text of Aristocles' quotation of B8 separately. As stated above, I take it that Simplicius' text is to be preferred.

Περὶ φύσεως ἢ περὶ τοῦ <ἐ>όντος <Μέλισσος Σάμιος τάδε λέγει περὶ φύσεως ἢ περὶ τοῦ ἐόντος.> εἰ μὲν μηδὲν ἔστι, περὶ τούτου τί ἂν λέγοιτο ὡς <ἐ>όντος τινός; εἰ δέ τι ἐστίν, (**B1**) ἀεὶ ἦν ὅ τι ἦν καὶ ἀεὶ ἔσται. εἰ γὰρ ἐγένετο, ἀναγκαῖόν ἐστι πρὶν γενέσθαι εἶναι μηδέν. εἰ <δὲ> τύχοι νῦν μηδὲν 5 ἐόν, οὐδαμὰ ἂν γένοιτο οὐδὲν ἐκ μηδενός. (**B2**) ὅτε τοίνυν οὐκ ἐγένετο, ἔστι τε καὶ ἀεὶ ἦν καὶ ἀεὶ ἔσται. καὶ ἀρχὴν οὐκ ἔχει οὐδὲ τελευτήν, ἀλλ' ἄπειρόν ἐστιν. εἰ μὲν γὰρ ἐγένετο, ἀρχὴν ἂν εἶχεν (ἤρξατο γὰρ ἄν ποτε γινόμενον) καὶ τελευτήν (ἐτελεύτησε γὰρ ἄν ποτε γινόμενον)· ὅτε δὲ μήτε ἤρξατο μήτε ἐτελεύτησεν, ἀεί τε ἦν καὶ ἀεὶ ἔσται, οὐκ ἔχει ἀρχὴν οὐδὲ τελευτήν· οὐ γὰρ 10 ἀεὶ εἶναι ἀνυστόν, ὅ τι μὴ πᾶν ἔστι. (**B3**) ἀλλ' ὥσπερ ἔστιν ἀεί, οὕτω καὶ τὸ μέγεθος ἄπειρον ἀεὶ χρὴ εἶναι. < ἄπειρον δ' ἐὸν ἓν ἐστίν> (**B5**) εἰ <γὰρ> μὴ ἓν εἴη, περανεῖ πρὸς ἄλλο, (**B4**) ἀρχήν δὲ καὶ τέλος ἔχον οὐδὲν οὔτε ἀίδιον οὔτε ἄπειρόν ἐστιν· <εἰ τοίνυν μὴ ἓν εἴη, οὔτ' ἀίδιον οὔτ' ἄπειρόν ἂν εἴη.> (**B6**) εἰ γὰρ εἴη, ἓν εἴη ἄν· εἰ γὰρ δύο εἴη, οὐκ ἂν δύναιτο ἄπειρα εἶναι, ἀλλ' 15 ἔχοι ἂν πείρατα πρὸς ἄλληλα. εἰ μὲν οὖν εἴη, δεῖ αὐτὸ ἓν εἶναι. (**B9**) ἓν δ' ἐόν, δεῖ αὐτὸ σῶμα μὴ ἔχειν. εἰ δὲ ἔχοι πάχος, ἔχοι ἂν μόρια, καὶ οὐκέτι ἓν εἴη. <εἰ τοίνυν ἕν ἐστιν, σῶμα οὐκ ἔχει. ἓν δὲ ἐὸν ὅμοιον εἶναι πάντῃ· εἰ γὰρ ἀνόμοιον εἴη, πλείω ἐόντα, οὐκ ἂν ἔτι ἓν εἶναι ἀλλὰ πολλά.> (**B7**) οὕτως οὖν ἀίδιόν ἐστι καὶ ἄπειρον καὶ ἓν καὶ ὅμοιον πᾶν. καὶ οὔτ' ἂν ἀπόλοιτο

---

1 <ἐ>όντος correxi: ὄντος codd.   2 addidi <ἐ>όντος correxi: ὄντος codd.
4 εἰ <δὲ> τύχοι νῦν μηδὲν ἐόν scripsi: εἰ τύχοι νῦν μηδὲν ἦν E: εἰ τύχῃ νῦν μηδὲν ἦν D: εἰ τε τὸ πρὶν μηδὲν ἦν CO   5 οὐδαμὰ DEF: οὐδαμῇ a οὐδὲν DE: μηδὲν aF ἔστι τε καὶ 29.22–3: ἔστι δέ 109.20: καὶ ἔσται 29.23   8 ἐτελεύτησε γὰρ ἄν ποτε γινόμενον aE: ἐτελεύτησε γὰρ ἄν ποτε γινόμενον ὄν F   8 ὅτε 29.25: εἰ 109.23   9 <καὶ> οὐκ ἔχει suppl. Kranz: ἔχει DE: ἔχον aF   11 ἀεὶ ἄπειρον D   11 <ἄπειρον δ' ἐὸν ἓν ἐστιν> addidi εἰ om. E <γὰρ> addidi περανοῖ E ἀρχήν δὲ aE: ἀρχήν τε DF   13 <εἰ τοίνυν μὴ ἓν εἴη, οὔτ' ἀίδιον οὔτ' ἄπειρόν ἂν εἴη> addidi εἰ γὰρ <ἄπειρον> εἴη Burnet suppl.   14 mg. γράφεται ἄλλως· εἰ γὰρ οὕτως ἦν ἔσται, δύναιντ' ἂν ἄπειρα εἶναι ἀλλ' ἔχοι ἂν πείρατα πρὸς ἄλληλα E²   16 οὖν EF: ὂν aD   17 <εἰ τοίνυν ἕν ἐστιν, σῶμα οὐκ ἔχει> addidi <ἓν δὲ ἐὸν ὅμοιον εἶναι πάντῃ· εἰ γὰρ ἀνόμοιον, πλείω ἐόντα, οὐκ ἂν ἔτι ἓν εἶναι ἀλλὰ πολλά> addidi cf. *MXG* 974a14–15   19 ἀπόλοιτο aF: ἀπόλλοιτο E: ἀπολλύοι τι CO: ἀπολλύοιτο τι LO

20 οὔτε μεῖζον γίνοιτο οὔτε μετακοσμέοιτο οὔτε ἀλγεῖ οὔτε ἀνιᾶται· εἰ γάρ τι
τούτων πάσχοι, οὐκ ἂν ἔτι ἓν εἴη. εἰ γὰρ ἑτεροιοῦται, ἀνάγκη τὸ ἐὸν μὴ
ὁμοῖον εἶναι, ἀλλὰ ἀπόλλυσθαι τὸ πρόσθεν ἐόν, τὸ δὲ οὐκ ἐὸν γίνεσθαι. εἰ
τοίνυν τριχὶ μιῆ μυρίοις ἔτεσιν ἑτεροῖον γίνοιτο τὸ πᾶν, ὀλεῖται πᾶν ἐν τῷ
παντὶ χρόνῳ. ἀλλ' οὐδὲ μετακοσμηθῆναι ἀνυστόν· ὁ γὰρ κόσμος ὁ
25 πρόσθεν ἐὼν οὐκ ἀπόλλυται οὔτε ὁ μὴ ἐὼν γίνεται. ὅτε δὲ μήτε
προσγίνεται μηδὲν μήτε ἀπόλλυται μήτε ἑτεροιοῦται, πῶς ἂν
μετακοσμηθέν τι τῶν ἐόντων εἴη; εἰ μὲν γάρ τι ἐγίνετο ἑτεροῖον, ἤδη ἂν
καὶ μετακοσμηθείη. οὐδὲ ἀλγεῖ· οὐ γὰρ ἂν πᾶν εἴη ἀλγέον· οὐ γὰρ ἂν
δύναιτο ἀεὶ εἶναι χρῆμα ἀλγέον· οὐδὲ ἔχει ἴσην δύναμιν τῷ ὑγιεῖ· οὐδ' ἂν
30 ὁμοῖον εἴη, εἰ ἀλγέοι· ἀπογινομένου γάρ τευ ἂν ἀλγέοι ἢ προσγινομένου,
κοὐκ ἂν ἔτι ὁμοῖον εἴη. οὐδ' ἂν τὸ ὑγιὲς ἀλγῆσαι δύναιτο· ἀπὸ γὰρ ἂν
ὄλοιτο τὸ ὑγιὲς καὶ τὸ ἐόν, τὸ δὲ οὐκ ἐὸν γένοιτο. καὶ περὶ τοῦ ἀνιᾶσθαι
ωὑτὸς λόγος τῷ ἀλγέοντι. οὐδὲ κενεόν ἐστιν οὐδέν· τὸ γὰρ κενεὸν οὐδέν
ἐστιν· οὐκ ἂν οὖν εἴη τό γε μηδέν. οὐδὲ κινέεται· ὑποχωρῆσαι γὰρ οὐκ ἔχει
35 οὐδαμῇ, ἀλλὰ πλέων ἐστίν. εἰ μὲν γὰρ κενεὸν ἦν, ὑπεχώρει ἂν εἰς τὸ κενεόν·
κενεοῦ δὲ μὴ ἐόντος οὐκ ἔχει ὅκη ὑποχωρήσει. πυκνὸν δὲ καὶ ἀραιὸν οὐκ ἂν
εἴη. τὸ γὰρ ἀραιὸν οὐκ ἀνυστὸν πλέων εἶναι ὁμοίως τῷ πυκνῷ, ἀλλ' ἤδη
τὸ ἀραιόν γε κενεώτερον γίνεται τοῦ πυκνοῦ. κρίσιν δὲ ταύτην χρὴ
ποιήσασθαι τοῦ πλέω καὶ τοῦ μὴ πλέω· εἰ μὲν οὖν χωρεῖ τι ἢ εἰσδέχεται,
40 οὐ πλέων· εἰ δὲ μήτε χωρεῖ μήτε εἰσδέχεται, πλέων. ἀνάγκη τοίνυν πλέων
εἶναι, εἰ κενεὸν μὴ ἔστιν. εἰ τοίνυν πλέων ἐστίν, οὐ κινέεται. (B10) <οὐδὲ
διαιρετόν ἐστιν.> εἰ γὰρ διήρηται τὸ ἐόν, κινέεται· κινούμενον δὲ οὐκ ἂν εἴη.
(B8) μέγιστον μὲν οὖν σημεῖον οὗτος ὁ λόγος ὅτι ἓν μόνον ἔστιν· ἀτὰρ καὶ
τάδε σημεῖα. εἰ γὰρ ἦν πολλά, τοιαῦτα χρὴ αὐτὰ εἶναι οἷόν περ ἐγώ φημι
45 τὸ ἓν εἶναι. εἰ γὰρ ἔστι γῆ καὶ ὕδωρ καὶ ἀὴρ καὶ πῦρ καὶ σίδηρος καὶ
χρυσός, καὶ τὸ μὲν ζῶν τὸ δὲ τεθνηκός, καὶ μέλαν καὶ λευκὸν καὶ τὰ ἄλλα,
ὅσα φασὶν οἱ ἄνθρωποι εἶναι ἀληθῆ, εἰ δὴ ταῦτα ἔστι, καὶ ἡμεῖς ὀρθῶς
ὁρῶμεν καὶ ἀκούομεν, εἶναι χρὴ ἕκαστον τοιοῦτον οἷόν περ τὸ πρῶτον
ἔδοξεν ἡμῖν, καὶ μὴ μεταπίπτειν μηδὲ γίνεσθαι ἑτεροῖον, ἀλλὰ ἀεὶ εἶναι
50 ἕκαστον οἷόν πέρ ἐστιν. νῦν δέ φαμεν ὀρθῶς ὁρᾶν καὶ ἀκούειν καὶ συνιέναι·
δοκεῖ δὲ ἡμῖν τό τε θερμὸν ψυχρὸν γίνεσθαι καὶ τὸ ψυχρὸν θερμὸν καὶ τὸ
σκληρὸν μαλθακὸν καὶ τὸ μαλθακὸν σκληρὸν καὶ τὸ ζῶν ἀποθνήσκειν καὶ
ἐκ μὴ ζῶντος γίνεσθαι, καὶ ταῦτα πάντα ἑτεροιοῦσθαι, καὶ ὅ τι ἦν τε καὶ ὃ
νῦν οὐδὲν ὁμοῖον εἶναι, ἀλλ' ὅ τε σίδηρος σκληρὸς ἐὼν τῷ δακτύλῳ
55 κατατρίβεσθαι ὁμουρέων, καὶ χρυσὸς καὶ λίθος καὶ ἄλλο ὅ τι ἰσχυρὸν
δοκεῖ εἶναι πᾶν, ἐξ ὕδατός τε γῆ καὶ λίθος γίνεσθαι· <ὥστε συμβαίνει

---

23 τριχὶ μιῆ aD: τρι^{x} μὴ ἢ Ε: τριχν μη (sine acc.) F   27 μετακοσμηθέντῶν
ἐόντων DF   27 ἢ codd.: εἴη correxit MU   29 πῶς ἂν μετακοσμηθείη τι τῶν ἐόντων
HE   32 ὄλοιτο MU   33 ὡυτὸς DF: ὁ αὐτὸς aE   35 κενὸν κενοῦ codd.
37 πλέον   38 κενεώτερον aD: κενώτερον F: κοινότερον E   41 κενὸν codd.: κενεὸν
a   41 οὐδὲ διαιρετόν ἐστιν addidi   46 ζῶν DE²: ζῶον AE   51 θερμὸν ψυχρὸν
DE: θερμὸν καὶ ψυχρὸν A   52 ζῶν D   56 ὥστε συμβαίνει μήτε ὁρᾶν μήτε τὰ ὄντα

μήτε ὁρᾶν μήτε τὰ ὄντα γινώσκειν.> οὐ τοίνυν ταῦτα ἀλλήλοις ὁμολογεῖ. φαμένοις γὰρ εἶναι πολλὰ καὶ ἀίδια καὶ εἴδη τε καὶ ἰσχὺν ἔχοντα, πάντα ἑτεροιοῦσθαι ἡμῖν δοκεῖ καὶ μεταπίπτειν ἐκ τοῦ ἑκάστοτε ὁρωμένου. δῆλον
60 τοίνυν, ὅτι οὐκ ὀρθῶς ἑωρῶμεν οὐδὲ ἐκεῖνα πολλὰ ὀρθῶς δοκεῖ εἶναι· οὐ γὰρ ἂν μετέπιπτεν, εἰ ἀληθῆ ἦν· ἀλλ' ἦν οἷόν περ ἐδόκει ἕκαστον τοιοῦτον. τοῦ γὰρ ἐόντος ἀληθινοῦ κρεῖσσον οὐδέν. ἦν δὲ μεταπέσῃ, τὸ μὲν ἐὸν ἀπώλετο, τὸ δὲ οὐκ ἐὸν γέγονεν. οὕτως οὖν, εἰ πολλὰ εἴη, τοιαῦτα χρὴ εἶναι οἷόν περ τὸ ἕν.

Aristocles *apud* Eusebius, *Praeparat. Evang.* (2 Mullach), cf. F7 Chiesara

εἰ γὰρ ἔστι γῆ, καὶ ὕδωρ, καὶ ἀὴρ, καὶ πῦρ, καὶ σίδηρος, καὶ χρυσός· καὶ τὸ μὲν ζῶν, τὸ δὲ τεθνηκός, καὶ μέλαν, καὶ λευκὸν, καὶ τὰ ἄλλα πάντα ὅσα φασὶν εἶναι ἄνθρωποι ἀληθῶς, ἢ καὶ ἡμεῖς ὀρθῶς ὁρῶμεν καὶ ἀκούομεν, εἶναι ἐχρῆν καὶ τὸ ὂν τοιοῦτον, οἷον πρῶτον ἔδοξεν ἡμῖν εἶναι, καὶ μὴ μεταπίπτειν, μηδὲ γίνεσθαι ἕτερον, ἀλλ' εἶναι ὅμοιον, οἷόν πέρ ἐστιν ἕκαστον. νῦν δέ ἔφαμεν ὀρθῶς ὁρᾶν, καὶ ἀκούειν, καὶ συνιέναι. δοκεῖ δὲ ἡμῖν τὸ θερμὸν, καὶ ψυχρὸν γίνεσθαι· καὶ τὸ ψυχρὸν, θερμὸν, καὶ τὸ σκληρὸν, μαλθακὸν, καὶ τὸ μαλθακὸν, σκληρὸν.

Appendix 2

How Much Do We Have of Melissus' Book?

The proposed reconstruction of Melissus' treatise amounts to less than a thousand words. How much of his original work can we reasonably expect this to represent? The surviving remains of early Greek philosophy are typically treated as meagre scraps, gesturing towards its innovative ideas while reminding us of how much has been lost.

Several features of Melissus' work set it apart. It is significant that all our evidence suggests that the fragments derive from a single work. Thus there is no worry, as there is, say, for those who take Empedocles to have composed more than one work, about assigning the fragments to the respective, proper treatise. It is also important that all of the fragments are found in the same source, Simplicius' commentaries on Aristotle, though of course we find a version of B8 in Aristocles. So we can be reasonably confident that all the fragments come from the same edition of Melissus' text, making possible a reconstruction of the kind proposed above.

A third factor is the existence of the two, possibly independent, paraphrases found in Simplicius and the *MXG*. As we have noticed, all the material found in them is corroborated by the extant verbatim quotations or obviously a derivation

γινώσκειν, ἐξ ὕδατός τε γῆ καὶ λίθος γίνεσθαι codd.: ἐξ ὕδατός τε γῆ καὶ λίθος γίνεσθαι prior ὥστε transp. Karsten: ὥστε συμβαίνει μήτε ὁρᾶν μήτε τὰ ὄντα γινώσκειν secl. BA et KRS   **58** φαμὲν οἷς A   **61** μεταπίπτει A   **62** μὲν ἐὸν BR: μέσον ADEF

thereof; this suggests, though it does not confirm, that no additional, genuine Melissan material was known to either paraphrast.[1] Indeed, with one exception, we do not find *any* doxographical material that attributes theses to Melissus that are not evident (either directly or as a derivation) in the verbatim fragments.[2] This exception is found in Diogenes Laertius' biography of Melissus in *The Lives of Philosophers* book IX, chapter 24. It is here that Melissus is said to have claimed that one ought not to speak about the gods because there is no knowledge of them. Above it was argued that such an epistemic commitment fits in nicely with Melissus' claim that what-is is unique and that it encompasses the whole of what there is; however, the context and language of Diogenes' report suggests that it is likely anecdotal and not an explicit claim of something Melissus' book contained. The hypothesis, i.e. if what-is is indeed *all* that there is, requires either the identification of what-is with the divine, or the acceptance of atheism. So, on the one hand, Melissus would be able to accept a sceptical view of direct human knowledge of the divine, while also maintaining that, out of necessity, that what-is is itself divine. This is a prime example of what Melissus gains by using the inferential model he adopts: the deductive security it affords can even overcome, or indeed accommodate, a pessimistic view about the capabilities of human knowledge. In any case, if we assume that such an argument is lost from the collection of verbatim fragments, it would likely amount to only a small fraction of total word count of the reconstructed treatise.

These factors suggest, contrary to the usual assumption about Presocratic fragments, that it is plausible that we possess the majority of Melissus' treatise, with the enticing possibility that what we have is an entire work with only the small gaps we have identified and filled. The reconstructed text is undoubtedly short but not uniquely so. In the Hippocratic corpus, which includes works that have some historical connection with Melissus, it is not uncommon to find works containing fewer than 2,000 words. The Littré edition of *De Corde*, for example, is a mere 1,062 words and *De Alimento* is only slightly longer at 1,339. We even find the treatise *De Anatome*, at a mere 260 words the shortest in the corpus, although it is probably fourth century in date.[3]

We may look as well to Melissus' fellow Eleatics. Undoubtedly, we have lost some of Parmenides *Way of Truth* but, even taking this into account, the extant 100 or so lines probably make up the bulk of this section of the poem.[4] After all,

---

[1] This accepts, of course, that the dilemmatic elements in both paraphrases are products of the imposition of interpretative matrices. [2] I set aside the connection scholars have occasionally made between Aristotle's remarks at *Generatione et Corruptione* 325a13–23 and Melissus. Here there is a summary of an argument for the infinity of what-is on the basis of the fact that what is finite would terminate in the void. Melissus requires no such additional argument for spatial infinity. I take it to be entirely possible, and indeed likely, that Aristotle is providing an interpretation of a Melissan argument and not a report of its original formulation. [3] See Craik 2006: 162–8. [4] It seems probable, though not certain, that the *Doxa* was the longer half of the poem. We

one of Simplicius' explicitly stated reasons for quoting Parmenides (*In Phys.* 144.25–8) is to preserve the *Way of Truth* in the face of possible loss and, as such, it follows that Simplicius provided as much as he had access to.

The length of Zeno's book and the number of arguments it contained are more obscure. By the time of Proclus, Zeno was thought to be the author of a work called *The Forty Logoi*, although how much genuine Zenonian material it contained is difficult to reconstruct.[5] While we cannot safely derive any conclusions about Zeno's original book from the possible length of *The Forty Logoi*, Proclus in his commentary on Plato's *Parmenides* provides us with an interesting comparison between the respective lengths of his edition of Parmenides and this Zenonian work. As Proclus was undoubtedly more familiar with ancient philosophical books than we can hope to be, the comparison might be of some value:

> ὅσα γὰρ ὁ Παρμενίδης ἀγκύλως καὶ συνεσπειραμένως ἀπεφθέγγετο, ταῦτα ἀνελίττων οὗτος καὶ εἰς παμμήκεις λόγους ἐκτείνων παρεδίδου· (684.16–18)

> For what Parmenides uttered in an intricate and concentrated style, Zeno unfolded and transmitted to us in an extended discourse. (Trans. Morrow and Dillon, slightly modified)

If we accept the conjecture that Simplicius' verbatim quotations of Zeno derive from the same edition Proclus had, we can make an approximate guess about the length of the work he comments upon.[6] Let us take one of Zeno's fragments which is presented unambiguously in his own words by Simplicius:

> εἰ πολλά ἐστιν, ἀνάγκη τοσαῦτα εἶναι ὅσα ἐστὶ καὶ οὔτε πλείονα αὐτῶν οὔτε ἐλάττονα. εἰ δὲ τοσαῦτά ἐστιν ὅσα ἐστί, πεπερασμένα ἂν εἴη. εἰ πολλά ἐστιν, ἄπειρα τὰ ὄντα ἐστίν· ἀεὶ γὰρ ἕτερα μεταξὺ τῶν ὄντων ἐστί, καὶ πάλιν ἐκείνων ἕτερα μεταξύ. καὶ οὕτως ἄπειρα τὰ ὄντα ἐστί. (DK29B3)

Now, according to Proclus, each of the forty *logoi* argued against those who posit many beings by demonstrating that such a hypothesis entails attributing to each of the many opposing attributes.[7] As such, the passage quoted above is an obvious candidate for inclusion as one of the forty. If we were

---

can, for example, point to positions presumably deriving from the *Doxa* (e.g. the identification of the evening star with the morning star) ascribed to Parmenides by later authors that have no analogue in the verbatim fragments.   [5] Dillon (1986) takes a positive view. Tarrant (1990) is more sceptical. See Tarrant, p. 23, for the view that this allegedly Zenonian work may have even been known to pre-Plotinian philosophers.   [6] Dillon (1986: 41) is fairly sympathetic to this conjecture. If Simplicius did quote from a different text in roughly contemporary circulation, it is odd that he would not make note of this fact.   [7] 631.25ff. Simplicius confirms that Zeno put forward many different arguments against plurality (*In Phys.* 139.5–6).

to accept that this *logos* is representative of the average length of each of the forty, we could approximate that *The Forty Logoi* ran to about 2,000 words. Of course, B3 might be a particularly short example of a *logos* and skew our approximation. We might, if so, take this estimate as indicative of the lower end of the range.

We may look, as well, to Zeno's B1 and B2, which seem to work together to establish that if there were a plurality, they would be so small as to have no magnitude and so large as to be infinite in magnitude.

> ʻεἰ γὰρ ἄλλῳ ὄντι', φησί, ʻπροσγένοιτο, οὐδὲν ἂν μεῖζον ποιήσειεν· μεγέθους γὰρ μηδενὸς ὄντος, προσγενομένου δέ, οὐδὲν οἷόν τε εἰς μέγεθος ἐπιδοῦναι. καὶ οὕτως ἂν ἤδη τὸ προσγινόμενον οὐδὲν εἴη. εἰ δὲ ἀπογινομένου τὸ ἕτερον μηδὲν ἔλαττον ἔσται μηδὲ αὖ προσγινομένου αὐξήσεται, δῆλον ὅτι τὸ προσγενόμενον οὐδὲν ἦν οὐδὲ τὸ ἀπογενόμενον. (DK29B2)

> ʻεἰ μὴ ἔχοι μέγεθος τὸ ὄν, οὐδ' ἂν εἴη', ἐπάγει ʻεἰ δὲ ἔστιν, ἀνάγκη ἕκαστον μέγεθός τι ἔχειν καὶ πάχος καὶ ἀπέχειν αὐτοῦ τὸ ἕτερον ἀπὸ τοῦ ἑτέρου. καὶ περὶ τοῦ προύχοντος ὁ αὐτὸς λόγος. καὶ γὰρ ἐκεῖνο ἕξει μέγεθος καὶ προέξει αὐτοῦ τι. ὅμοιον δὴ τοῦτο ἅπαξ τε εἰπεῖν καὶ ἀεὶ λέγειν· οὐδὲν γὰρ αὐτοῦ τοιοῦτον ἔσχατον ἔσται οὔτε ἕτερον πρὸς ἕτερον οὐκ ἔσται. οὕτως εἰ πολλά ἐστιν, ἀνάγκη αὐτὰ μικρά τε εἶναι καὶ μεγάλα· μικρὰ μὲν ὥστε μὴ ἔχειν μέγεθος, μεγάλα δὲ ὥστε ἄπειρα εἶναι. (DK29B1)

Even if these two quotations fail to represent the whole of Zeno's paradox, they provide an indication of the length of a more complex piece of argumentation than what we find in B3. As such, we might speculate that these two passages are representative of the upper range of the length of the *Logoi*, and estimate that an edition of the *Forty Logoi* consisting of arguments of such a length would stretch to 5,000 words. It seems plausible, then, to give a range of 2,000–5,000 words as an educated guess of the length of Proclus' copy of Zeno.

Proclus' repeated characterisation of *The Forty Logoi* as both long and containing a rich variety of arguments (cf. 684.16–18 with 631.25–632.15) targeting the many, and revealing its opposing attributes, suggests that its length is very much at the upper end of his editions of Eleatic philosophical treatises. This helps put Melissus' treatise in context. The hypothesis that his original treatise contained around 1,000 words, though undoubtedly on the shorter end of the spectrum, does not seem *prima facie* implausible if Zeno's 2,000–5,000-word book is understood to be an extended and painstaking work.

What we may conclude here is that there is a better case for thinking that we possess a significant continuous, running text for Melissus than any other Presocratic. While there is the possibility that some of the original text is lost (e.g. a section outside of the main string of arguments on the model of B8), we have good reason to appreciate our good luck in inheriting the fragments of Melissus, as we have them.

Appendix 3

Melissus and the Eleatics: A Map of Melissus

Melissus' fragments together form a deductive chain of arguments. The character of these arguments and the relations between the fragments we have explored in the above reconstruction. An important conclusion that has emerged is that not every assertion or conclusion is equal in status for Melissus; some are fundamental insofar as they are repeatedly invoked while others play a supplemental role, adducing additional support for claims already deduced. The arguments against the veracity of sense experience and against division, for example, belong on my account to the latter category.

In what follows I offer a map of Melissus' general strategy to clarify what has been argued in the reconstruction and commentary. The aims are to provide a representation of the argument that clarifies the relations between the fragments and to make the essential character of the chain of demonstrations evident. The strongly deductive nature of the work that I have emphasised will of course emerge, but also apparent will be the change in strategy from strict linear deduction to more general explication that I have suggested begins in line 17 (B7) (now that a text of Melissus has been given as a whole, I refer to its line numbers with the Diels-Kranz 'B' numbers in parentheses). There will also be occasional, and in no way comprehensive, notes on how Melissus updates and refines his Eleatic patrimony. These suggestions will support what I take, roughly speaking, to be the character of Melissus' reception of Parmenides: where the latter is difficult to grasp with certainty and subject to controversy, the former disambiguates and clarifies.

In the following, the underlined and emboldened portions represent what I take to be the positive claims Melissus makes about what-is. Those only in bold type indicate arguments made that are not necessarily indicative of his position in the final analysis. The arrows designate the movement from one argument to another and the small roman numerals list the reasons or arguments given in support of arguments provided in bold lettering.

Nature/What-is (Περὶ φύσεως ἢ περὶ τοῦ <ἐ>όντος)

The inclusion of this title marks Melissus' first improvement on Parmenides. The evidence for the authenticity of the generic title ascribed to the latter's poem (Περὶ φύσεως, according to Sextus Empiricus, *Ad Math.* vii. 111) is far weaker than what we have canvassed in Melissus' case.[8] We have seen that Melissus' deductive strategy probably began from the title, where the subject of the treatise (what-is, identified with nature) was raised; the rhetorical question found in Q then works to confirm that such a topic is something we can truly speak about. It

---

[8] It is possible that Parmenides, in B1.29–30, uses ἀληθείης and δόξας, to refer, respectively, to each half of his poem. Certainly, other works were called *Aletheia*, including ones by Antiphon, Protagoras, Antisthenes, and Simmias, suggesting that it was a standard title along the same lines as Περὶ φύσεως.

is difficult to resist the thought that such a title works as a clarification of Parmenides, much like, as I have suggested, the distinctively predicational use of εἶναι in **Q**. Whatever we make of the details of Parmenides' *Doxa* (his account of mortal beliefs about the natural world), it is clear that the status of that section of his poem is inferior (epistemically or otherwise) to his account of τὸ ἐόν in the *Way of Truth*. Indeed the *Doxa* is called deceptive (ἀπατηλόν) at B8.52, picking up B1.30, where mortal beliefs are characterised as lacking conviction. Melissus' title suggests that he rejected any such contrast between an enquiry into nature and an enquiry into what-is: nature and what-is are identical.

Why must we suppose what-is is something and not nothing?

Q, lines 2–3, picking out the predicative function of the verb 'to be' as fundamental, asks rhetorically what we could say about what-is were it nothing, i.e. it had no predicates. The upshot of the question is that the cost of accepting such a nihilistic view is the loss of philosophical enquiry itself: we could no longer say anything about what-is. Melissus then raises for consideration the fundamental hypothesis 'what-is is something' and explores what predicates we can attach to it.

What-is is something we can attach predicates to

Sempiternity

(i) Coming-to-be ex nihilo is impossible

(ii) Destruction in nihil is impossible

What-is is sempiternal

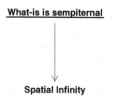

Spatial Infinity

(i) What-is is sempiternal

Melissus' characteristic use of deductive reasoning often means that reasons or arguments were themselves deduced immediately above in the chain of reasoning, e.g. sempiternity is demonstrated, then deployed as a premise in the argument for spatial infinity. Spatial infinity too is demonstrated and immediately invoked as a premise in the argument for uniqueness.

(ii) Spatial beginnings and ends could be reasonably attributed to what-is only if it had come-to-be

Superficially, this marks one of the clearest instances where Melissus departs from Parmenides' poem and, as such, it is often pointed out by commentators (e.g. Graham 2010: 480–1 and Palmer 2004: 26–7). Above, it was suggested that the contrast breaks down on further inspection. What limits achieve for Parmenides is precisely what their absence does for Melissus: completeness (i.e. what-is encompasses or exhausts what there is). This does not mean that Melissus and Parmenides are found in harmony: Parmenides posits a πεῖρας πύματον while Melissus uses the privative ἄπειρόν. What I submit is that *motivation* for both (demonstrating the completeness of what-is) can be construed along the same lines.

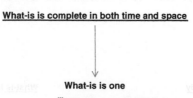

What-is is complete in both time and space

What-is is one

(i) What-is is spatially infinite
(ii) What-is is sempiternal

Melissus' commitment to monism of this type (i.e. that what-is is numerically one) is widely accepted and often thought to represent a deviation from Parmenides. See Barnes (1982: 204–13) for a consideration of whether Parmenides did, in fact, argue for a 'real' monist position as tradition ascribes to him. Barnes suggests that nothing in the surviving fragments forces us to attribute numerical monism or even homogeneity to Parmenides. There are a great many variegated interpretations of Parmenides' poem and how it coheres with the tradition that makes him a proponent of the 'One' or that 'what-is is one'. Palmer (2009: 1–45) has a thorough account of the literature. I take no concerted position here (doing so would inevitably beg the question). Rather I want to suggest that on monism just as on spatial infinity what we find is not necessarily a criticism or eristic reworking of Parmenides but a clarification of what Melissus took him to mean, schematised into a deductive chain of arguments. This is not to say that one could, let alone ought to, find

Melissus and Parmenides in harmony, but I do think that it is perfectly possible that their respective accounts were intended by Melissus to amount collectively to a unified position.

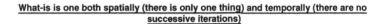

What-is is one both spatially (there is only one thing) and temporally (there are no successive iterations)

It here, on my account, that the strict linearity of Melissus' deductions stops and the treatise begins to branch out. Next, bodilessness and homogeneity will be established in parallel (i.e. neither demonstration takes logical priority). Then, in the remainder of the text, further arguments will be made that again work in parallel and not in succession. Therefore, once the character of the 'Eleatic One' is made clear (i.e that it is one, homogeneous, spatially infinite, and sempiternal), Melissus can articulate what he takes these twin claims to amount to. In his final argument, for example, Melissus takes a different tack, via sense experience, to reinforce his claim that what-is is one and that plurality is impossible.

What-is lacks a body   **What-is is homogeneous**

That these two arguments (that what-is has no body and that what-is is homogeneous) work in tandem has not been heretofore suggested, although Palmer (2003: 9) does make the important point that lines 14–17 (B9) seem to belong prior to lines 17–37 (B7). However, it makes a great deal of sense. Both arguments obviously proceed from the premise 'what-is is one' and both work to eliminate internal demarcations (parts in the case of corporeality, qualitative differentiation in the case of heterogeneity) within what-is. It is also worth noting that parts and heterogeneity are sorts of potentially stable differentiation, while alteration, rearrangement, pain and anguish, and motion represent unstable processes threatening Melissus' characterisation of the Eleatic One.

226

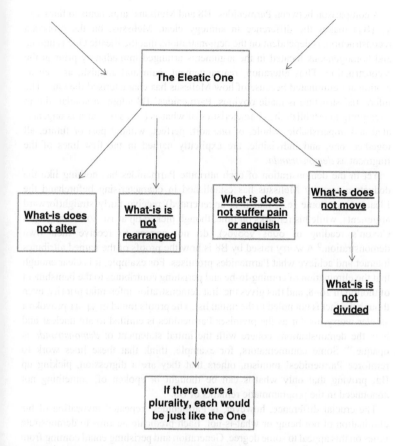

The structure of the argument, as it is presented above, is Melissus' greatest advance on Parmenides. Substantively, I find no compelling instance in which Melissus unambiguously targets a Parmenidean position. For every occurrence of disharmony superficially present (e.g. on the extent of what-is), I have maintained that the difference is probably best interpreted as a refinement or disambiguation in service of a similar end.

But this conclusion is not what I primarily wish the reader to take away. What is crucial is how Melissus, beginning from his title, deductively develops his demonstration of the Eleatic One and reaches a crescendo in the proofs of uniqueness and unity. This characterisation of the Eleatic One is then used to eliminate species of change as well as the testimony of sense experience. The two aims are decidedly Parmenidean, but it is Melissus' argumentative structure that is both novel and effective.

A comparison between Parmenides' B8 and Melissus' arguments in lines 17–37 (B7) makes the difference in strategy clear. Melissus, on the proposed reconstruction, is dependent on the demonstrations that the Eleatic One is unique and homogeneous located in the arguments arranged immediately prior in the reconstruction. Thus alteration, rearrangement, pain and anguish, as well as motion are eliminated because of how Melissus has characterised the One. The inferential structure is made obvious. Parmenides' B8 adopts a similar aim in attempting to establish the characteristics of what-is (τὸ ἐόν): that it is ungenerated and imperishable, whole, of one sort, perfect, without past or future, all together, one, and indivisible, are explicitly named in the first lines of the fragment as *demonstranda*.

Yet in the demonstration of each attribute Parmenides has nothing like the deductive security Melissus has established in characterising beforehand the Eleatic One. Some (e.g. that it is ungenerated) receive fairly straightforward arguments, while his remarks on time, though picked up at 19–20 and at 36 (on Coxon's reading of οὐδὲ χρόνος), do not appear to receive their own demonstration.[9] A worry raised by B8 is how the proofs of the named attributes interact and achieve what Parmenides promises. For example, it is clear enough that the elimination of coming-to-be and perishing contributes to the banishment of motion in 26–8, and this gives the first demonstration inferential priority, even though the fact is not noted in the initial list. The proofs found in 34–41 provoke a similar worry insofar as the premises Parmenides is entitled to are unclear and how the demonstrations cohere with the initial statement of *demonstranda* is opaque.[10] Some commentators, for example, think that these lines work to reinforce Parmenides' monism, others that they are a digression, picking up B2, proving that only what-is can be thought or spoken of, something not announced in the programmatic remarks of B8.[11]

The crucial difference, however, is Parmenides' repeated invocation of his elimination of not-being or what-is-not. Each predicate he aims to demonstrate relies on this appeal to some degree. Generation and perishing entail coming from or dying into not-being. Division in 22–5 is countered by showing that what-is is perfectly continuous without any degrees of being, i.e. some intermixed not-being. Motion is denied because it entails generation and perishing and because what-is is held, by necessity, in the bonds of a limit. The latter point suggests that not-being would be necessary for motion to be possible. Whether this means that not-being is understood as available space to move (i.e. void), or simply some incompleteness that would permit motion, is irrelevant for our present purposes. What is clear is that it is on the basis of the prohibition of not-being that

---

[9] Sedley (1999: 118) makes this point.

[10] This is not to say that they do not have a place within the programme announced at the beginning of B8, only to say that Parmenides does not make it obvious what this is. [11] Sedley 1999: 119–21 for the former, McKirahan 2008: 202–5 for the latter.

Parmenides grounds his argument. The appeal to this premise is continued in 34–41 and is used to support both pieces of the argument for perfection in 44–9.

By contrast, not-being plays no role for Melissus. He *does* identify void with not-being in lines 29–30, but this does not amount to an endorsement of the exclusion of 'is not' from philosophical discourse. In place of Parmenides' constant re-invoking of the same premise, we find a linear, deductive structure, culminating in the characterisation of the Eleatic One in lines 11–16. The above map is intended to make this inferential structure clear by illustrating how Melissus deduces a predicate and then, in turn, uses that interim conclusion as a premise for the following argument. Thus 'something is' leads to sempiternity, which leads to spatial infinity, which leads to monism with its attendant attributes of partlessness and homogeneity, established in two corollary arguments. With this structure in place, change in all its forms is eliminated by arguing that it threatens the unity and uniqueness of the Eleatic One.

Thus we find in Melissus' use of a deductive inferential structure of the kind described a striking departure from Parmenides. This is not to say that a family resemblance is not apparent; deductive arguments are evident in both. Rather it is to say that Melissus demonstrates an affinity for argumentative clarity by creating a deductive structure more obvious and robust than what Parmenides offers. And it is this point about structure that characterises what I take to be Melissus' primary and distinctive contribution to Eleaticism.

BIBLIOGRAPHY

Albertelli, P. (1939) *Gli Eleati.* Bari: Laterza e Figli.

Apelt, O. (1886) 'Melissos bei pseudo-Aristoteles'. *Neue Jahrbücher für classische Philologie.* 729–66.

(1888) *Aristoteles: De Plantis Alia.* Leipzig: Teubner.

Baltussen, H. (2002) 'Philology or Philosophy? Simplicius on the Use of Quotations' in *Epea and Grammata: Oral and Written Communication in Ancient Greece.* I. Worthington and J. M. Foley (eds.). Leiden: Brill. 173–89.

(2008) *Philosophy and Exegesis in Simplicius: The Methodology of a Commentator.* London: Duckworth.

Barnes, J. (1981) 'Reply to Professor Mourelatos'. *Philosophical Books* 22. 77–80.

(1982) *The Presocratic Philosophers.* London: Routledge.

(2011) *Zenone e l'infinito.* L. Rosetti and M. Pulpito (eds.). Sankt Augustin: Academia Verlag.

Bauslaugh, R. A. (1979) 'Thucydides IV 8.6 and the South Channel of Pylos'. *Journal of Hellenic Studies* 99. 1– 6.

Bertelli, L. (2001) 'Hecataeus: From Genealogy to Historiography' in *The Historian's Craft in the Age of Herodotus.* N. Luraghi (ed.). Oxford: Oxford University Press. 67–94.

Bicknell, P. (1982) 'Melissus' Way of Seeming?' *Phronesis* 27. 194–201.

Booth, N. B. (1958) 'Did Melissus Believe in Incorporeal Being?' *American Journal of Philology* 79. 61–5.

Bostock, D. (1991) 'Aristotle on the Continuity of *Physics* VI' in *Aristotle's Physics: A Collection of Essays.* L. Judson (ed.). Oxford: Oxford University Press. 179–212.

(2006) *Space, Time, Matter, and Form.* Oxford: Oxford University Press.

Brandis, C. A. (1813) *Commentationum Eleaticarum pars I: Xenophanis, Parmenidis et Melissi doctrina exposita.* Altona: Hammerich.

Breglia, L. (2005) 'Melisso: problemi di una incerta biografia' in *Da Elea a Samo.* L. Breglia and M. Lupi (eds.). Naples: Arte Tipografica Editrice. 59–83

Brémond, M. (2016) 'Lectures de Mélissos: édition, traduction et interprétation des témoignages sur Mélissos de Samos'. Doctoral thesis, Paris IV-Sorbonne and LMU München.

Broadie, S. (1999) 'Rational Theology' in *The Cambridge Companion to Early Greek Philosophy.* A. A. Long (ed.). Cambridge: Cambridge University Press. 205–24.

Brown, E. A. (1997) 'Plato's Argument for the Immortality of the Soul'. *Apeiron* 30. 211–38.

Bibliography

Brown, L. (1986) 'Being in the *Sophist*'. *Oxford Studies in Ancient Philosophy* 4. 49–70.

(1994) 'The Verb "To Be" in Greek Philosophy: Some Remarks' in *Language*. S. Everson (ed.). Cambridge: Cambridge University Press. 212–36.

Burnet, J. (1930) *Early Greek Philosophy*, fourth edition. London: Adam and Charles Black.

Caston, V. (2002) 'Gorgias on Thought and its Objects' in *Presocratic Philosophy: Essays in Honour of Alexander Mourelatos*. V. Caston and D. W. Graham (eds.). Aldershot: Ashgate. 205–32.

Cherniss, H. (1935) *Aristotle's Criticism of Presocratic Philosophy*. Baltimore: Johns Hopkins University Press.

Chiesara, M. L. (2001) *Aristocles of Messene: Testimonies and Fragments*. Oxford: Oxford University Press.

Cosgrove, M. R. (2014) 'What Are "True" *doxai* Worth to Parmenides'. *Oxford Studies in Ancient Philosophy* 46. 1–31.

Covotti, A. (1898) 'Melissi Samii Reliquiae'. *Studi Italiani di Filologia Classica* 6. 213–27.

Coxon, A. H. (2009) *The Fragments of Parmenides*. R. McKirahan (ed.). Las Vegas: Parmenides Publishing.

Craik, E. M. (2006) *Two Hippocratic Treatises: On Sight and On Anatomy*. Leiden: Brill.

Curd, P. (1993) 'Eleatic Monism in Zeno and Melissus'. *Ancient Philosophy* 13. 1–22.

(1998) *The Legacy of Parmenides*. Princeton: Princeton University Press.

(2007) *Anaxagoras of Clazomenae*. Toronto: University of Toronto Press.

Denniston, J. D. (1959) *The Greek Particles*. Oxford: Oxford University Press.

Diels, H. (1879) *Doxographi Graeci*. Berlin: G. Reimer.

(1882) *Commentaria in Aristotelem Graeca*. Volume ix. Berlin: G. Reimer.

Diels, H., and Kranz, W. (1951) *Die Fragmente der Vorsokratiker*, sixth edition. Berlin: Weidmannsche Verlagsbuchhandlung.

Dillon, J. (1986) 'Proclus and the Forty Logoi of Zeno'. *Illinois Classical Studies* 9. 35–41.

Fehling, D. (1975) 'Zur Funktion und Formgeschichte des Proömiums in der älteren griechischen Prosa' in *ΔΩPHMA: Hans Diller zum 70. Geburtstag*. K. Vourveris and A. Skiadas (eds.). Athens: Griechische Humanistische Gesellschaft. 61–75.

Ferrari, F. (2005) 'Melisso e la scuola eleatica' in *Da Elea a Samo*. L. Breglia and M. Lupi (eds.). Naples: Arte Tipografica Editrice. 85–94.

Fortenbaugh, W. W. et al. (eds.) (1992) *Theophrastus of Eresus: Sources for his Life, Writings, Thought and Influence*. Leiden: Brill.

Fowler, R. (2001) 'Early *Historiē* and Literacy' in *The Historian's Craft in the Age of Herodotus*. N. Luraghi (ed.). Oxford: Oxford University Press. 95–115.

Furley, D. (1967) *Two Studies in the Greek Atomists*. Princeton: Princeton University Press.

Bibliography

(1989) 'Melissus of Samos' in *Ionian Philosophy*. K. J. Boudouris (ed.). Athens: International Association for Greek Philosophy.

Gendler, T. S. (2000) *Thought Experiment: On the Powers and Limits of Imaginary Cases*. New York: Garland.

Gershenson, D. E., and Greenberg, D. A. (1961) 'Melissus of Samos in a New Light: Aristotle's *Physics* 186a10–16'. *Phronesis* 6. 1–9.

Gilbert, O. (1911) *Griechische Religionsphilosophie*. Leipzig: Wilhelm Engelmann.

Gleede, B. (2012) '*Creatio ex nihilo*: A Genuinely Philosophical Insight Derived from Plato and Aristotle? Some Notes on the *Treatise on the Harmony between the Two Sages*'. *Arabic Sciences and Philosophy* 22. 91–117.

Gomperz, H. (1932) 'ΑΣΩΜΑΤΟΣ'. *Hermes* 32. 155–67.

Gomperz, T. (1906) *Greek Thinkers: A History of Ancient Philosophy*. Trans. Laurie Magnus. London: John Murray.

Goodwin, W. W. (1889) *Syntax of the Moods and Tenses of the Greek Verb*. London: Macmillan.

Graeser, A. (1972) *The Argument of Melissus*. Athens: Hellenic Society for Humanistic Studies.

Graham, D. W. (1999) *Aristotle* Physics *VIII*. Oxford: Oxford University Press.

(2006) *Explaining the Cosmos*. Princeton: Princeton University Press.

(2010) *The Texts of Early Greek Philosophy*. Cambridge: Cambridge University Press.

(2013) *Science before Socrates: Parmenides, Anaxagoras, and the New Astronomy*. Oxford: Oxford University Press.

Guthrie, W. K. C. (1962) *A History of Greek Philosophy*. Volume I. Cambridge: Cambridge University Press.

(1965) *A History of Greek Philosophy*. Volume II. Cambridge: Cambridge University Press.

Hankinson, R. J. (1998) *Cause and Explanation in Greek Thought*. Oxford: Clarendon Press.

Harriman, B. 'The Beginning of Melissus' *On Nature, or On What-is*: A Reconstruction'. *Journal of Hellenic Studies* 135. 19–34.

Heiberg, I. L. (1893) *Commentaria in Aristotelem Graeca*. Volume VII. Berlin: G. Reimer.

Heidel, W. A. (1913) 'On Certain Fragments of the Pre-Socratics'. *Proceedings of the American Academy of Arts and Sciences* 48. 681–734.

(1943) 'Hecataeus and Xenophanes'. *American Journal of Philology* 64: 255–77.

Herrmann, F. G. (2007) *Words and Ideas: The Roots of Plato's Philosophy*. Swansea: The Classical Press of Wales.

Hintikka, J. (1973) *Time and Necessity*. Oxford: Oxford University Press.

Hoffmann, P. (1987) 'Simplicius' Polemics' in *Philoponus and the Rejection of Aristotelian Science*. R. Sorabji (ed.). London: Duckworth. 57–83.

Bibliography

Holmes, B. (2010) *The Symptom and the Subject*. Princeton: Princeton University Press.

Huby, P. M. (1973) 'Concerning Nature': Review of Schmalzriedt, E. (1970) *Peri Physeos. Classical Review* 23. 206–8.

Huby, P. M., and Taylor, C. C. W. (2011) *Simplicius: On Aristotle* Physics 1.3–4. London: Bristol Classical Press.

Hussey, E. (1983) *Aristotle* Physics *Books III and IV*. Oxford: Clarendon Press.

(2004) '*On Generation and Corruption* 1.8'. *Aristotle's On Generation and Corruption I*. F. de Haas and J. Mansfeld (eds.). Oxford: Clarendon Press. 243–65.

Jacoby, F. (1913) 'Herodotus'. *Real-Encyclopädie der classischen Altertumswissenschaft*, Suppl. 2. 205–520.

Jaeger, W. (1947) *The Theology of the Early Greek Philosophers*. Oxford: Clarendon Press.

Jones, W. H. S. (1923) *Hippocrates*. Volume II. Cambridge, MA: Harvard University Press.

Jori, A. (1996) *Medicina e medici nell'antica Grecia: saggio sul peri technes ippocratico*. Naples: Il Mulino.

Jouanna, J. (1965) 'Rapports entre Mélissos de Samos et Diogène d'Apollonie, à la lumière du traité hippocratique *De natura hominis*'. *Revue des Études Anciennes* 67. 306–23.

(1975) *Hippocrate, De natura hominis*. Corpus Medicorum Graecorum, Volume 1.1.3. Berlin: Akademie Verlag.

Kahn, C. H. (1960) *Anaximander and the Origins of Greek Cosmology*. New York: Columbia University Press.

(1966) 'The Greek Verb "To Be" and the Concept of Being'. *Foundations of Language* 2. 245–65.

(2004) 'A Return to the Theory of the Verb *Be* and the Concept of Being'. *Ancient Philosophy* 24. 381–405.

(2009) *Essays on Being*. Oxford: Oxford University Press.

Kerferd, G. B. (1975) 'A Vindication of Melissus'. Critical notice of G. Reale (1970) *Melisso: Testimonianze e frammenti. Classical Review* 25: 186–7.

Kirk, G. S. (1962) *Heraclitus: The Cosmic Fragments*. Cambridge: Cambridge University Press.

Kirk, G. S., and Raven, J. E. (1957) *The Presocratic Philosophers*. Cambridge: Cambridge University Press.

Kirk, G. S., Raven, J. E., and Schofield, M. (1983) *The Presocratic Philosophers*, second edition. Cambridge: Cambridge University Press.

Kirk, G. S., and Stokes, M. C. (1960) 'Parmenides' Refutation of Motion'. *Phronesis* 5. 1–4.

Lausberg, H. (1998) *Handbook of Literary Rhetoric: A Foundation for Literary Study*. D. E. Orton and R. D. Anderson (eds.). Leiden: Brill.

Lear, J. (1988) *Aristotle: The Desire to Understand*. Cambridge: Cambridge University Press.

Bibliography

Lee, H. D. P. (1936) *Zeno of Elea*. Cambridge: Cambridge University Press.

Lesher, J. H. (1991) 'Xenophanes on Inquiry and Discovery: An Alternative to the "Hymn to Progress" Reading of Fr. 18'. *Ancient Philosophy* 11. 229–48.

(1992) *Xenophanes of Colophon*. Toronto: University of Toronto Press.

Liddell, H. G., Scott, R., and Jones, H. S. (1940) *A Greek–English Lexicon*, ninth edition. Oxford: Oxford University Press.

Littré, É. (1849) *Œuvres complètes d'Hippocrate*. Paris: J. B. Baillière.

Lloyd, G. E. R. (1966) *Polarity and Analogy*. Cambridge: Cambridge University Press.

Loenen, J. H. M. M. (1959) *Parmenides, Melissus, Gorgias*. Assen: Royal Van Gorcum.

Long, A. A. (1976) Critical notice of G. Reale (1970) *Melisso: Testimonianze e frammenti. Gnomon* 48. 645–50.

(1996) 'Parmenides on Thinking Being'. *Proceedings of the Boston Area Colloquium in Ancient Philosophy* 12. 125–51.

Longrigg, J. (1993) *Greek Rational Medicine: Philosophy and Medicine from Alcmaeon to the Alexandrians*. London: Routledge.

Makin, S. (1993) *Indifference Arguments*. Oxford: Blackwell.

(2005) 'Melissus and his Opponents: The Argument of DK 30 B8'. *Phronesis* 50. 263–88.

(2014) 'Parmenides, Zeno, and Melissus' in *The Routledge Companion to Ancient Philosophy*. J. Warren and F. Sheffield (eds.). London: Routledge. 34–48.

Malcolm, J. (1991) 'On Avoiding the Void'. *Oxford Studies in Ancient Philosophy* 9. 75–94.

Mann, J. E. (2012) *Hippocrates, On the Art of Medicine*. Leiden: Brill.

Mansfeld, J. (1979) 'The Chronology of Anaxagoras' Athenian Period and the Date of his Trial'. *Mnemosyne* 32. 39–69.

(1985) 'Historical and Philosophical Aspects of Gorgias' "On What Is Not"' in *Gorgia e la Sofistica, Siculorum Gymnasium* 38 *(1985)*. L. Montoneri and F. Romano (eds.). Catania: Facoltà di Lettere e Filosofia, Università di Catania. 243–71.

(1986) 'Aristotle, Plato, and the Preplatonic Doxography and Chronology' in *Storiografia e dossografia nella filosofia antica*. G. Cambiano (ed.). Turin: Tirrenia. 1–59.

(1987) 'Theophrastus and the Xenophanes Doxography'. *Mnemosyne* 40. 286–312.

(1990) 'De Melisso Xenophanes Gorgia: Pyrrhonizing Aristotelianism' in *Studies in the Historiography of Greek Philosophy*. Assen: Van Gorcum. 200–37.

(1992) 'Physikai doxai and Problēmata physika from Aristotle to Aëtius (and Beyond)' in *Theophrastus: His Psychological, Doxographical, and Scientific Writings*. W. W. Fortenbaugh and D. Gutas (eds.). Rutgers

Bibliography

University Studies in Classical Humanities 5. New Brunswick: Transaction Publishers. 63–111.

(2016) *Melissus between Miletus and Elea*. M. Pulpito (ed.). Sankt Augustin: Academia Verlag.

Mansfeld, J., and Runia, D. T. (1997) *Aëtiana: The Method and Intellectual Context of a Doxographer*. Volume I. Leiden: Brill.

McDowell, J. (1973) *Plato: Theaetetus*. Oxford: Clarendon Press.

McKirahan, R. D. (1994) *Philosophy before Socrates*. Indianapolis: Hackett.

(2008) 'Signs and Arguments in Parmenides B8' in *The Oxford Handbook of Presocratic Philosophy*. P. Curd and D. W. Graham (eds.). Oxford: Oxford University Press. 189–229.

Merrill, B. L. (1998) 'Melissus of Samos: A Commentary on the Sources and Fragments'. PhD thesis, University of Texas (Austin).

Mourelatos, A. P. D. (1965) 'The Real, Appearances and Human Error in Early Greek Philosophy'. *Review of Metaphysics* 19. 346–65.

(1970) *The Route of Parmenides*. New Haven: Yale University Press.

(1981) 'Pre-Socratic Origins of the Principle that There Are No Origins from Nothing'. *Journal of Philosophy* 78. 649–65.

(1987) 'Quality, Structure, and Emergence in Later Pre-Socratic Philosophy' in *Proceedings of the Boston Area Colloquium in Ancient Philosophy*. Volume II. John J. Cleary (ed.). New York: University Press of America. 127–94.

Mullach, F. W. A. (1883) *Fragmenta Philosophorum Graecorum*. Paris: Ambrosio Firmin Didot.

Natorp, P. (1890) 'Aristoteles und die Eleaten'. *Philosophische Monatshefte* 26. 147–69.

Obertello, J. (1984) 'Melissus of Samos and Plato on the Generation of the World'. *Dionysius* 8. 3–18.

Osborne, C. (1987) *Rethinking Early Greek Philosophy: Hippolytus of Rome and the Presocratics*. London: Duckworth.

(1987) 'Empedocles Recycled'. *Classical Quarterly* 37. 24–50.

(2006) *Philoponus: On Aristotle's Physics* 1.1–3. London: Duckworth.

Owen, G. E. L. (1958) 'Zeno and the Mathematicians'. *Proceedings of the Aristotelian Society* 58. 143–65.

(1960) 'Eleatic Questions'. *Classical Quarterly* 10. 84–102.

(1965) 'Aristotle on the Snares of Ontology' in *New Essays on Plato and Aristotle*. R. Bambrough (ed.). London: Routledge. 69–95.

(1966) 'Plato and Parmenides on the Timeless Present'. *The Monist* 50. 317–40.

(1971) 'Plato on Not-Being' in *Plato: I Metaphysics and Epistemology*. G. Vlastos (ed.). Garden City, NY: Anchor Books. 223–67.

Pabst, A. (1889) *De Melissi Samii Fragmentis*. Bonn.

Palmer, J. (2003) 'On the Alleged Incorporeality of What Is in Melissus'. *Ancient Philosophy* 23. 1–10.

Bibliography

(2004) 'Melissus and Parmenides'. *Oxford Studies in Ancient Philosophy* 26. 19–54.

(2009) *Parmenides and Presocratic Philosophy*. Oxford: Oxford University Press.

Pellegrin, P. (1999) *Aristote: Physique*. Paris: Flammarion.

Pendrick, G. J. (2002) *Antiphon the Sophist: The Fragments*. Cambridge: Cambridge University Press.

Porciani, L. (1997) *La forma proemiale: storiografia e pubblico nel mondo antico*. Pisa: Scuola Normale Superiore.

Prantl, C. (1854) *Aristoteles' Acht Buecher* Physik. Leipzig.

Prior, A. (1967) *Past, Present and Future*. Oxford: Oxford University Press.

Pruss, A. R. (2006) *The Principle of Sufficient Reason: A Reassessment*. Cambridge: Cambridge University Press.

Rapp, C. (2006) 'Zeno and the Eleatic anti-pluralism' in *La costruzione del discorso filosofico nell'età dei Presocratici*. Maria Michela Sassi (ed.). Pisa: Edizioni della Normale. 161–82.

(2013) 'Melissos aus Samos' in *Grundriss der Geschichte der Philosophie, Philosophie der Antike*, Bd. 1: *Frühgriechische Philosophie*. D. Bremer, H. Flashar, and G. Rechenauer (eds.). Basel: Schwabe Verlag. 573–98.

Rashed, M. (1995) 'Alexandre d'Aphrodise et la "Magna Quaestio", rôle et indépendance des scholies dans la tradition byzantine du corpus aristotélicien'. *Études Classiques* 63. 295–351.

(1997) 'A "New" Text of Alexander on the Soul's Motion' in *Aristotle and After*. R. Sorabji (ed.). London: Insititute of Classical Studies. 181–95.

(2005) *Aristote: De la génération et la corruption*. Paris: Les Belles Lettres.

Raven, J. E. (1948) *Pythagoreans and Eleatics*. Cambridge: Cambridge University Press.

Reale, G. (1970) *Melisso: Testimonianze e frammenti*. Florence: La Nuova Italia.

Reinhardt, K. (1916) *Parmenides und die Geschichte der griechischen Philosophie*. Bonn: Friedrich Cohen.

Renehan, R. (1979) 'The Meaning of ΣΩΜΑ in Homer: A Study in Methodology'. *California Studies in Classical Antiquity* 12. 269–82.

(1980) 'On the Greek Origins of the Concepts Incorporeality and Immateriality'. *Greek, Roman, and Byzantine Studies* 21. 105–38.

Ritter, H., and Preller, L. (1888) *Historia Philosophiae Graecae*, seventh edition. Gotha: Friedrich Andreas Perthes.

Robbiano, C. (2011) 'What Is Parmenides' Being?' in *Parmenides: Venerable and Awesome*. N. L. Cordero (ed.). Las Vegas: Parmenides Publishing. 213–31.

Ross, W. D. (1924) *Aristotle's Metaphysics*. Oxford: Clarendon Press.

(1936) *Aristotle's Physics*. Oxford: Oxford University Press.

Schiefsky, M. J. (2005) *Hippocrates: On Ancient Medicine*. Leiden: Brill.

Schmalzriedt, E. (1970) *Peri Physeos: Zur Frühgeschichte der Buchtitel*. Munich: Fink Verlag.

Bibliography

Schofield, M. (1970) 'Did Parmenides Discover Eternity?'. *Archiv für Geschichte der Philosophie* 52. 113–35.

(2003) 'The Presocratics' in *The Cambridge Companion to Greek and Roman Philosophy*. David Sedley (ed.). Cambridge: Cambridge University Press. 42–72.

Sedley, D. (1977) 'Diodorus Cronus and Hellenistic Philosophy'. *Proceedings of the Cambridge Philological Society* 23. 74–120.

(1982) 'Two Conceptions of Vacuum'. *Phronesis* 27. 175–93.

(1999) 'Parmenides and Melissus' in *The Cambridge Companion to Early Greek Philosophy*. A. A. Long (ed.). Cambridge: Cambridge University Press. 113–33.

(2007) *Creationism and its Critics in Antiquity*. Berkeley: University of California Press.

Smyth, H. W. (1956) *Greek Grammar*. Cambridge, MA: Harvard University Press.

Solmsen, F. (1969) 'The "Eleatic One" in Melissus'. Reprinted in F. Solmsen 1982: 137–49.

(1982) *Kleine Schriften III*. Hildesheim: Georg Olms Verlag.

Sorabji, R. (1980) *Necessity, Cause, and Blame*. London: Duckworth.

(1983) *Time, Creation and the Continuum*. London: Duckworth.

(1988) *Matter, Space and Motion*. London: Duckworth.

Tannery, P. (1930) *Pour l'histoire de la science hellène*. Paris: Gauthier-Villars.

Tarán, L. (1965) *Parmenides: A Text with Translation, Commentary, and Critical Essays*. Princeton: Princeton University Press.

(1986) 'The First Fragment of Heraclitus'. *Illinois Classical Studies* 11. 1–15.

(1987) 'The Text of Simplicius' Commentary on Aristotle's *Physics*' in *Simplicius: sa vie, son œuvre, sa survie*. I. Hadot (ed.). Berlin: Walter de Gruyter. 246–66.

Tarrant, H. (1990) 'More on Zeno's Forty Logoi'. *Illinois Classical Studies* 15. 23–37.

Thomas, R. (2000) *Herodotus in Context*. Cambridge: Cambridge University Press.

Untersteiner, M. (1955) *Senofane: Testimonianze e frammenti*. Florence: La Nuova Italia.

Verdenius, W. J. (1948) 'Notes on the Presocratics'. *Mnemosyne* 1. 8–14.

Vitali, R. (1973) *Melisso di Samo: sul mondo o sull'essere*. Urbino: Argalìa Editore.

Vitelli, H. (1888) *Philoponi in Physicorum Octo Libros Commentaria*. Berlin: G. Reimer.

Vlastos, G. (1953) Critical Notice of Raven, J. E. (1948) *Pythagoreans and Eleatics*. *Gnomon* 53. 29–35.

Wardy, R. (1990) *The Chain of Change: A Study of Aristotle's Physics VII*. Cambridge: Cambridge University Press.

Warren, J. (2007) *Presocratics*. Stocksfield: Acumen.

Bibliography

Waterlow, S. (1982) *Passage and Possibility*. Oxford: Oxford University Press.

Węcowski, M. (2004) 'The Hedgehog and the Fox: Form and Meaning in the Prologue of Herodotus'. *Journal of Hellenic Studies* 124. 143–64.

West, M. L. (1995) 'The Date of the *Iliad*'. *Museum Helveticum* 52. 203–19.

Wicksteed, P. H., and Cornford, F. M. (1934) *Aristotle: The Physics*. Cambridge, MA: Harvard University Press.

Williams, C. J. F. (1982) *Aristotle's* De Generatione et Corruptione. Oxford: Clarendon Press.

Zeller, E. (1919) *Die Philosophie der Griechen in ihrer geschichtlichen Entwicklung*. W. Nestle (ed.). Leipzig: O. R. Reisland.

INDEX

Index

Index

Index